AF706109

COMPUTER-GENERATED EVIDENCE UNDER NIGERIAN LAW

CASES, MATERIALS AND COMMENTARIES

COMPUTER-GENERATED EVIDENCE UNDER NIGERIAN LAW

CASES, MATERIALS AND COMMENTARIES

Professor Ibrahim Abdullahi, SAN
Department of Private and Business Law,
Faculty of Law, Usmanu Danfodiyo University,
Sokoto, Nigeria

malthouse MP

Malthouse Press Limited

Lagos, Benin, Ibadan, Jos, Port-Harcourt, Zaria

First Published 2025
ISBN 978-978-60617-0-2

Published by Malthouse Press Limited

Lagos Port Harcourt Zaria

5 Adele Road, Off Warehouse Road,
Apapa, Lagos Mainland, Nigeria
E-mail: malthouselagos@gmail.com
Facebook:@malthouselagos
Twitter:@malthouselagos
Instagram:@malthouselagos
Tel: 0802 600 3203

DEDICATION

This book is dedicated to all the victims of terrorism in Nigeria.

ACKNOWLEDGEMENTS

For sparing my life and for His never – ending grace and mercies, I give thanks to Allah (SWT). This book is based on a research conducted out of the digital age we find ourselves and in which our judex operate in the administration of justice. I am therefore grateful to a number of personalities who inspired me to start this surgical journey, persevere with it and finally publish it. My indebtedness goes to my beloved parents for their inspiration and love. To Professor A.S.R Matazu, Professor Muftau Rufai, Professor Mansur Ibrahim Said, Professor M.L. Ahmadu, Professor M.J. Umaru and Professor S. O. Rabiu, I am grateful for the mentorship, expert advice and encouragement throughout. My gratitude also extends to my amiable colleague Associate Professor Balkisu Saidu, an erstwhile Senior Special Assistant in the office of the Vice President of the Federal Republic of Nigeria, all the Justices of the Court of Appeal of Nigeria sitting at Sokoto and all the Judges of the Superior and Inferior courts in Sokoto State, for their encouragement and believe. To other colleagues in the Faculty of Law UDUS, your encouragement is acknowledged. Most of all, I want to thank my wife and soul mate, the best person I know for her incredible patience and understanding, love and as in all things, her invaluable support. To the entire members of my family comprising of my children, brothers, sisters as well as my in-laws to mention but a few. **I love you all.** To my juniors in chambers and readers of my publications, thank you for sticking to my writings. I would also like to thank my brilliant, exceptional and truly outstanding publishers – Malthouse Press Ltd. For all those who have touched my life in any way, you all know who you are, and I am truly grateful for all you have done. May the Almighty Allah bless you all. ***Aameen.***

PREFACE

That the world is changing from analogue to digital is no longer news but a truism. We are living in an age where most of the things we used to do manually are now done on computers, computer-like devices, or with the aid of computers and computer networks (such as the Internet). For instance, using a debit card, the customer can use an Automated Teller Machine (ATM) to obtain access to his account, and to withdraw money anywhere in the world. With an Internet-enabled cell phone, a customer can authorize the transfer of money to anybody anywhere in the world at any time, as well as making purchases using the same Internet-enabled cell phone. Thence, the rapid growth in technology especially in the area of Information and Communications Technology (ICT), has led to the entire constellation of mostly wireless audio, video, communication and photographic devices together with the computer which corporate and physical entities rely on for record keeping, data storage, communication and this has eased commercial and financial transactions in Nigeria and the world over.

Computer generated evidence otherwise known as electronic evidence has therefore steadily assumed a very important position in the adjudication of disputes or cases; be they criminal or civil and anything done on the computer or the Internet usually leaves traces or digital footprints which can serve as evidence in legal proceedings.

In the year 2011, Nigeria recognised the need to amend its laws to accommodate evidence generated or obtained through computer technology thus necessitating the amendment of the hitherto Evidence Act 1990. One of the innovative provisions relates to the provision for admissibility of statements in documents produced by computers thereby making electronic and computer-generated evidence as a statutorily recognised form and means of proof before the law courts. In the course of trial however, problems relating to the admissibility of electronically-generated evidence, relevance, authenticity, integrity, and confidentiality of such evidence have always sprang up for determination and documents have often than not been rejected for lack of proper grasps of the conditions for the admissibility of documents produced electronically or computer-generated. To add more impetus to computer-generated evidence, the Evidence Act 2011 has been amended by the Evidence (Amended) Act 2023 which introduced far reaching provisions in the area of admissibility of computer-generated evidence in Nigeria.

Judicial pronouncements on computer-generated evidence are happily steadily developing in Nigeria. There are, however, dearth of legal literature on the subject matter which necessitates a resource guide towards the citation of authorities and knowing what changes have taken place in the law especially in the area of practice and procedures of courts before which these electronically generated pieces of evidence are tendered. Conflicting decisions of the Court of Appeal of Nigeria in the area of computer-generated evidence and or electronic evidence further makes the need to have a resource book that will serve as a quick guide in spelling out issues that borders on practice and procedures as pronounced by the superior courts of records in Nigeria which will act as a guide to the Bar and the Bench.

This book highlights in a most condensed but comprehensive manner, judicial pronouncements by the superior courts of records as it relates to practice and procedures in the area of computer-generated evidence in Nigeria and made commentaries on same. As usual, the book is not a magic wand for all the practice and procedures as it relates to all the issues relating to electronic evidence in Nigeria but merely a token contribution to the enhancement of practical information and understanding and to break the barrier that often leads to otherwise admissible evidence to be rejected at the altar of wrong application of practice and procedures thus leading to losing a good case whose foundation lies on computer-generated evidence.

This pioneering effort of mine will no doubt not be free from blemishes and human errors. Some are due to the limits of human knowledge and others as a result of frailty. I take personal responsibility for possible errors, inaccuracies and shortcomings noticeable in this book and would very much appreciate if these are brought to our knowledge to avoid future repetition. This book is intended to be a reference guide.

- Professor Ibrahim Abdullahi, SAN
Department of Private and Business Law,
Faculty of Law, Usmanu Danfodiyo University,
Sokoto, Nigeria.

FOREWORD

I have had the privilege of reading in advance a draft copy of this book entitled, *Computer-Generated Evidence Under Nigerian Law: Cases, Materials and Commentaries*, which the author invited me to write this Foreword.

Reading through the pages of this book written by an erudite scholar and writer in person of Professor Ibrahim Abdullahi **SAN,** I found ample evidence of the writer's deep understanding and mastery of the subject matter to the extent that the legal nitty-gritty relating to the thorny issues of computer generated evidence. His brilliant exposition and intelligent analysis shows the expositions of the judex in this area of the law.

This book presents an opportunity for people of diverse backgrounds within and outside the legal and judicial circles to read and appreciate the law relating to computer-generated evidence in Nigeria especially now that we are in a digital age. This book is in a class of its own and I found it to be a unique contribution and uncommon enterprise in the province of the exposition of burning legal issues that are of immense relevance to the need of judges, legal practitioners, law teachers, security agents and law students.

Actually, the book is a testimony of the writer's academic dexterity and penchant for the promotion of the law and legal development which he aptly demonstrated in the way and manner he presented legal principles in a lucid and simple manner in the area of computer generated evidence in Nigeria.

Let me hasten to say, in no uncertain terms, that I have benefited immensely from the rich and thought – provoking discussions advanced in this book and I have no hesitation in recommending this essential and must read legal literature to all Nigerians within and outside the legal profession.

Professor Mansur Ibrahim Sa'id
Former Deputy Vice Chancellor Administration,
Usmanu Danfodio University, Sokoto.

TABLE OF CASES

Abidoye & Anor v. Dosunmu & Anor (2019) LPELR-47719 (CA); 27
Abubakar v. Chuks (2007) 18 NWLR (Pt. 1066) 386; 127
Abubakar v. Joseph (2008) All FWLR (Pt. 432) Pg 1065; 105
Adelodun v. FRN (2017) LPELR-42356(CA); 131
Adeyemo Abiodun v. Federal Republic of Nigeria (2018) LPELR-43838 (SC); 94
Adie v. The State (1980) 1-2 SC 116 5
African Newspaper v. Nigeria (1985) 2 NWLR (Pt. 6) 137; 115
A.G. of Bendel State v. Aiyedan (1989) 4 NWLR 646; 59
AG, Federation v. Abubakar (2007) All FWLR (PT 375) 405, 555; 99
A.G., Oyo v. Fairlakes (1989) 5 NWLR Pt. 121 Pg 255; 25
Agagu v. Dawodu (1990) 7 NWLR (Pt. 160) 56 CA; 23
Agip Nigeria Limited v. Agip Pet. Int'l (2010) 5 NWLR (1187); 57
Ahmed v. Nigerian Navy (2017) LPELR-44025(CA); 67
Ahmed v State (2001) 18 NWLR (PT. 746) 622; 6
Aihenvba v. State (2016) LPELR-40134(CA); 5
Ajayi v. Fisher 1 F.S.C. 97; 69
Akeredolu & Anor v. Mimiko & Ors. (2013) LPELR-20532(CA); 32

Akunne v Ekwuno & Ors. (1951) 14 WACA 59; 72
Alade v. Olukade (1976) SC 183; 69, 72, 134
Aladejobi v. NBA (2013) 5-7 MJSC (Pt. 11) 20 – 207; 133
Alao v. Akano (2005) 4 SCNJ 65 at 74; 29
Alashe v. Ilu (1964) 1 All NLR 390; 69, 72, 134
Alashe & Ors. V Olori Ilu & Ors. (1962) NMLR 66 at 67; 105
Alhadi v Allie (1951) 13 WACA 323; 71
Anatogu & ors v. Igwe Iweka II & ors (1995) 8 NWLR Part 415 page 547; 14, 23, 30
ANPP v. Usman (2008) 12 NWLR Pt. (1100) p. 1 at 72 – 73; 101
Anyaebosi v. R.T. Briscoe (Nig.) Ltd. (1987) 3 NSWLR (Pt. 59) 84; 27, 45, 57
Anyagbosi v. R.T. Briscoe Ltd. (1987) 3 NWLR (Pt. 59) 108; 80
Anyaokoro v. Obiakor (1990) 2 NWLR (PT.130); 52
Araka v. Egbue (2003) 17 NWLR Pt. 848 Pg. 1 at 18; 25,
Archibong v. The State (2006) LPELR (537) 1 at 27 SC; 129, 130
Arum v. Nwobodo (2013) LPELR-20390(SC) Per Aka'ahs J.S.C. at P.40, paras A-B; 2
Ashakacem Plc v. Asharatul Mubashshurun Investment Ltd (2019) LPELR-46541(SC); 132
Asiniola v. Fatodu (2009) 6 NWLR (Pt 1136) 184 at 198; 22
Attorney General of the Federation v. Princewell Ugonna Anuebunwa (SC); 63, 64
Azu v. State (1993) 7 SCNJ PT 1 151; 99
Bajulaiye v. State (2012) LPELR-7995(CA); 4
Barnayi v. A.G.F (2001) 468 @ 480; 57
Beamans Ltf. V Metroplitan Police District Receiver (1961) 1 WLR 634; 71
Berende v. FRN (2019) LPELR-48376(CA); 94

Brila Energy Ltd v. FRN (2018) LPELR-43926(CA); 107
Cavalotti Govianni v. Bonaso Luigi, SC.402; 67, 69, 72
Chief J.A Ajao v Ambrose Family & Ors. (1969) 1 NMLR 25 at 30; 13, 15
Chukwura Akunne v. Mathias Ekwunno and Ors. (1952) 14 WACA 59; 69
Chudi Vertical Co. Ltd v Ifesinachi Industries (Nig) Ltd & Anor (2018) LPELR-44701(SC); 3, 10
C.M & E.S Ltd v. Pazan Services Nig. Ltd (2020) 1 NWLR (PT. 1704) P. 70; 80
Citizens International Bank Ltd. v. SCOA Nigeria Ltd. & Anor. (2006) LPELR-5509(CA); 2
Compact Manifold & Energy Services Ltd v. Pazan Services (Nig.) Ltd (2017) LPELR-41913 (CA); 84
Consortium Ltd. V. Shambilat Shelter (NIG.)(Ltd.) (2018) LPELR-43902(SC); 84
Continental Sales Limited v. R. Shipping Inc. (2012) LPELR - 7905 (CA); (2013) 4 NWLR (PT. 1343) P. 67; 83, 85
Continental Sales Ltd v. R. Shipping Inc (2012) LPELR-7905(CA); 78
Daggash v. Bulama (2004) All FWLR (Pt.212) 1666 CA; 18,
Dalyop v. C.O.P, Plateau State Command (2019) LPELR-47031(CA); 108
Dantata v. Dantata (2002) 4 NWLR (pt. 756) 144, 162; 22
Darma v. Batagarawa (2002) 17 NWLR (pt 769) 243, 259; 22
David v, Edinburgh Magistrates (1953) SC; 34, 40, 99
Davou v. C.O.P Plateau State Command (2019) LPELR-47040 (CA); 43
Delta State House of Assembly & Anor v. DPP & Ors (2014) LPELR-22808(CA); 17,

Dickson v. Chief Timipre Marilin Sylva & ors (2016) LPELR – 41257; 19
Dickson v. Sylva (2017) 8 NWLR (PT 1567) 167; 51, 90, 111, 126, 128
DPP v. Mckeown (1997) 1 All ER 737
Dumina v. State (1995) NWLR (pt 415) 539, 540; 22
Ebu v. Obun (2004) 14 NWLR (PT. 892) 76 at 88; 16
Elias v. FRN & Anor (2016) LPELR-40797(CA); 20,
Elukpo v. FHA (1991) 3 NWLR Pt. 179 322; 96
EmmanueL v. FRN (2018) LPELR-45235(CA); 103
ENL Consortium Ltd. v. Shambilat Shelter (Nig.) Ltd (2018) LPELR- 43902 (SC).
Esso West Africa Inc. v. Oyegbola (1969) All 196 NMLR 44. 45, 69, 78, 123
Etumionu v. A-G Of Delta State (1994) LPELR-14361(CA); 5
Eze v. Okoloagu & Ors (2009) LPELR-3922(CA); 1
Fasina v. Agunkayode (2005) All FWLR (Pt. 283) 116 at 131 paragraphs C-E; 29
Fed. Milit Governor v Sani (No. 2)(1989) 4 NWLR (Pt. 117) 684; 2
Federal Republic of Nigeria v. Femi Fani-Kayode (2010) 14 NWLR (Pt. 1214) 481 at 506 paragraphs E-H 45; 123
Federal Polytechnic, Ede & Ors v. Oyebanji (2012) LPELR-19696(CA); 80
FRN V. Fani-Kayode (2010) 14 NWLR (Pt. 1214) 481 at 506; 80
FRN v. Ojo & Anor (2018) LPELR-45541(CA); 18,
Gilbert v. Endean (1878) 9 Ch. D.259; 69
Glaxosmithkline Consumer Nigeria Plc 92019) LPELR-47498 (CA) at pp.57-62; 87
GTB Plc v. Abiodun (2017) LPELR-42551(CA); 18

Goodwill & Trust Investment Ltd v. Witt & Bush Ltd. (2011) All FWLR (Pt. 576) 517, 34 WRN 1; 31, 90

Guobadia v. The State (2004) LPELR – 1344 SC; 133

Habib Nig. Bank v. Koya (1992) 7 NWLR Pt. 251 Pg. 43 Pg. 55-56; 25

Haruna v. Moddibbo (2004) 16 NWLR (Pt. 900) p. 487 at 544-6 para F-D; 22

IBTC Bank v. Long Term Bglobal Capital Ltd & Ors (2021) LPELR – 55610 (CA); 64

Idudhe v. Eseh (1996) 5 NWLR pt. 451 750 at 758; 95

Idudueko v. Pfzier Products Ltd (2014) 12 NWLR (Pt. 1420) 96 at 122; 133

Igori v. Igori & Ors (2013) LPELR-21027(CA) ; 25

Iheonu v. Obiukwu (1994) 1 NWLR Pt. 322 Pg. 594 at 601-603; 25

Ikenye v. Ofunne (1985)2 NWLR (PT. 501); 134

INEC v. AC (2009) 2 NWLR (Pt. 1126) 524 at 595; 33

International Bank of West Africa Ltd. V Imano (2001) 3 SCNJ Pg. 160; 25

Inyang v. APC & Ors (2019) LPELR-47538(CA); 86

Isibor v. The state (1970) 1 ALL MLR 248; 23

Isitor v. Fakarode (2008) 1 NWLR (PT. 1069) 602 AT P. 626, PARA. F; 26,

Islam Rafiqul v. FRN (2018) LPELR-44520(CA); 128

Jacker v. International Cable Co. Ltd. (1888) LT.R. 13; 69

Jarman v. Lambert and Cooke (Contractors) Ltd. (1051) 2 All ER 255; 71

Jubril v. FRN (2018) LPELR-43993(CA); 97

Kassim v. State (2017) LPELR – 42586 (SC); 89

Kate Enterprises Ltd. V. Daewoo Nig. Ltd. (1985) 2 NWLR; 73

Kayili v. Yilbuk (2015) LPELR – 24323 (SC); 30

Kubau v. Rilwanu (2013) LPELR-22346(CA); 13,
Kubor & Anor v. Dickson & Ors (2012) LPELR-9817(SC); 21, 50, 87
Kubor v. Dickson (2013) All FWLR(pt. 676) 392 at 429; 19, 29, 51, 103, 106, 121, 128, 131
Lawal v Union Bank of Nigeria Plc. (1995) 2 NWLR (Pt.378) 407; 2
Loben Investment Co-Operative Multipurpose Society Ltd v. FRN (2019) LPELR-47325(CA); 116
Lufthansa German Airlines v. Ballanyne (2012) LPELR-7977(CA); 44
Lumatron (Nig) Ltd & Anor v. FCMB (2016) LPELR-41409(CA); 56
Maduekwe v. Okoroafor (1992) 9 NWLR (Pt. 263) 69; 33
Maranro v. Adebisi (2008) 26 WRN 182 at p. 200; 23
MD Zahirul Islam v. FRN (2018) LPELR-44529(CA); 33
Miliar v. State (2005) 8 NWLR (PT. 932) 236; 6
Military Governor of Ondo State v. Adewunmi (1988) 2 NWLR (Pt. 82) 280; 59
Minister of Internal Affairs & Ors v. Okoro & Ors (2003) LPELR-7264(CA); 74
Mirchandani v. Pinheiro (2001) 3 NWLR (Pt. 701) 552 at 573; 85
MD Zahrul Islam v. FRM (2018) LPELR-44529 (CA); 33
Minister of Housing and Local Government v. Lambert (1969) 2 WLR 447; 114
Mobil Nig. Plc v. IAL 36 Inc. (2000) FWLR (Pt. 10) 1632; 114
Mrs Elizabeth Anyaebosi v. R.T. Briscoe (Nig.) Ltd. (1987) 6 SC 15; 41, 55, 67
MV Delos v. Ocean Steamship (Nig.) Ltd (2004) 17 NWLR (PT 901) AT PG. 103 PARAS E-F; 12

NEC v. Zuogu (1993) 2 NWLR (Pt. 275) 270; 114
Nomany v. FRN (2018) LPELR-44546(CA); 129
Northwest Energy Nigeria Ltd & Anor v. Ibafon Oil Ltd (2014) LPELR-24133(CA); 17
Nwaeze v. The State (1996) LPELR (2091) 1 at 33 SC; 129, 130
Nwanji v. Coastter Services (2004) All FWLR Pt. 219 Pg. 1150 at 1162; 25
Nweke v. The State (2001) LPELR-2119 (SC); 5
Nwankwo & Anor. v. FRN (2002) LPELR-7089(CA); 5
OANDO Nig. Plc v. Adijere W/A Ltd (2013) 5 NWLR (Pt. 1377) 374; 125
Obatuga & Anor v. Oyebokun & Ors (2014) LPELR-22344 (CA) ; 24
Obembe v. Ekene (2001) 10 NWLR (Pt.722) 677; 127
Obi v. INEC (2007) NWLR (Pt. 1046) p. 565 at 643; 120
Obot v. State (2019) LPELR-48172(CA); 3
Odua v. Fed. Rep. of Nig.(2002) 5 NWLR (PT 761) AT 634 Paras A-C (2002) LPELR-7166(CA); 27
Odogwu v. Odogwu (2006) 2 SCNJ 96 at 114; 57
Odunewu v. Agoro (2022) 7 NWLR (PT 1830) 545 AT 573 – 574, PARAS F – A; 133
Odwuola v. Aina (2001) 12 NWLR (PT. 741) 1; 22
Ofuma v. IBWA (1988) 1 NWLR PART 73 at 658; 121, 131
Ogbunyinya v. Okudo (1979) 1 ANRR 10; 23, 59
Oghoyone v. Oghoyone (2010) LPELR-4689(CA); 121, 130
Ogiale v. SPDC (Nig) Ltd (1997) 3 NWLR (Pt. 480) 165; 99
Ogunsanya v. Taiwo (1970) 1 All NLR p. 147 at p. 151; 30,
Oguonzee v. State (1998) 5 NWLR (PT 551) 60; 99
Ojengbede v. Esan (2001) 18 NWLR (pt 746) 771, 790; 22
Ojo v. Gharoro (1999) 1 NWLR (PT. 615) 374; 4, 10
Okafor v. Okafor & Ors (2014) LPELR-23561(CA); 11

Okeke v. Obidife (1965) NMLR 113.; 72, 134
Okesuji v. Lawal (1991) 2 SCNJ 1 at 13; 59
Okiki II v. Jagun (2000) 5 NWLR (Pt.655) 19 at pp. 27 – 28; 23
Okirinta Ugbola & Ors. V Awo Okorie & Ors (1972) 12 SC 1 at pp13-14; 71
Olatunji v. State (2019) LPELR-48027(CA); 37
Olokologbe v. Alami (1987) 3 NWLR (Pt. 61) 377 SC; 115
Omisore & Anor v. Aregbesola & Ors (2015) LPELR-24803(SC); 51, 106, 111, 132
Onochie v. Ikem (1989) 4 NWLR (Pt. 116) p. 458 at p. 465; 30
Onwuzulike v. State (2017) LPELR-41889 (CA) at. pp110-123; 67, 112,
Onwuzuruike v. Edoziem & Ors (2016) LPELR-26056(SC); 26
Orogun & Anor v. Fidelity Bank (2018) LPELR-46601(CA); 65
Owale v. Shell Petroleum Development Company Ltd (1997) NWLR Pt. 480 page 148 at 183; 100
Owoyin v. Omotosho (1961) 1 All NLR 304; 69, 71, 105, 134
Oyekanmi v. FRN (2019) LPELR-47323(CA); 31, 108
Oyeyemi v. Commissioner for Local Government, Kwara State (1992) 2 SCNJ (Pt. 2) 266; 114
P. D. Hallmark Contractors Nigeria Ltd & Anor v. Gomwalk (2015) LPELR-24462 (CA); 57
PML (Nigeria) Ltd v. FRN (2014) LPELR-22767(CA); 11
PML Securities Company Ltd v. FRN (2014) LPELR-22768(CA); 30
R v. Shephard (1991) 93 Cr. App.R 139; 97, 126
R v. Shepherd (1993) 1 All ER 225, 231; 106, 107
R v. Silverlock (1894) 2 Q. B. 766; 99

R v. Singh (2006) 1 WLR 1564; 66, 82
Rabiu Nafiu v. Kano State (1980) FNLR 509 at 524; 59
Raimi v. Akintoye (1986) 3 NWLR (PT. 26); 97, 134
Rankia v. Maigemu (2003) 6 NWLR (pt. 817) 496, 517; 22
Re: Glaxosmithkline Consumer Nigeria Plc (2019) LPELR-47498 (CA); 87
Rosehill Ltd v. GTB (2016) LPELR-41665(CA); 117
Rowaye v. FRN & ORS (2018) LPELR-45650(CA); 75, 92
Samual & Ors. v. Nigerian Army (2006) LPELR-11751(CA); 6
SDV (Nig) Ltd v. Ojo & Anor (2016) LPELR-40323 (CA); 123
Shonubi v. People of Lagos State (2015) LPELR-24807(CA); 86
Sowemimo v. State (2004) All FWLR PT 203 951; 99
SPDC Ltd v. Farah and Ors (1995) 3 NWLR (Pt. 382); 99
SPDC v. Otoko (1990) 6 NWLR (PT. 159) 693; 99
Stanbic Ibtc Bank v. Longterm Global Capital Ltd & Ors (2021) LPELR – 55610 (CA); 33, 36
Tamkeyar v. Bussa & Ors (2017) LPELR-42987 (CA); 29,
Tarka & Ors. V D.p.p (1961) NLRNLR 63; 115
The State v. Ogbubunjo (2001) LPELR-3223 1 at 40-41 SC; 129, 130
Torti v. Ukpabi (1984) 1 SC 370; 127
Trade Bank Plc. V Chami (2003) 13 NWLR (Pt. 836) 216; 45, 78, 80
Tukur v. Uba & Ors. (2012) LPELR-9337 (SC); 1
Tumionu v. A-G of Delta State (1994) LPELR-14361 (CA); 4
U.B.N. Plc v. Agbontaen & Anor (2018) LPELR-44160 (CA); 47
Udenkwo v. Nwosu (2014) LPELR – 24290 (CA); 30

Udoh & Ors v. Orthopaedic Hospitals Management Board & Anor (1993) 7 SCNJ /(Pt. 2) 436; 59
Udoro & Ors v. The Governor, Akwa Ibom State & Ors. (2008) LPELR-4094(CA); 37
Ukorah v. The State (1977) 4 SC 167; 5
Uli Microfinance Bank (Nig) Ltd v. Norbert (2018) LPELR-44953(CA); 38
Uli Microfinance Bank (Nig) Ltd v. Okwuchukwu (2018) LPELR-44956(CA); 52
Umar & Anor v. Kwari & Ors (2019) LPELR-49454(CA); 108
Umogbai v. Aiyemhoba (2002) FWLR (Pt. 132) 192 CA; 18,
UNICAL & Ors v. Effiong & Ors (2019) LPELR-47976(CA); 110
Usman v. State (2018) LPELR-46568(CA); 3
Uwua Udo v. The State /92016) 2-3 SC (Pt. 111) 29; 90
Uzoma v. Asodike (2009) LPELR-8421(CA); 18,
Uzor v. Delta Freeze Nig. Ltd & Ors (2010) LPELR-9114 (CA); 12, 16,
Waziri v. The State (1997) 3 NWLR (PT. 496) AT 689; 101
Yahaya v. Oparinde (1997) 10 NWLR (PT.523) 126; 4, 10
Yashin v. Barclays Bank DCO (1968) 1 All NLR 171; 72, 73, 105, 134
Yassin v. Barclays Bank DC0 (2001) FWLR (Pt. 44) 21; 21, 69, 70
Yesufu v. ACB (1976) LPELR – SC.542/1975; 21, 80

TABLE OF STATUTES

1999 Constitution, section 233(1); 133
Evidence Act, Cap. 62
Evidence Act
  Ss1 62
  Ss2 62
Ss1, Section 96 70
Ss2, section 96 70
Ss(2)(a) – (d); 110
Section 2e; 131
Section 41; 107
Section 51; 131, 132
Section 52; 131, 132
Section 96(1) ; 70
Section 96(2); 70
Section 97 (1)(h); 131
Section 97(2)e; 131
Section 2(1); 46
Section 2 (2)(a); 86
Section 82(2); 103
Section 83(1)-(5); 61
Section 83(3); 134, 135
Section 84; 66, 67, 82, 91, 117, 129
Section 84(4)(a) 91, 110
Section 84(4)(b); 92, 110

Section 84(1)-(4); 62, 132
Section 84(2); 51, 52, 132
Section 84(2)(b); 92
Section 84(2)(c; 93
Section 84(3); 92, 132
Section 84 (4); 33, 34, 103, 107, 115, 128, 129, 132
Section 84(4)c; 92, 93
Section 84(5); 115
Section 84(5)c; 109
Section 87(a)-e; 60
Section 84(1)(d); 67
Section 89(a); 61
Section 90(1)(c; 87
Section 90(2) 71
Section 90(3); 71
Section 91(a)-(c); 61
Section 94 66, 82
Section 94(1) 82
Section 94 (2) 82
Section 96 72
Section 96(1) 45
Section 96(1)(b) 73
Section 96(2) 45
Section 97(1) 45
Section 97 (2) 45
Section 97(2)(a) 46
Section 97 (2)e 46, 130, 131
Section 102(b) 86, 87
Section 125 66, 82
Section 126 66, 82
Section 226(1); 71
Section 251(1); 128, 129

Section 258 91
Section 258(1); 59, 107
Section 258(1)(a); 58
Section 258(1)(d) 65, 81
Evidence Act, 2004
Section 37; 123
Section 97; 123
Evidence Act, 1990 15
Evidence Act, 2011; 10, 20, 21, 25, 28
Part III; 41
Ss1; 39, 41, 47
Ss1 of Section 84; 118
ss2; 39, 40, 44, 47
ss2 (a) – (d) 44
ss2 of Section 84; 116, 119, 121
ss4 of Section 84; 118
ss5 of Section 84; 118
Section 34(i)(b); 131
Section 41; 126
Section 51; 47, 56, 126
Section 68; 95, 102
Section 89(1)(h); 47
Section 90(1)(e) 47
Section 83; 112, 123
Section 84; 35, 36, 43, 44, 49, 50, 51, 63, 75, 97, 104, 106, 108, 109, 110, 112, 121, 122, 124
Section 84 (4) (a) and (b); 44, 105
Section 84(5)(a); 83
Section 84(5)c; 83
Section 84(1); 39, 50, 117, 119, 123
Section 84(2); 50, 52, 104, 105, 108, 111, 117, 119, 124
Section 84(3)(d) 115

Section 84 (1) – (5), 2; 36, 39, 52
Section 84 (4); 35, 103, 111
Section 84 (4) – (5); 34, 35
Section 84(4)(a); 106, 116
Section 84(4)(b); 106,
Section 84(b)(i); 116
Section 84/(5)(a); 76, 116
Section 84(5)c; 76, 116
Section 84 (5)c; 44
Section 85; 88, 90
Section 86; 88, 90
Section 86(1)-(4); 60
Section 86(4); 89
Section 87; 88
Section 102; 88
Section 103; 88
Section 89(1)(h); 50
Section 90(1)e ; 50
Section 96(1); 73
Section 96(2); 73
Section 124(1); 41
Section 124(1) – (3); 39, 52
Section 125; 39, 52
Section 126(a) –(d); 39, 52
Section 140; 56
Section 258; 111
Section 258(1); 42, 55, 57, 59, 124
Section 258(1); 39
Evidence (Amendment Act) 2023
Inheritance (Family Provision) Act, 1938 7
National Library Act
Section 2(2)(a); 88, 89

Section 4(1); 88, 89
Section 4(7)c; 88
Section (7)(c); 88
UK Police and Criminal Evidence Act, 1984
Section 69; 97, 125
Section 69(1); 107, 108
UK Youth Justice and Criminal Evidence Act, 1999
Section 60
Housing Act, 1957
Section 113(4); 113
Fugitive Offenders Act, 1881
Section 10; 113
Nigerian Evidence Act, 2011
Ss1; 164, 169, 180, 183, 190, 197, 203, 205, 215, 220
Ss2; 169, 171, 172, 197
Ss2(a); 170
Ss4; 168
Section 3; 176
Section 7; 217
Section 36(4); 215
Section 39; 159
Section 59; 164
Section 60; 164
Section 61; 164
Section 62; 164
Section 68; 165
Section 76; 165
Section 78; 167
Section 82; 167
Section 89; 179
Section 89(a); 175
Section 90; 179

Section 91; 174
Section 102; 174
Section 135; 197
Section 140; 197
Section 148; 202
Section 155; 179, 202
Section 175; 220
Section 180; 212
Section 182(1); 214
Section 192; 216
Section 199; 217
Section 201; 218
Section 204; 218
Section 208; 220
Section 217; 212
Section 218; 212
Section 219; 212
Section 221; 212
Section 222; 212
Section 223; 212
Section 224; 212
Section 225; 212
Section 226; 212
Section 231; 212
Section 290; 159
Section 291; 159
Section 300; 212
Section 301; 212
Section 319; 159
Section 340; 212
Section 341; 212
Section 357; 212

Section 362; 212
Section 369; 212
Section 270; 212
Section 371; 212
Section 458; 213
Section (1); 137
Section (2); 137
Section (3); 137
Section (4) – (13); 137
Section (14) – (36); 137
Section (37) – (82); 138
Section (83) – (120); 140
Section (121) – (124); 141
Section (125) – (127); 141
Section (128) – (130); 141
Section 128; 194
Section 129; 194
Section (131) – (144); 142
Section (145) – (174); 142
Section (175) – (204); 142
Section (205) – (247); 144
Section (248) – (250); 146
Section (251); 146
Section (252) – (254); 146
Section (255) – (259); 146
Criminal Procedure Act
Ss1; 164, 169, 180, 183, 233, 235
Ss2; 169, 171, 172
Ss2(a); 170
Ss4; 168
Section 3; 176
Section 39; 159

Section 59; 164
Section 60; 164
Section 61; 164
Section 62; 164
Section 68; 165
Section 76; 165
Section 78; 167
Section 82; 167
Section 89; 179, 210
Section 89(a); 175
Section 90; 179, 210
Section 91; 174
Section 102; 174
Section 134; 237
Section 140; 237
Section 155; 179
Section 290; 159
Section 291; 159
Section 319; 159
Matrimonial Causes Act
Section 84; 205
Criminal Code Act
Ss1; 218, 229, 230, 231
Ss1. Section 51; 219
Section 40; 218
Section 41; 218
Section 42; 218
Section 97(1); 230
Section 180; 224
Section 191; 221, 226, 228
Section 208; 219
Section 209; 219

Section 223; 224
Section 224; 225, 232
Section 225; 232
Section 239; 229
Section 240; 229
Section 243; 230

TABLE OF CONTENTS

Dedication
Acknowledgements
Preface
Foreword
Table of Cases
Table of Statutes

CHAPTER 1: MEANING AND CLASSIFICATION OF EVIDENCE

- Meaning of Evidence - 1
  -Testimony, documents and tangible objects that tend to prove or disprove the existence of an alleged fact constitute evidence; 1
  -Evidence encompasses and includes the means employed for the purpose of proving a disputed fact; 2
  -Any species of proof, or probative matters legally presented at the trial can constitute evidence; 2
- Direct evidence as a classification of evidence - 3
- Direct evidence is the best evidence - 3
- Distinction between Circumstantial Evidence and Direct Evidence - 4

- Circumstantial evidence is a form of Indirect Evidence in the Classification of Evidence; 5

  - Circumstantial or Indirect Evidence is very often the Best Evidence; 5

  - Mathematical accuracy is required in circumstantial evidence
- Distinction between Circumstantial Evidence and Direct Evidence - 5
- Court's findings must be supported by concrete and real evidence - 6
- Commentary - 6

CHAPTER 2: PRIMARY AND SECONDARY DOCUMENTARY EVIDENCE

- How the contents of a document can be proved - 11
- Primary evidence means the document itself - 11
- Primary evidence of a public document is the document itself or a certified true copy of it - 12
- Proof of documents must strictly be by primary evidence except in cases where secondary evidence can then be tendered - 12
- The phrase "the only type of secondary evidence" does not exclude primary evidence from being admissible - 13
- Primary evidence needs not be certified before it can be admitted in evidence - 16
- Secondary evidence is admissible in law - 17
- Photocopy of a public document to be admissible in Evidence needs to be certified - 17

- A wrongly certified public document can be re-certified and re-tendered - 18
- Position of the law on dissimilarity in signatures - 18
- The purpose of a certificate is to authenticate the means of production - 18
- Categories of evidence that are inadmissible and the exceptions under Sections 89(h) and 90(1)(e) of the Evidence Act - 20
- Commentary - 21

CHAPTER 3: LAYING OF FOUNDATION FOR THE ADMISSIBILITY OF DOCUMENTARY/ ELECTRONIC EVIDENCE

- Document tendered in the nature of secondary evidence without any explanation of the whereabouts of the original would be rejected - 24
- Photocopies of a document is admissible when proper foundation has been laid for it - 25
- Foundations to be laid for the Admissibility of Secondary Evidence - 26
- What is required in laying proper foundation for admission of secondary evidence - 26
- Photocopies of documents are admissible in criminal trials without proper foundation in certain circumstances - **27**
- Proper foundation is required for the admissibility of a secondary document - 27
- Essence of laying proper foundation for the admissibility of documentary evidence - 29

- The contents of a document can only be proved by tendering the original document or secondary evidence thereof after laying the proper foundation - 30
- Instances where laying of foundation would not be needed for the admissibility of a private document - 31
- Failure to lay the necessary foundation regarding the condition of the electronic gadget or computer they were used is fatal to the extent of not fulfilling the conditions spelt out in section 84 of the Evidence Act - 32
- Electronic evidence without an accompanying certificate of identification as stipulated in Section 84 (4) of the Evidence Act - 33
- Computer-generated document tendered by a party whose computer did produce the document is admissible without need for certification as required by Section 84(4) of the Evidence Act, 2011 - 33
- Commentary - 35

CHAPTER 4: ADMISSIBILITY OF PHOTOGRAPHS/PICTURES, DIGITAL CAMERA(S) AND ELECTRONIC STATEMENT OF ACCOUNT

- Definition of the word "Photograph" - 37
- Pictures and photographs are admissible primary evidence - 37
- Court can take judicial notice of the fact that the appellant operates or carries on business with the aid of computers - 38

- If photographs are taken with a digital camera or produced from a digital camera, it becomes a computer -generated document by virtue of Section 84(5)(C) of The Evidence Act, 2011 - 43
- Conditions for the admissibility of a bank statement of account - 44
- Electronic ledger or statement of account derived electronically are not excluded, being documents derivable or generated from a computer - 47
- Judicial notice may be taken of the fact that many banks now operate their banking businesses through computer-generated documentary evidence - 52
- A statement of account, alone and without other or further evidence, oral or documentary, is not sufficient evidence to form or warrant a charge of liability of a person - 56
- Distinction between a "copy of a document" and a "document" - 57
- Commentary - 63

CHAPTER 5: ADMISSIBILITY OF SMS FROM GLOBAL SATELLITE MOBILE (GSM), TELEPHONE CONVERSATIONS, EMAILS, TAPE RECORDINGS AND ELECTRONIC SERVICE OF COURT PROCESSES

- A GSM gadget with useful information can be tendered in evidence together with the message or information stored by it - 65
- Position of the law on admissibility of telephone conversations/messages - 67

- Admissibility of recorded conversations of persons who are deceased - 67
- Distinction between an instrument and a telephone conversation - 74
- The test of admissibility of electronically generated documents such as an email is its authenticity and trustworthiness and the relevance of its content to the proceedings - 74
- Electronic evidence as a medium of service of court processes is admissible - 78
  -Electronic service of hearing notice is valid; 80
- Tape recordings fall under the category of evidence that is admissible upon the fulfilment of certain conditions - 80
- Commentary - 81

CHAPTER 6: ADMISSIBILITY OF FINGERPRINT EVIDENCE, ONLINE NEWSPAPER AND NEWSPAPER PUBLICATION

- When fingerprint evidence can be admissible - 86
- An online newspaper publication is a computer generated evidence is admissible under Section 84 of the Evidence Act - 86
- An Internet print out of a newspaper is admissible as a secondary evidence of same by virtue of sections 85 and 87(a) of the Evidence Act 2011 - 87
- Position of the law on admissibility of newspaper publication - 87
- Commentary -90

CHAPTER 7: EXPERT OPINION ON COMPUTER GENERATED EVIDENCE

- Who is an Expert? - 94
- When is the evidence of an expert necessary? - 94
- Position of the law with regard to opinion evidence - 94
- The reliability and functionality of a computer used in generating a document can be made by oral evidence - 97
- Commentary - 98

CHAPTER 8: CONDITIONS FOR THE ADMISSIBILITY OF COMPUTER GENERATED EVIDENCE

- Evidence in relation to the use of a computer must be called to establish the conditions set out under Section 84(2) of the Evidence Act, 2011 - 103
- Internet-generated documents are not the only form of documents caught by the admissibility requirements of Section 84 of the Evidence Act 2011 - 106
- Parole evidence of a person familiar with the operation of a computer can be given of its reliability and functionality in the absence of a certificate under Section 84(4) of the Evidence Act - 107
- A computer-generated evidence is not admissible in evidence in that it is not accompanied by Certificate of Compliance - 108
- The provision of Section 84(2) of the Evidence Act, 2011 is mandatory and allows for no discretion - 108

- Electronic evidence that offends Section 84 of the Evidence Act, 2011 are to be expunged - 109
- Section 84 of the Evidence Act 2011 consecrates two methods of proof, either by oral evidence under Section 84(1) and (2) or by a Certificate under Section 84(4) - 110
- In construing the provisions of Sections 83 and 84 of The Evidence Act, 2011, attention has to be given to each and every punctuation inserted between one section, subsection or paragraph to arrive at the intention of the Legislature - 112
- The provision of Section 84(2) of the Evidence Act, 2011 is mandatory and allows for no discretion - 116
- Evidence in relation to the use of a computer must be called to establish the conditions set out under Section 84(2) of the Evidence Act, 2011 - 117
- The Evidence Act provides an elaborate protocol for the receipt of electronic evidence - 123
- Commentary - 123

CHAPTER 9: APPEALS ON COMPUTER GENERATED EVIDENCE

- Wrongfully admitted/excluded evidence only cannot constitute a ground for reversing a decision on appeal - **128**
- Where wrongful admission and or rejection of electronic evidence will not make any difference to the decision reached, the wrongful admission shall not be a basis on which to reverse the decision of the Lower Court - **129**

- When a document has substantially complied with the provisions of Section 97(2)(E) of the Evidence Act and admitted without objection, a party cannot later raise objection to it on appeal - 130
- An objection cannot be raised on the admissibility of evidence which the court had ruled on - 131
- The Supreme Court cannot pronounce on an issue not raised at the court of appeal regarding the admissibility of a document electronic or otherwise - 132
- A document not tendered at the trial court due to the inadvertence of counsel can be tendered on appeal as fresh evidence - 133
- Commentary - 133

APPENDIX - Evidence Act 2011 (as amended by the Evidence Amendment Act, 2023) - 136

INDEX - 243

Chapter 1

MEANING AND CLASSIFICATION OF EVIDENCE

MEANING OF EVIDENCE

The Supreme Court of Nigeria in the case of *Tukur* v. *UBA & Ors.* (2012) LPELR-9337 (SC) Per Ariwoola, J.S.C. at Pp 44-45, paras E-A remarked thus:

> What then is Evidence? "Evidence, broadly defined, is the means from which an inference may logically be drawn as to the existence of a fact; that which makes evident or plain. 'Evidence' is the demonstration of a fact, it signifies that which demonstrates, makes clear, ascertains the truth of the very fact or point in issue, either on the one side or on the other. In legal acceptation, the term 'evidence' includes all the means by which any alleged matter of fact, the truth of which is submitted to investigation, is established or disproved. 'Evidence' has also been defined to mean any species of proof legally presented at the trial of an issue, by the act of the parties and through the medium of witnesses, records, documents concrete objects and the like.

Testimony, Documents and tangible objects that tend to Prove or Disprove the Existence of an alleged Fact Constitute Evidence

Tsamiya, J.C.A. at Pp. 24-25, paras. D-A in the case of *Eze v. Okoloagu & Ors* (2009) LPELR-3922(CA) posited thus:

As it is known, the term 'evidence' is defined as, the "facts; sign or objects that make you believe that something is true; or the information that is used in a court of law to try to prove something." See *Oxford Advance Learner's Dictionary* p. 398. While in Black's Law Dictionary, 7th Edition, pages 76, the term 'evidence' is defined to mean; something (including testimony, documents and tangible objects) that tends to prove or disprove the existence of an alleged fact. Case law authorities, defined 'evidence' as the means whereby the Court is informed as to the issues of facts as ascertained by the pleading; it is the testimony, whether oral or documentary or real, which is produce before a court, or tribunal some facts in dispute. See *Fed. Milit Governor* v. *Sani* (No.2) (1989) 4 NWLR (Pt.117) 684; *Lawal* v. *Union Bank of Nigeria Plc.* (1995) 2 NWLR (Pt.378) 407.

Evidence Encompasses and Includes the Means Employed for the Purpose of Proving a Disputed Fact

In further elucidating the definition of Evidence, the Supreme Court of Nigeria in the case of *Arum* v. *Nwobodo* (2013) LPELR-20390(SC) Per Aka'ahs, J.S.C. at P. 40, paras. A-B held as follows:

> In *Chukwuogor* v. *Obiora supra* Oputa J.S.C. defined Evidence in these words at pages 477 - 478. "In its broad sense, Evidence encompasses and includes the means employed for the purpose of proving a disputed fact."

Any Species of Proof, or Probative Matters Legally Presented at the Trial can constitute evidence

Salami, J.C.A. at P.28, Paras. E-G in the case of *Citizens International Bank Ltd.* v. *SCOA Nigeria Ltd. & Anor.* (2006) LPELR-5509(CA) posited thus:

> Evidence according to *Blacks' Law Dictionary* 5th Edition pg. 498 means - "Any species of proof, or probative matters

> legally presented at the trial of an issue by the act of the parties and through the medium of witnesses, records, documents, exhibits, concrete objects, etc., for the purpose of inducing belief on the minds of the court."

DIRECT EVIDENCE AS A CLASSIFICATION OF EVIDENCE

In the case of *Obot* v. *State* (2019) LPELR-48172 (CA), Shuaibu, J.C.A. at Pp. 10-11, Paras. C-A in dealing with the nature of direct evidence required to prove cause of death stated thus:

> Learned counsel for the respondent has submitted rightly that the guilt of the accused could be proved either by direct evidence or circumstantial evidence that creates no room for doubt or speculation. The direct evidence required to prove the cause of death must be such as would connect the death of the deceased person with the act of the accused. This may include the evidence of the medical officer who examined or performed post-mortem examination on the death and certifies that the injuries inflicted on the deceased by the accused are those that caused the death of the deceased, particularly if the deceased did not die in the course of the act of his assailant.

DIRECT EVIDENCE IS THE BEST EVIDENCE

In the case of *Usman* v. *State* (2018) LPELR-46568 (CA), *Abba Aji*, J.C.A. at P. 15, Paras. B-E held as follows:

> Direct evidence is said to be the best evidence. Section 126 of the Evidence Act, 2011, requires that oral evidence in all cases must be direct. Evidence is direct when, if the fact to be proved was seen, then by the witness who saw it. If it was heard, then it must be the evidence of the witness who heard it. See Per *Eko*, J.S.C in *Chudi Verdical Co. Ltd* v. *Ifesinachi Industries (Nig) Ltd & Anor* (2018) LPELR-44701(SC). Evidence

of a witness which the Court must act on is the direct oral evidence of a witness. That is what it takes to have a fact receivable as direct oral evidence of a witness. See *Yahaya* v. *Oparinde* (1997) 10 NWLR (PT. 523) 126; *Ojo* v. *Gharoro* (1999) 8 NWLR (PT. 615) 387.

DISTINCTION BETWEEN CIRCUMSTANTIAL EVIDENCE AND DIRECT EVIDENCE

In the case of *Tumionu* v. *A-G of Delta State (1994) LPELR-14361(CA),* Ige, J.C.A. at P. 17, paras. C-D remarked as follows:

> Circumstantial evidence usually is contrasted with direct evidence. By direct evidence as in this case, there must be the evidence of an eyewitness of the incident of murder. By circumstantial evidence it means indirect evidence or existence of some facts from which an inference of a true fact can be made.

CIRCUMSTANTIAL EVIDENCE IS A FORM OF INDIRECT EVIDENCE IN THE CLASSIFICATION OF EVIDENCE

Pemu, J.C.A at Pp. 30-31, paras. E-B in the case of *Bajulaiye* v. *State* (2012) LPELR-7995 (CA) remarked as follows:

> "Circumstantial evidence" has been defined in the *Blacks' Law Dictionary* 8th Edition as "evidence based on inference and not on personal knowledge or observation" Again it is described as "indirect evidence". That which is applied to the principal fact, indirectly or through the medium of other facts, by establishing certain circumstances or minor facts, already described as evidentiary, from which the principal facts is extracted and gathered by a process of special inference - Alexander M. Burrill, *A Treatise on the Natural Principles and Rules of Circumstantial Evidence.* 4 (1868). Again, it is defined by Williams P. Richardson, *The Law of Evidence* III at (3rd

Edition 1928) as "Evidence of some collateral fact from which the existence or non-existence of some fact in question may be inferred as a probable consequence, is termed circumstantial evidence."

Circumstantial or Indirect Evidence is very often the Best Evidence

Edozie, J.C.A at P. 46, Paras E-G in the case of *Nwankwo & Anor.* v. *FRN* (2002) LPELR-7089(CA) held thus:

> It has been said that circumstantial evidence is very often the best evidence. It is evidence of surrounding circumstances which by undesigned coincidence, is capable of proving a proposition with the accuracy of mathematics. It is no derogation of evidence to say that it is circumstantial; *R.* v. *Taylor, Weaver and Donovan* 21 Cr. App. R 20.

Mathematical Accuracy is required in Circumstantial Evidence

In the case *Aihenvba* v. *State* (2016) LPELR-40134(CA), Ogakwu, J.C.A. at Pp. 30-31, Paras. D-A held as follows:

> Let me make it clear that as held by the apex Court in *Nweke* v. *The State* (2001) LPELR-2119 (SC) 1 at 11:" Circumstantial evidence is very often the best. It is evidence of surrounding circumstances which, by undesigned coincidence, is capable of proving a proposition with the accuracy of mathematics. It is no derogation of evidence to say that it is circumstantial." See also *Adie* v. *The State* (1980) 1-2 SC 116 and *Ukorah* v. *The State* (1977) 4 SC 167.

DISTINCTION BETWEEN CIRCUMSTANTIAL EVIDENCE AND DIRECT EVIDENCE

In the case of *Etumionu* v. *A-G of Delta State* (1994) LPELR-14361(CA), Ige, J.C.A. at P. 17, paras. C-D held thus:

> Circumstantial evidence usually is contrasted with direct evidence. By direct evidence as in this case, there must be the evidence of an eyewitness of the incident of murder. By circumstantial evidence it means indirect evidence or existence of some facts from which an inference of a true fact can be made.

COURT'S FINDINGS MUST BE SUPPORTED BY CONCRETE AND REAL EVIDENCE

Augie, J.C.A. at P. 31, Paras. A-D in the case of *Samual & Ors.* v. *Nigerian Army (2006) LPELR-11751(CA)* posited as follows:

> ... it is trite law that a Court's findings must be supported by concrete and real evidence and not speculation - see *Millar* v. *State* (2005) 8 NWLR (pt 927) 236 & *Ahmed* v. *State* (2001) 18 NWLR (pt. 746) 622 where Ayoola, JSC said: "Our criminal justice system loses its essential requirement of proof by evidence beyond reasonable doubt if persons accused of crime are convicted on mere suspicion or mere speculation, however intelligent that may be notwithstanding the inadequacy of evidence. Whatever the reason for the inadequacy of evidence or absence of essential evidence may be it is immaterial to the duty of the Court not to convict an accused of an offence not proved by evidence."

COMMENTARY

Court decisions are to be based on truth founded on evidence and the primary duty of courts is to conduct proper proceedings so as to hear and consider evidence. The law of evidence is made up largely of procedural regulations concerning the proof and presentation of facts, whether involving the testimony of witnesses, the presentation of documents or physical objects, or the assertion of a foreign law. The many rules of evidence that have evolved under different legal systems have, in the main, been founded on experience and shaped by varying legal requirements of what constitutes admissible and sufficient proof.[1] Although evidence, in this sense, has both legal and technical characteristics, judicial evidence has always been a human rather than a technical problem. During different periods and at different cultural stages, problems concerning evidence have been resolved by widely different methods. Since the means of acquiring evidence are clearly variable and delimited, they can result only in a degree of probability and not in an absolute truth in the philosophic sense. Only Soviet doctrine, under the influence of philosophical materialism, expresses a belief that absolute, objective truth can be attained through evidence. In common law countries, civil cases require only preponderant probability and criminal cases, probability beyond reasonable doubt. In civil-law countries so much probability is required that reasonable doubts are excluded. In *Phipson on Evidence*,[2] evidence was defined in the following language:

> Evidence, as used in judicial proceedings, has several meanings. The two main senses of the word are: first, the means, apart from argument and inference, whereby the Court is informed as to the issues of fact as ascertained by the pleadings; secondly, the subject-matter of such means. The word is also used to denote that some fact may be admitted as proof and also in some cases that some fact has relevance to the issues of fact. In a real sense evidence is that which may be placed before the Court in order that it may decide the issues of fact. There also are other shades of meaning that it is not necessary to discuss here. Thus it has been held that "evidence" in the Inheritance (Family Provision) Act, 1938

[1] See *The New Encyclopedia, Britannica Macropedia*, Vol. 7 at p. 1.

[2] *Phipson on Evidence*, 12th Edition at pp 2-3 paragraphs 3-5

> covers all the material that persons outside a Court of law take into consideration when deciding how to act. Evidence, in the first sense, means the testimony, whether oral, documentary or real, which may be legally received in order to prove or disprove some fact in dispute. Facts: No satisfactory definition of the term "fact" has been or perhaps can be given. Broadly it applies to whatever is the subject of perception or consciousness. But juridically it has generally to be distinguished from law, sometimes from opinion, and sometimes from testimony and documents. It is not possible always to apply these distinctions consistently...

The subject of evidence is not one which lends itself readily either to definitions or divisions. Few of its terms have acquired settled or unambiguous meanings, and no to writers adopt the same classification. The following divisions or distinctions, however, which are commonly observed in practice or by writers, comprise all that are really essential to be noticed: Direct, indirect and real evidence[3]. By direct evidence is meant that the existence of a given thing or fact is proved either by its actual production, or by the testimony or admissible declaration of someone who has himself perceived it. By indirect or presumptive evidence is meant that other facts are thus proved, from which the existence of the given fact may be logically inferred. The two forms are equally admissible, and the testimony, whether to the *factum probandum* or the *facta probantia,* is equally direct; but the superiority of the former is that it contains at most only one source of error, fallibility of assertion, while the latter has, in addition, fallibility of inference. Little is to be gained from a comparison of their weight, since, save in the case of actual production, both forms admit of every degree of cogency

[3] Ibid.

from the lowest to the highest. Real Evidence on its part is material objects other than documents, produced for inspection of the Court, is commonly called real evidence. This, when available, is probably the most satisfactory kind of all, since, save for identification or explanation, neither testimony nor inference is relied upon. Unless its genuineness is in dispute, the thing speaks for itself. Unfortunately, however, the term "real evidence" is itself both indefinite and ambiguous, having been used in three divergent senses: (1) Evidence from things as distinct from persons. (2) Material objects produced from the inspection of the Court. This is the second and most widely accepted meaning of "real evidence".

It must be borne in mind that there is a distinction between a document used as a record of a transaction, such as a conveyance, and a document as a thing. It depends on the circumstances in which classification it falls. On a charge of stealing a document, for example, the document is a "thing". The best evidence rule stipulates that admissible evidence to prove any fact or relevant fact in dispute is to come from vital witnesses or documentary exhibits depending on the nature of the proceedings. The *New Encyclopaedia, Britannica*,[4] reads as follows:

> THE CLASSIC MEANS OF PROOF: According to Anglo-American law, the classic means of proof are witnesses, documents, and real evidence (derived from the actual inspection of objects). As a result of historical development, the status of witness was accorded to experts and to the parties in a civil lawsuit, and even to the accused in criminal proceedings. The development of continental European law has taken a different course. Parties cannot be witnesses, and

[4] The *New Encyclopaedia, Britannica*, Vol.7, p.3.

> evidence by experts is subject to special procedural rules. Consequently, there are essentially five separate sources of evidence: witnesses, parties, experts, documents, and real evidence.

Direct evidence is said to be the best evidence. Section 126 of the Evidence Act, 2011, requires that oral evidence in all cases must be direct. Evidence is direct when, if the fact to be proved was seen, then by the witness who saw it. If it was heard, then it must be the evidence of the witness who heard it[5]. Evidence of a witness which the Court must act on is the direct oral evidence of a witness. That is what it takes to have a fact receivable as direct oral evidence of a witness and is generally regarded as the best evidence.[6]

---

[5] Per Eko, J.S.C in *Chudi Verdical Co. Ltd* v. *Ifesinachi Industries (Nig) Ltd & Anor* (2018) LPELR-44701(SC).

[6] See the cases of *Yahaya* v. *Oparinde* (1997) 10 NWLR (PT. 523) 126; *Ojo* v. *Gharoro* (1999) 8 NWLR (PT. 615) 387.

Chapter 2

PRIMARY AND SECONDARY DOCUMENTARY EVIDENCE

HOW THE CONTENTS OF A DOCUMENT CAN BE PROVED

Commenting on how the contents of a document can be proved, Lokulo-Sodipe, J.C.A. at P. 24, paras. A-C in the case of *PML (Nigeria) Ltd* v. *FRN* (2014) LPELR-22767(CA) held thus:

> The content of a document can only be proved by tendering the original document or secondary evidence thereof after laying the proper foundation. See *Goodwill* & *Trust Investment Ltd* v. *Witt & Bush Ltd* (2011) All FWLR (Pt. 576) 517, (2011) 34 WRN 1. Hence the content of a document cannot ordinarily be established *viva voce*. See *Ogundele* v. *Agiri* (2010) 9 WRN 1.

PRIMARY EVIDENCE MEANS THE DOCUMENT ITSELF

Bolaji -Yusuff, J.C.A. at P. 36, para. G in the case of *Okafor* v. *Okafor & Ors* (2014) LPELR-23561(CA), held as follows:

> Primary evidence means the document itself produced for the inspection of the Court.

PRIMARY EVIDENCE OF A PUBLIC DOCUMENT IS THE DOCUMENT ITSELF OR A CERTIFIED TRUE COPY OF IT

In *MV Delos* v. *Ocean Steamship (Nig.) Ltd* (2004) 17 NWLR (PT 901) AT PG. 103 Paras E-F, Chukwuma-Eneh JCA posited as follows:

> If I may observe, primary evidence of a public document is the document itself or a certified true copy of it; in this instance, only the document itself or its certified true copy can be used to prove the contents of the counter-claim. Again, it is not proper to rely on Clause 50 as stipulated in exhibit FA3 (a public document) as the basis for the said charter party and the arbitration clause when exhibit FA3 is not a certified true copy; nor is the deposition in paragraph 6 of the supporting affidavit to the application even though on oath of any assistance as the proof of the contents of the counter-claim and in other words, the arbitral award of the arbitration filed before the New York arbitration panel.

PROOF OF DOCUMENTS MUST STRICTLY BE BY PRIMARY EVIDENCE EXCEPT IN CASES WHERE SECONDARY EVIDENCE CAN THEN BE TENDERED

In the case of *Uzor* v. *Delta Freeze Nig. Ltd & Ors* (2010) LPELR-9114(CA), Thomas, J.C.A. at P. 47, paras. C-E held thus:

> It is settled law that the proof of documents must strictly be by primary evidence except in cases stipulated under section 97 of the Evidence Act where secondary evidence can then be tendered and will be accepted. Under Section 94(1) of the Act, the meaning of primary evidence is defined. It reads as follows: "s.94 (1) Primary evidence means the document itself produced for the inspection of the court."

THE PHRASE "THE ONLY TYPE OF SECONDARY EVIDENCE" DOES NOT EXCLUDE PRIMARY EVIDENCE FROM BEING ADMISSIBLE

Commenting on the above, *Orji-Abadua*, J.C.A. at Pp. 41-45, paras. B-F in the case of *Kubau* v. *Rilwanu* (2013) LPELR-22346(CA) remarked thus:

> ...With the greatest respect possible to my Lord, Salami, JCA, I do not agree with the view expressed by His Lordship that only certified copies of public documents are admissible. My Lord, Salami, JCA, seems to have relied on the case of Obadina family and Executors of *Chief J.A. Ajao* v. *Ambrose Family & Ors.* (1969) 1 NMLR 25 at 30, where the Supreme Court, per Coker, J.S.C. stated as follows:
>
> "The combined effect of the subsection is that in the case of public documents, the only type of secondary evidence permissible is a certified true copy of the document and none other. The document now marked exhibit "2" is not a certified copy but a Photostat copy and it is therefore inadmissible as secondary evidence of a public document which it purports to be. There was no objection to its admissibility when it was produced but it is not within the competence of parties to a case to admit by consent or otherwise a document which, by law, is inadmissible."
>
> A critical examination of that case shows that what His Lordship, Coker, J.S.C. was considering was the admissibility of various types of secondary evidence and in particular a certified copy and a photocopy came to the conclusion that among the various types of secondary evidence of a public document, the only type that is in admissible is a certified true copy thereof. The consideration was not between the original, i.e., primary and secondary evidence of a public document. The phrase "the only type of secondary evidence" does not seem to me to exclude primary evidence from being admissible. Section 93 of the Evidence Act, provides that: "the

contents of documents may be proved either by primary or secondary evidence." Section 94(1) defines primary evidence as "the document itself". Section 96 of the Evidence Act provides that "documents must be proved by primary evidence," except in the Cases to be mentioned later. There is no section of the Evidence Act that provides that no primary evidence of a public document is admissible. Section 112 of the Act allows certified true copy to be produced in proof of the contents of public document or part of public document. I do not think the provision of section 112 of the Act renders the primary evidence of public document inadmissible in evidence. In my view, the net effect of sections 91(1)(a), 93, 94(1), 95, 97(1)(e) and 112 of the evidence is that the contents of public documents such as the report and the white paper in question may be proved by producing the originals themselves for the court to inspect as primary evidence. If the maker of the statement, as in this case had personal knowledge of the matter dealt with by the statement, i.e. DW1, or prove by the production of their certified true copies as secondary evidence, the two documents being public documents. By virtue of section 96 of the Evidence Act, it is my view that public documents are provable by their originals. It says: "Documents must be proved by primary evidence except in the cases herein after mentioned." Although section 112 allows certified true copies thereof to be used as well. It does not make original inadmissible. These sections of the Evidence Act in summary lay down that in proving the contents of documents; the emphasis is on the production of their originals, i.e. their primary evidence. They however go on to provide that if the contents are to be proved by secondary evidence, a restricted type of secondary evidence only may be accepted i.e. certified copies in the case of public documents. In *Anatogu & ors* v. *Igwe Iweka II & ors.* (1995) 8 NWLR Part 415 page 547 at 572, The Supreme Court, per Uwais, J.S.C. (as he then was) talking on the mode for tendering public documents in Court stated *inter alia*, as follows:

"In my opinion, the documents could only be admitted in evidence if they satisfied the provisions of section 90 subsection 1 or section 112 of the Evidence Act quoted above.

The latter section allows for certified copies of the documents to be produced, but even then what were sought to be tendered in this case were not certified copies but the original public documents. Had the procedure under sections 110 and 111 been adhered to by the Respondents, the certified copies of the documents would have automatically become admitted in evidence by the trial Judge without P.W.1 giving evidence of them. In other words, the documents would have been directly admissible without any foundation being laid."

It should be noted that sections 90 and 111 being referred to above are now sections 91 and 112 of the Evidence Act, Cap. 112 of the Laws of the Federation, 1990. What the Lord Chief Justice of Nigeria is saying as quoted above is that public documents could be admitted in evidence either under section 91(1) or section 112 of the Evidence Act. If a party intends to tender under section 91(1) he must comply with the procedure under section 91(1) by producing the original document, provided the maker of the statement therein who had personal knowledge of the matters dealt with by the statement is called; or by complying with the provisions section 111 by producing a certified true copy of the document and tender it under section 112 of the Evidence Act. It seems to me in the circumstance that the authority i.e. the case of *Lawson* v. *Afani Continental Co. (Nig.) Ltd* (*supra*) relied upon by the tribunal is very much incongruous and inconsistent with the two cases of the Supreme Court, namely:- Obadina family and Executors of Chief J.A. Ajiao v. Ambrose family & 7 ors (supra) and *Philip Antagu* v. *Igwe Iweka II* (*supra*). In the instant case on appeal, the Appellant as 1st Respondent at the trial tribunal, call DW1 as witness. DW1 was the Chairman of the Administrative Panel of Inquiry set up by the Borno State Government to investigate Revenue Generation and Utilization of the Maiduguri Metropolitan Council. He gave unchallenged evidence that he was the Chairman of the Panel of Inquiry set by the Borno State Government. He gave the names of all the members of the panel and stated how they carried out the assignment given to them. Indeed, he laid very good foundation for tendering of both the report of the panel and the Government white paper thereon accepting some of the recommendations of the panel. He has complied with guidelines for tendering original public documents contained in the case of *Philip Anatogu & ors,* v. *Igwe Iweka II & ors.* (*supra*). In that regard, I am of the view that both original report of the panel and original Government White Paper thereon are admissible and majority members of the tribunal were in grave error when they rejected the two documents." It is evident that this Court in *Daggash.* v. *Bulama* (*supra*) overruled itself, meaning, therefore, that its earlier decision in *Lawson* v. *Afani Continental Co. Ltd* (*supra*) cannot take precedence over the latter decision of the Court.

PRIMARY EVIDENCE NEEDS NOT BE CERTIFIED BEFORE IT CAN BE ADMITTED IN EVIDENCE

In *Uzor* v. *Delta Freeze Nig. Ltd & Ors* (2010) LPELR-9114 (CA), Galadima, J.C.A. at Pp. 26-27, paras. E-D held thus:

It is for the foregoing reasons that I shall hold that Exhibit 'B' being primary evidence under Section 94 is admissible without the need for certification by virtue of Sections 93 and, 96 of the Evidence Act. With due respect to the learned trial Judge he was in error in holding that Exhibit 'B' ought to have been certified. It does not require to be certified to render it admissible in evidence. In the case of *Ebu* v. *Obun* (2004) 14 NWLR (pt. 892) 76 at 88, Learned counsel for the Respondent argued that original of public documents ought to be certified to make them admissible. In response to this argument this court held per Opene JCA thus: "I do not know how the Learned counsel came about this argument when a copy of a document is certified, it is certified to be a true copy of the original, if then the original is to be certified, what will it be certified to be? Will it be certified as a true copy of itself (original)?" In conclusion, his Lordship held that the documents were wrongly rejected and ought to have been admitted in evidence. Clearly in view of this decision, I hold that Exhibit 'B' was wrongly rejected and ought to have been considered by the Learned Trial Judge in his judgment instead of treating it as if it had never been admitted.

SECONDARY EVIDENCE IS ADMISSIBLE IN LAW

In *Northwest Energy Nigeria Ltd & Anor* v. *Ibafon Oil Ltd* (2014) LPELR-24133(CA), Obaseki-Adejumo, J.C.A at Pp. 13-14, paras. D-A held as follows:

> Section 90(1)(c) provides that secondary evidence admissible in respect to the original documents referred to the several paragraphs of Section 89 as it relates to paragraph (e) or (f), a certified copy of the document, but no other secondary evidence is admissible. Section 89(d) of the Evidence Act, 2011 provides to the effect that: Secondary evidence may be given to the existence, condition or contents of a document when- a. .... b. .... c. .... d. .... e. the original is a public document within the meaning of section 102.

PHOTOCOPY OF A PUBLIC DOCUMENT TO BE ADMISSIBLE IN EVIDENCE NEEDS TO BE CERTIFIED

Ogunwumiju, J.C.A. at Pp. 39-40, paras. E-A in the case of *Delta State House of Assembly & Anor* v. *DPP & Ors* (2014) LPELR-22808(CA) remarked as follows:

> In this case at hand, I agree with learned appellant's counsel that the substance of the 1st and 2nd respondents case was that the 3rd respondent had defected to another political party. They relied very strongly on a photocopy of the letter dated September 17, 2012 addressed to the 2nd appellant as well as the proceeding of the 1st appellant (attached to the affidavit in support of the originating summons as exhibit RON 4) to establish this critical fact. These documents are public documents within the meaning of S.89 and 90 of the Evidence Act (as amended) and as such only certified copies of them are

> admissible and can be countenanced. In the absence of any certification, the documents are hereby declared inadmissible.

A WRONGLY CERTIFIED PUBLIC DOCUMENT CAN BE RE-CERTIFIED AND RE-TENDERED

In stating the position of the law, Eko, J.C.A. at P. 18, paras. D-F in the case of *Uzoma* v. *Asodike (*2009) LPELR-8421(CA) stated thus:

> It is now settled that a wrongly certified or even an uncertified public document can be re-certified and re-tendered in evidence. See *Umogbai* v. *Aiyemhoba* (2002) FWLR [Pt.132] 192 CA, (2002) 8 NWLR (Pt.770) 687, and also *Law of Evidence in Nigeria* - S.T. Hon at page 287. Poor certification is generally treated as mere irregularity, and the court can order the document to be properly certified by curing the defect complained of.

POSITION OF THE LAW ON DISSIMILARITY IN SIGNATURES

In the case of *GTB Plc* v. *Abiodun* (2017) LPELR-42551(CA), Elechi, J.C.A. at P. 40, Para. A) stated thus:

> It is also settled that mere dissimilarity of the signatures is not conclusive evidence. It is not proof that they were not made by the same person. See also: *Daggash* v. *Bulama* (2004) All FWLR (pt 212) 1666 at 1712.

THE PURPOSE OF A CERTIFICATE IS TO AUTHENTICATE THE MEANS OF PRODUCTION

In the case of *FRN* v. *Ojo & Anor (*2018) LPELR-45541(CA), Obaseki-Adejumo, J.C.A. at Pp. 21-23, Paras. E-E stated thus:

Heavy weather has being made on Section 84(2) of the Evidence Act in respect of a certificate issued by relevant person who did generate computer production. Exhibit Q and R was tendered through PW10 an EFCC Operative head of the Telephone forensic unit he testified on the process of extraction of phone contents with the aid of a computer he extracted text messages from the phones and printed them out through a system in the standard format he identified the document exhibit Q & R but confirmed he did not sign the document as he is not required to sign it after printing. See page 898 of the record vol. 11. There was no certificate covering the computer in line with Section 84 (2) of the Evidence Act. Sections 84 (1) & (2) is reproduced below: "in any proceeding a statement contained in a document produced by a computer shall be admissible as evidence of any fact stated in it of which direct oral evidence would be admissible, if it is shown that the conditions in Subsection (2) of this section are satisfied in relation to the statement and computer in question. (2) The conditions referred to in Subsection (1) of this section are: (a) that the document containing the statement was produced by the computer during a period over which the computer was used regularly to store or process information for the purposes of any activities regularly carried on over that period, whether for profit or not, by anybody, whether corporate or not, or by any individual; (b) that over that period there was regularly supplied to the computer in the ordinary course of those activities information of the kind contained in the statement or of the kind from which the information so contained is derived. The correct interpretation to be given to this Section 84 of the Evidence Act where electronically generated document is sought to be demonstrated is that such electronically generated evidence must be certified and must comply with preconditions laid down in Section 84(2). See *Dickson* v. *Chief Timipre Marilin Sylva & Ors* (2016) LPELR - 41257 (SC); *Kubor* v. *Dickson* (2013) ALL FWLR (PT.676) 392 at 429. Therefore, in the light of the above, Exhibit Q7 & R not having been backed up is inadmissible. The purpose of a certificate is to authenticate the means of production. They are expunged from the records.

CATEGORIES OF EVIDENCE THAT ARE INADMISSIBLE AND THE EXCEPTIONS UNDER SECTIONS 89 (H) AND 90(1) (E) OF THE EVIDENCE ACT

In the case of *Elias* v. *FRN & Anor* (2016) LPELR-40797(CA), Sankey, J.C.A. at pp. 64-67, Paras. E-B held as follows:

> It is trite law that there are certain types of evidence, such as hearsay and unstamped and unregistered documents, which are inadmissible per se and which cannot form the basis for a decision. An objection to these may be taken at any stage of a trial by any of the parties or at the instance of the Court, or even on appeal. However, Section 90 creates an exception wherein it makes certain documents admissible under certain conditions. With particular reference to Section 89(h) and 90(1)(e), copies of entries in banker's books are admissible in evidence under certain conditions. The fulfilment of that condition shall be by oral or affidavit evidence showing that the Exhibits are extracts from a Banker's book, kept by the banker and that the figures copied out had been compared with the original and found to be correct. In considering the admissibility of entries in books of or statements of account, Sections 51, 84, 89 and 90 of the Evidence Act, 2011 are relevant. Section 51 of the Act makes admissible entries in books of account or electronic records regularly kept in the course of business admissible whenever they refer to a matter into which the Court has to inquire. However, the same section provides that such statements alone shall not be sufficient evidence to charge any person with liability. Under Section 89(h), secondary evidence of the existence, condition or contents of an entry in a banker's book is also admissible. The admissibility of such an entry is, however, subject to the fulfilment of the conditions stipulated under Section 90(1)(e). Section 84 allows for the admissibility of a statement contained in a document produced by a computer, banking practices having emerged from the days of parchment and weighty

paper and thus entries in account books to computer or electronic records. It follows therefore that all statements of accounts emanating from banks these days are invariably computer generated. It has been held that in an attempt to satisfy the conditions stated in Section 90(i)-(iv), the evidence of such is not required to be a verbatim reproduction of the facts in the section. It is sufficient that the provisions are substantially complied with. In *Yesufu* v. *ACB* (1976) LPELR-SC.542/1975; (1976) NSCC 202 at 206, the Supreme Court, per Fatayi-Williams, JSC, held thus: It is not the length of evidence given in tendering a bank statement of account that matters but the substance of the evidence given; nor is it compulsory that the precise words set out in Section 97(2) (e) should be used by the witness or the judge taking down his evidence. It is enough that substantially the requirements of the section are observed. Section 97(2) (e) of the Evidence Act referred to therein, is *in pari materia* with Section 90(1) (e) of the Evidence Act, 2011. See also *Kubor* v. *Dickson* (2012) LPELR-9817(SC); *Yassin* v. *Barclays Bank DCO* (2001) FWLR (Pt. 44) 21.

COMMENTARY

Primary evidence means the document itself produced for the inspection of the court.[1] That is the language of section 89(1) of the Evidence Act. By virtue of the provisions of section 83 of the Evidence Act, documents may be proved either by primary or by secondary evidence. However, section 83(1)(b) of the Evidence Act provides that:

> 83(1) - In any civil proceedings where direct oral evidence of a fact would be admissible, any statement made by a person in a document and tending to establish that fact, shall on production of

---

[1] See Y. B Nimpar and S. S. Obende, *Documentary Evidence: The Law Practice and Procedure,* Jos University Press Ltd, (1998), Pp10 to 32.

> the original documents be admissible as evidence of that fact if the following conditions are satisfied...
>
> (b) If the maker of the statement is called as a witness in the proceedings...

Where the maker was not called as a witness in the proceedings and did not show that he has satisfied the proviso of the section of the law permitting a document to be admitted even though the maker was not called to testify, such a document is not admissible since it failed to satisfy the requirement of the law.[2]

In *Asiniola* v. *Fatodu,*[3] Nwaeze JCA, held, *inter alia*, as follows:

> It is axiomatic that English Language is the *lingua franca* of the superior courts in Nigeria. Hence, a document written in the dialect of the parties and which is not translated into the English Language, is of no evidential value and should be discountenanced, *Odwuola* v. *Aina* (2001) 12 NWLR (pt 741) 1, 22, as it is inadmissible, *Dantata* v. *Dantata* (2002) 4 NWLR (pt 756) 144, 162. "For such a document to be admissible, it must be translated into English Language, *Rankia* v. *Maigemu* (2003) 6 NWLR (pt. 817) 496, 517. The translation must be done either by a competent witness called by the party to the proceedings who need to prove his case or by the official interpreter of the court. This is not court's responsibility, *Ojengbede* v. *Esan* (2001) 18 NWLR (pt 746) 771, 790; *Darma* v. *Batagarawa* (2002) 17 NWLR (pt 769) 243, 259, *Dumina* v. *State* (1995) NWLR (pt415) %13, 539, 540; see generally C.C. Nweze, *Contentious issues and Responses in Contemporary Evidence Law in Nigeria* (vol. one) (Enugu: Institute for Development Studies, (University of Nigeria, Enugu Campus, 2003) 340.

---

[2] See *Haruna* v. *Moddibbo* (2004) 16 NWLR (Pt 900) p. 487at 544-6 para F-D.

[3] (2009) 6 NWLR (Pt 1136) 184 at 198.

It has been held in a number of cases that a duly certified public document would be admissible in evidence without laying foundation and that the issue of proper custody and related matters will not arise.[4] It can even be tendered from the bar by or through counsel who is not even a party in the case.[5] The cases of *Maranro* v. *Adebisi* [6] and *Okiki II* v. *Jagun*,[7] are to the effect that a witness who is not a party to a public document can tender the duly certified true copy of the said public document. A public document duly certified is presumed to be genuine. The presumption is though rebuttable as was held in the cases of *Anyaokoro* v. *Obiakor*[8] cited with approval in *Daggash* v. *Bulama*.[9]

---

[4] See the case of *Anatogu* v. *Iweka II* (1995) 2 SCNJ 1 and *Agagu* v. *Dawodu* (1990) 7 NWLR (Pt.160) 56 CA.

[5] See the cases of *Isibor* v. *The state* (1970) 1 ALL MLR 248; *Magaji* v. *Nigerian Army* (2005) ALL FWLR (Pt.257) 1511 and *Ogbunyinya* v. *Okudo* (1979) 1 ANRR 10.

[6] (2008) 26 WRN 182 at p. 200.

[7] (2000) 5 NWLR (Pt.655) 19 at pp. 27 - 28.

[8] (1990) 2 NWLR (PT.130) 52.

[9] (2004) ALL FWLR (Pt.212) 1666 CA.

Chapter 3

LAYING OF FOUNDATION FOR THE ADMISSIBILITY OF DOCUMENTARY AND ELECTRONIC EVIDENCE

DOCUMENT TENDERED IN THE NATURE OF SECONDARY EVIDENCE WITHOUT ANY EXPLANATION OF THE WHEREABOUTS OF THE ORIGINAL WOULD BE REJECTED

Owoade, J.C.A. at pp. 84-85, paras. G-F held in the case of *Obatuga & Anor* v. *Oyebokun & Ors* (2014) LPELR-22344(CA) as follows:

> The first is the contention of the learned senior counsel for the appellants that the document in issue was wrongly rejected. In deciding this issue, I noted that the learned senior counsel conceded in his brief of argument that the document tendered but rejected is not a public document and clearly therefore there was no requirement of certification. The document is indeed a private document but was rightly rejected on the basis that proper foundation was not laid. The document is a certified photocopy of a letter written by the 4tn defendant (appellant) himself to some of the kingmakers. The primary evidence of the document is the letter itself addressed to the kingmakers. Also by virtue of the provision of Section 94 of the Evidence Act Cap 112 LFN 1990, the executed counterparts or other numbers of the document made by one uniform process would still qualify as primary evidence of such a document. The document tendered however is in the nature of secondary evidence without any explanation of the whereabouts of the

original in accordance with the provision of section 97 of the Evidence Act. The learned trial judge was thus right to have held that no proper foundation was laid for its admissibility as Exhibit.

PHOTOCOPIES OF A DOCUMENT IS ADMISSIBLE WHEN PROPER FOUNDATION HAS BEEN LAID FOR IT

In the case of *Igori* v. *Igori & Ors* (2013) LPELR-21027(CA), Ogunwumiju, J.C.A. at Pp 13-14, Paras E-E held as follows:

> Thus the court has a duty to reject inadmissible evidence arising from its duty to act only legal evidence. See *International Bank of West Africa Ltd.* v. *Imano* (2001) 3 SCNJ Pg. 160; (2001) 3 SC Pg. 182. Primary evidence is the production of the document itself. S. 86(1) EA, 2011. Secondary evidence requires foundation if not little weight attaches to it. See *A.G., Oyo* v. *Fairlakes* (1989) 5 NWLR Pt. 121 Pg. 255; S.88 of the Evidence Act 2011. Thus, photocopies of a document are admissible when proper foundation has been laid for it. See *Habib Nig. Bank* v. *Koya* (1992) 7 NWLR Pt. 251 Pg. 43 Pg. 55-56 where a photocopy has been pleaded by the plaintiff and admitted by the defendant, it is admissible. If the defendant wants to debunk its correctness, he must tender the original. See *Nwanji* v. *Coaster Services* (2004) All FWLR Pt.219 Pg. 1150 at 1162. In any event every public document must be proved by producing a Certified True Copy of the said document. See S.112 of the Evidence Act Cap 112 and S.105 of the Evidence Act 2011. In *Lawal* v. *Magaji & Ors.* This court upheld the fact that a photocopy of a Certified True Copy is not admissible as against the decision in *Iheonu* v. *Obiukwu* (1994) 1 NWLR Pt. 322 Pg. 594 at 601-603. In *Araka* v. *Egbue* (2003) 17 NWLR Pt. 848 Pg. 1 at 18 the Supreme Court re-emphasized that by virtue of S. 97(2)(c) of the Evidence Act now S.90(1)(c) of the Evidence Act 2011, the only acceptable secondary evidence of a public document is a certified true copy of the document and none other.

FOUNDATIONS TO BE LAID FOR THE ADMISSIBILITY OF SECONDARY EVIDENCE

The Supreme Court of Nigeria per Onnoghen, J.S.C. at Pp. 7-8, Paras. B-A in the case of *Onwuzuruike* v. *Edoziem & Ors (*2016) LPELR-26056(SC) posited as follows:

> It should be noted that the issue as to whether a document needs certification relates to admissibility of secondary evidence of the original document Under the provisions of Section 94(1) of the Evidence Act the original of a document is what is known as primary evidence while a copy of the original document is known as secondary evidence of the original - see Section 97(1) *supra*. It is settled law that documents must be proved by primary evidence except in certain circumstances provided under Section 97 of the Evidence Act. The exceptions where secondary evidence may be given and admitted of the existence, condition or contents of the original document (a) the original is shown or appears to be in the possession or power of the person against whom the document is sought to be proved, or of any person legally bound to produce it and does not produce it despite being served with notice as stated in Section 98 of the Act or the original is a public document within the meaning of Section 109 of the Evidence Act, *supra,* in which case the secondary evidence admissible is a certified true copy.

WHAT IS REQUIRED IN LAYING PROPER FOUNDATION FOR ADMISSION OF SECONDARY EVIDENCE

In the case of *Isitor* v. *Fakarode* (2008) 1 NWLR (Pt. 1069) 602 AT P. 626, Para. F, Jega, JCA held thus:

> What is required for the purpose of laying proper foundation for the admission of a secondary evidence is an explanation to the satisfaction of the court to enable the admissibility of the

secondary evidence and not a justification. [*Opawole* v. *Tunbi* (2004) 11 NWLR (Pt.884) 290.

PHOTOCOPIES OF DOCUMENTS ARE ADMISSIBLE IN CRIMINAL TRIALS WITHOUT PROPER FOUNDATION IN CERTAIN CIRCUMSTANCES

In the case of *Odua* v. *Fed. Rep. of Nig.* (2002) 5 NWLR (PT 761) AT 634 Paras A-C (2002) LPELR-7166 (CA), Chukwuma-Eneh JCA stated thus:

> Coming to the 2nd Issue, the question to answer revolves on sustaining the conviction on exhibits 1-10 (photocopies and exhibits 65, 66 and 67 as they were inadmissible documentary evidence. On record exhibits 1-10 represent the letters by fax sent by the appellant to Mr. Fausing. There can be no disputing the fact that exhibits 1-10 were photocopies of fax messages and that as the law stands today they are no better than secondary evidence in contrast to primary evidence and it would offend against best evidence rule to admit secondary evidence. See *Anyaebosi* v. *R. T. Briscoe (Nig.) Ltd.* (1987) 3 NWLR (Pt.59) 84. In other words, exhibits 1-10 being photocopies are inadmissible in a criminal trial without laying proper foundation. See section 96 of the Evidence Act, 1990 for tendering photocopies. This recognises the distinction between primary and secondary evidence.

PROPER FOUNDATION IS REQUIRED FOR THE ADMISSIBILITY OF A SECONDARY DOCUMENT

In *Abidoye & Anor* v. *Dosunmu & Anor (*2019) LPELR-47719(CA), Saulawa, J.C.A. at Pp. 28-31, Paras. F-D posited as follows:

> The PW1 equally stated under cross-examination that he could identify his signature in Exhibit 1, the content of which he knew nothing about. The signature of the PW2 (Joseph Ayinla Awoniyi) is the last on the second page of Exhibit 1. Curiously, however, it is obvious on the face of Exhibit 1, that

the name against which the PW2 signed was not his but that of one Chief Awoniyi Afolagbiye. Undisputably, the PW2 on the face of Exhibit 1 signed against the name of an entirely different person. As aptly posited by the 1st Respondent's learned counsel in paragraph 6.19 at page 14 of the brief thereof: My Lords, PW2, who is Joseph Ayinla Awoniyi signed for another person, i.e. one Chief Awoniyi Afolagboye: Pw2 never said he also known (sic) as chief Awoniyi Afolagboye. Joseph Awoniyi is different from Chief Awoniyi Afolagboye. They cannot be one and the same person. Thus, this curious anomaly has undoubtedly put the purported genuineness of Exhibit 1 to question. Exhibit 1 was never interpreted to the PW2. Not surprisingly, the PW2 admitted under cross-examination to the effect thus: "I am an illiterate...I cannot read English or speak unless interpreted to me. I cannot read Yoruba even though I can speak it. I don't know what is in Exhibit 1." Exhibit 1, the purported agreement for rotation to commence in the future is obviously a photocopy, thus a secondary document. No proper foundation was laid by the Appellants prior to the tendering of Exhibit 1. Notwithstanding, the fact that Exhibit 1 was not objected at the material time it was tendered, the said exhibit could not by any stretch of imagination fulfil the pre-condition for its admissibility under the provisions of Sections 87, 89 and 90 of the Evidence Act, 2011. Not surprisingly, the Court below aptly rejected the said exhibit in its findings at page 545 of the record: On Exhibit 1, PW1, Chief Ayinla Awoniyi clearly signed for another person. He signed for chief Awoniyi Aforlagboye Exhibit 1 was not interpreted to him and he never said the document was read to him before he signed. Under cross examination, he said the document was read to him before he signed. Under cross examination he said he did not know the content of Exhibit 1; there was no proper foundation laid for its admissibility as it is a photocopy. I have no iota of doubt in my mind, that the above findings of the Court are in tandem with the well settled principle regarding admissibility of evidence. In my considered view, Exhibit 1 being a photocopy of the original thereof, is essentially a secondary document. Ironically, no proper foundation has been laid for its admissibility as required by law. Indeed, the law is settled, that photocopies of documents are inadmissible without proper foundation being laid for their admission. Thus, where the law declared a document inadmissible, as in the instant case, such document cannot by any stretch of imagination be admitted in evidence even in the absence of an objection or by consent of parties to its admission. See *Fasina* v. *Agunkayode* (2005) All FWLR (Pt. 283) 116 at 131 paragraphs C - E; *Alao* v. *Akano* (2005) 4 SCNJ 65 at 74; *Kubor* v. *Dickson* (2013) ALL FWLR (676) 393 at 430 paragraphs E - G.

ESSENCE OF LAYING PROPER FOUNDATION FOR THE ADMISSIBILITY OF DOCUMENTARY EVIDENCE

In the case of *Tamkeyar* v. *Bussa & Ors* (2017) LPELR-42987 (CA), Omoleye, J.C.A. at Pp. 16-18, Paras. C-F, remarked as follows:

> In the instant case, the letter being sought to be tendered in evidence by the Appellant is a photocopy. Parties and indeed the trial Court were in agreement that the said Letter was pleaded and also relevant. The bone of contention is the procedure allowed by law for it to be tendered in evidence being a photocopy. I am at one with the stance of the learned counsel for the Respondents that pursuant to Section 89 of the Evidence Act, a proper foundation must first be laid by the party seeking to tender the photocopy, stating the condition of its original to the satisfaction of the Court. This is notwithstanding the fact that the learned counsel for the Appellant, with due respect to him, appeared to be scattered on the position or state of the original of the Letter in dispute. In the brief of argument of the Appellant, the learned counsel stated in Paragraph 4.2.1 at page 8 and 4.2.4 at page 9, that the original of the Letter is in the custody of the Appellant. While in Paragraphs 4.2.8 at page 9 of the said brief, he made a sudden last minute U-turn and stated that the said original of the Letter is not in the custody of the Appellant. However, in the Ruling being appealed against, the learned trial Judge observed that the original of the Letter in question is with the

Respondents. Failure to lay the foundation stating the state of the original, the Court may refuse to admit the photocopy being secondary evidence. For by virtue of Section 88 of the Act, ordinarily, documents ought to be proved by primary evidence except as otherwise provided in the Act. What this means is that, for the secondary evidence of a document to be admissible, a foundation must be laid to explain why the primary evidence is unprocurable and its secondary evidence is being resorted to. See cases of: (1) *Ogunsanya* v. *Taiwo* (1970) 1 All NLR p. 147 at p.151; (2) *Onochie* v. *Ikem* (1989) 4 NWLR (Pt. 116) p. 458 at p. 465; (3) *Anatogu* v. *Iweka* II (1995) LPELR - 484 (SC); (4) *Udenkwo* v. *Nwosu* (2014) LPELR - 24290 (CA) and (5) *Kayili* v. *Yilbuk* (2015) LPELR - 24323 (SC). In this matter both "Identification A" and the Letter, its photocopy the Appellant sought to tender through PW6 are both photocopies. I hold pursuant to the foregoing postulations that a proper foundation having not been laid regarding the state of its original, the learned trial Judge was right in refusing to admit the said photocopy in evidence. However, the position of the law is that in a situation like the instant case, the said photocopy of the Letter must not be marked "rejected" since it is not intrinsically inadmissible having been pleaded and relevant and may still be represented to the Court after proper foundation must have been laid to secure its admissibility. The learned trial Judge was therefore within the orbit of law by merely refusing in evidence the photocopy of the said Letter for failure to comply with the relevant procedure laid down by the Evidence Act and not marking it "rejected".

THE CONTENTS OF A DOCUMENT CAN ONLY BE PROVED BY TENDERING THE ORIGINAL DOCUMENT OR SECONDARY EVIDENCE THEREOF AFTER LAYING THE PROPER FOUNDATION

Lokulo-Sodipe, J.C.A. at P. 24, paras. B-C in the case of *PML Securities Company Ltd* v. *FRN (*2014) LPELR-22768(CA), held as follows:

The content of a document can only be proved by tendering the original document or secondary evidence thereof after laying the proper foundation. See *Goodwill & Trust Investment Ltd* v. *Witt & Bush Ltd* (2011) All FWLR (Pt. 576) 517, (2011) 34 WRN 1. Hence the content of a document cannot ordinarily be established viva voce. See *Ogundele* v. *Agiri* (2010) 9 WRN 1.

INSTANCES WHERE LAYING OF FOUNDATION WOULD NOT BE NEEDED FOR THE ADMISSIBILITY OF A PRIVATE DOCUMENT

Obaseki-Adejumo, J.C.A. at Pp. 40-41, Paras. B-A in the case of *Oyekanmi* v. *FRN* (2019) LPELR-47323(CA) held as follows:

> With respect to the airway bill, it is not in dispute that the document sought to be tendered is a photocopy and it is my view that unless proper foundation is laid, which was not done in the instant case, same cannot be admitted by the Court. I agree with the Respondent's counsel that the Appellant's counsel submission that there was no need to lay foundation for the document merely because the same photocopy was once attached to a process at the High Court, hence a public document, is not well founded. The document remains a private document as it does not come within the definition of public document as defined by Section 102 of the Evidence Act. I share similar sentiments with the Respondent's counsel that if the Court process, which the photocopy of the airway bill forms part of, was properly certified and tendered as public document, then the Court can admit same under Section 102 and it will not be necessary for any foundation to be laid. Therefore, the learned trial judge rightly rejected Exhibit P36 which was retendered as Exhibit D3.

FAILURE TO LAY THE NECESSARY FOUNDATION REGARDING THE CONDITION OF THE ELECTRONIC GADGET OR COMPUTER THAT WERE USED IS FATAL TO THE EXTENT OF NOT FULFILLING THE CONDITIONS SPELT OUT IN SECTION 84 OF THE EVIDENCE ACT

Commenting on this all-important area of the law, Jombo-Ofo, J.C.A. at pp. 29-30, paras. B-F in the case of *Akeredolu & Anor* v. *Mimiko & Ors.* (2013) LPELR-20532(CA) held as follows:

> It is specifically provided in section 84 of the Evidence Act as it relates to admissibility of statement in document produced by computers that: 84 (1) In any proceeding a statement contained in a document produced by a computer shall be admissible as evidence of any fact stated in it of which direct oral evidence will be admissible, if it is shown that the conditions in subsection (2) of this section are satisfied in relation to the statement and computer in question. The conditions referred to in subsection (1) of this section are:- (a)That the document containing the statement was produced by the computer during a period over which the computer was used regularly to store or process information for purposes of any activities regularly carried on over that period whether for profit or not, or by any individual; (b) That over that period there was regularly supplied to the computer in the ordinary course of those activities information of the kind contained in the statement or of the kind from which the information so contained is derived; (c) That throughout the material part of that period the computer was operating properly or, if not, that in any respect in which it was not operating properly or was out of operation during that part of that period was not such as to affect the production of the document or the accuracy of its contents; and (d) that the information contained in the statement is reproduced or is derived from information supplied to the computer in the ordinary course of those activities. Going by the foregoing provision it is discernible that

> the appellants who were desirous of demonstrating electronically the content of Exhibits P50A and P50B failed to lay the necessary foundation regarding the condition of the electronic gadget or computer they were going to use. To the extent that those conditions as spelt out in section 84 supra were unfulfilled the demonstration ought not be allowed. See the cases of: (i) *Maduekwe* v. *Okoroafor* (1992) 9 NWLR (Pt.263) 69 (ii) *INEC* v. *AC* (2009) 2 NWLR (Pt.1126) 524 at 595.

ELECTRONIC EVIDENCE WITHOUT AN ACCOMPANYING CERTIFICATE OF IDENTIFICATION AS STIPULATED IN SECTION 84 (4) OF THE EVIDENCE ACT.

Ogakwu, J.C.A. at Pp. 22-23, Paras. E-A in the case of *MD Zahirul Islam* v. *FRN* (2018) LPELR-44529(CA), held as follows:

> Undoubtedly, Exhibit P23 is computer-generated evidence. From the Records, the said Exhibit P23 was admitted without an accompanying certificate of identification as stipulated in Section 84 (4) of the Evidence Act. (See pages 183-184 of the Records). The said Exhibit P23 was therefore wrongfully admitted in evidence and ought to be expunged. See *Kubor* v. *Dickson* (*supra*) and *Dickson* v. *Sylva* (*supra*).

COMPUTER–GENERATED DOCUMENT TENDERED BY A PARTY WHOSE COMPUTER DID PRODUCE THE DOCUMENT IS ADMISSIBLE WITHOUT NEED FOR CERTIFICATION AS REQUIRED BY SECTION 84(4) OF THE EVIDENCE ACT, 2011

In the case of *Stanbic IBTC Bank* v. *Longterm Global Capital Ltd & Ors* (2021) LPELR – 55610 (CA), the Court of Appeal posited thus:

> It is, therefore, suggested that the law should not be too strict on a party whose computer did not produce the

electronic document and it becomes impossible for him to produce same. This should be treated as an exception to Section 84(4) in the interest of justice. This is because, it will amount to a denial of justice if the authentic document is kept out of consideration of the Court by reason of the fact that a certificate is not produced by a party who cannot possibly secure its production. In this technological age, nothing more unjust can be conceived. By happenstance, a party may wish to rely on or be a proponent of a document which germinates from a computer that is outside his control. In that wise, it is obvious that he will lack the capacity and capability to attest to the continuous proper operation, in the ordinary course of business/activity, of the mother computer/device or provide an endorsed certificate showcasing the manner of production of the document he proposes to furnish to the Court. To compel him to do either evinces a natural and evidential impossibility – *Lex non mogit ad impossibili.* Such compulsion will eclipse the very ends of justice – the attainment of which is the primary duty of the Court. It is deducible from the records, the bible of the appeal, that the trilogy of the appellant, the second and third respondents were involved in the generation of the exhibit L2 in question. Put differently, the first respondent was not particeps in the chain of production that midwife the CSR – exhibit L2. Indeed, evidence on this galore. Neither the first respondent not its computer was involved in its production. Therefore, the first respondent was/is not in control of the computer, which gave birth to it, to equip it with the knowledge that will enable it authenticate its continuous workability. Nor can it properly issue a certificate disclosing the process of its production. To laden this burden on it will be tantamount to foreclosing or shutting the document out of the temple of justice. It, certainly, cannot be the intention of the legislature that Section 84 of the Evidence Act, 2011 should strip a party, who is not the owner/maker of a computer–generated document of his right to present electronic evidence, meant for the prosecution or defence of his case in a Court of law. In effect, the lower Court was firma terra in law when it admitted the first respondent's Credit Status Report

(CSR) as an exhibit – exhibit L2. I too, welcome the document to the appeal. I deck it with the deserved cap of admissibility.

COMMENTARY

Sections 84(4)-(5) of the Evidence Act 2011 stipulates the foundation or procedure to be laid for tendering a computer-generated or processed statement in evidence. Section 84(4) provides thus:

> In any proceedings where it is desired to give a statement in evidence by virtue of this section, a certificate doing any of the following things, that is to say: (a) Identifying the document containing the statement and describing the manner in which it was produced; (b) Giving such particulars of any device involved in the production of that document as may be appropriate for the purpose of showing that the document was produced by a computer; (c) Dealing with any of the matters to which the conditions mentioned in subsection (2) above relate, and purporting to be signed by a person occupying a responsible position in relation to the operation of the relevant device or the management of the relevant activities, as the case may be, shall be evidence of the matter stated in the certificate, and for the purpose of this subsection it shall be sufficient for a matter to be stated to the best of the knowledge and belief of the person stating it.
>
> (5) For the purposes of this section:
>
> (a) Information shall be taken to be supplied to a computer if it is supplied to it in any appropriate form and whether it is supplied directly or (with or without human intervention) by means of any appropriate equipment;
>
> (b) Where, in the course of activities carried on by any individual or body, information is supplied with a view to its being stored or processed for the purposes of those activities by a computer operated otherwise than in the course of those activities, that information, if duly supplied to that computer, shall be taken to be supplied to it in the course of those activities.

(c) A document shall be taken to have been produced by a computer whether it was produced by it directly or (with or without human intervention) by means of any appropriate equipment.

Thence, a statement contained in a document produced by a computer shall be admissible as evidence of any fact stated in it of which direct oral evidence would be admissible, if it is shown that the conditions in subsection (2) of this section (Section 84(1)-(5))[1] are satisfied in relation to the statement and computer in question. Therefore, a party who seeks to tender documentary evidence in Court to prove or disprove a fact in issue has to plead whether such document was processed or generated by "one uniform process, as in the case of printing, lithography, photography, computer or other electronic or mechanical process," for "each shall be primary evidence of the contents of the rest" of the document under Section 84(4) of the Act.

With the decision in *Stanbic IBTC Bank* v. *Longterm Global Capital Ltd & Ors*,[2] where a person who is not the maker of the computer generated evidence, and the maker is not willing to testify, such a party can tender the computer generated evidence without a certificate of compliance. If the party is a customer of a bank, the bank customer can tender it without the certificate.

---

[1] Ibid.

[2] (2021) LPELR – 55610 (CA).

Chapter 4

ADMISSIBILITY OF PHOTOGRAPHS/PICTURES, DIGITAL CAMERA(S) AND ELECTRONIC STATEMENT OF ACCOUNT

DEFINITION OF THE WORD "PHOTOGRAPH"

In the case of *Udoro & Ors* v. *The Governor, Akwa Ibom State & Ors* (2008) LPELR-4094 (CA), Orji-Abadua, J.C.A. at pp.12-13, paras. F-B stated thus:

> The *Oxford Advance Learners Dictionary* at p. 868 defined "photograph" thus: "A picture formed by means of the chemical action of light on film, and then transferred to specially prepared paper" The same Dictionary at p. 1327 described video cassette thus: "A film, etc., recorded on a video tape. Video is said to be: "the process of recording, reproducing or broadcasting films on magnetic tape using a special camera and a television, or to record moving pictures on video tape."

PICTURES AND PHOTOGRAPHS ARE ADMISSIBLE PRIMARY EVIDENCE

In the case of *Olatunji* v. *State* (2019) LPELR-48027(CA), Danjuma, J.C.A. at pp. 26-28, Paras. F-B stated thus:

It is trite that Exhibits A, A1, A2 and A3 pictures and photographs are not secondary evidence as submitted by the Appellant's counsel. They are indeed primary evidence; it is also not correct that the digital camera used in the photography was the primary evidence of the Exhibits- that were produced by the Digital camera. Each of those objects are primary evidence on their own - and may be so tendered as they are, where they are relevant to a relevant fact. It is a different thing where it is argued that the technology for the production of the photographs is not explained. The digital camera was shown as not using film or negatives and the fact of evidence as to how it works and whether it was in good working condition to produce the document photographs so that their authenticity may be assessed could not be gone into because the photographer was said to be unavailable to testify upon explanation. In any case, here was not a case of tendering a secondary evidence of a document produced by mechanical process which authenticity had to be vouched or ascertained. It was simply a case of showing that a corpse was found of the victim of the Appellant's act committed with his co -conspirators as seen on the photographs. The Exhibits A, A1, A2, A3 were only to corroborate the evidence of the prosecution witnesses of the death of a human being and the existence of a corpse and at a place where some witnesses were led to through the investigations appertaining the Appellant's joint acts with other persons. The said Exhibits were relevant primary evidence that were admissible without more.

COURT CAN TAKE JUDICIAL NOTICE OF THE FACT THAT THE APPELLANT OPERATES OR CARRIES ON BUSINESS WITH THE AID OF COMPUTERS

Tur, J.C.A. at pp. 2-11, Paras. A-D held in the case of *Uli Microfinance Bank (Nig) Ltd* v. Norbert (2018) LPELR-44953 (CA) thus:

The appellant is a Microfinance Bank, incorporated under the Banks and Other Financial Institutions Act Cap. B3, Laws of the Federation of Nigeria, 2004 to carry on "banking business" under Section 61 of the Banks and Other Financial Institutions Act No.25 of 1991 and has "banker's books" which is defined to include "ledger, day books, cash books and all other books used in the banking business." See Section 258(1) of the Evidence Act, 2011. The appellant operate the banking business with computers. A "computer" is defined in Section 258(1) of the Evidence Act, 2011 as "...any device for storing and processing information, any reference to information being derived from other information is a reference to its being derived from it by calculation, comparing or any other process." This Court can take judicial notice of the fact that the appellant operates or carries on business with the aid of computers as most banks do in this generation. Section 84(1)-(5), 124(1)-(3), 125 and 126(a)-(d) of the Evidence Act, 2011 provides as follows: "84(1) In any proceedings a statement contained in a document produced by a computer shall be admissible as evidence of any fact stated in it of which direct oral evidence would be admissible, if it is shown that the conditions in Subsection (2) of this section are satisfied in relation to the statement and computer in question. (2) The conditions referred to in Subsection (1) of this section are: (a) That the document containing the statement was produced by the computer during a period over which the computer was used regularly to store or process information for the purposes of any activities regularly carried on over that period, whether for profit or not, by anybody, whether corporate or not, or by any individual; (b) That over that period there was regularly supplied to the computer in the ordinary course of those activities or of the kind from which the information so contained is derived; (c) That throughout the material part of that period the computer was operating properly or, if not, that in any respect in which it was not operating properly or was out of operation during that part of that period was not such as to affect the production of the document or the accuracy of it contents; and (d) That the information contained in the statement reproduces or is derived from information supplied to the computer in the ordinary course of those activities. (3) Where over a period the function of storing or processing information for the purposes of any activities regularly carried on over that period as mentioned in Subsection (2): (a) of this section was regularly performed by computers, whether (b) by a combination of computers operating over that period; or (c) by different computers operating in succession over that period, or (d) by different combinations of computers operating in succession over that period; or (e) in any other manner involving the successive operation over that period, in whatever order, of one or more computers and one or more combinations of computers, all the computers used for that purpose during that period shall be treated for the purposes of this section as constituting a single computer; and references in accordingly." (4) In any proceedings where it is desired to give a statement in evidence by virtue of this section...: (a) Identifying the document containing the statement and describing the manner in which it was produced; (b) Giving such particulars of any device involved in the production of that document as may be appropriate for the purpose of showing that the document was produced by a computer; (c) Dealing with any of the matters to which the conditions mentioned in Subsection (2) above relate, and purporting to be signed by a person occupying a responsible position in relation to the operation of the relevant device or the management of the relevant activities, as the case may be, shall be evidence of the matter stated in the certificate, and for the purpose of this subsection it shall be sufficient for a matter to be stated to the best of the knowledge and belief of the person stating it. (5) For the purposes of this section: (a) Information shall be taken to be supplied to a computer if it is supplied to it in any appropriate form and whether it is supplied directly or (with or without human intervention) by means of any appropriate equipment; (b) Where, in the course of activities carried on by any individual or body, information is supplied with a view to its being stored or processed for the purposes of those activities by a computer operated otherwise than in the course of those activities, that information, if duly supplied to that computer, shall be taken to be supplied to it in the course of those activities. (c) A document shall be taken to have been produced by a computer whether it was produced by it directly or (with or without human intervention) by means of any appropriate equipment. xxxxxxxx 124(1) Proof shall not be required of a fact the knowledge of which is not reasonably open to question and which is: (a) Common knowledge in the locality in which the proceeding is being held, or generally; or (b) Capable of verification by reference to a document the authority of which cannot reasonably be questioned. (2) The Court may acquire, in any manner it deems fit, knowledge of a fact to which Subsection (1) of this section refers, and shall take such knowledge into account. (3) The Court shall give to a party to any proceeding such opportunity to make submission, and to refer to a relevant information, in relation to the acquiring or taking into account of such knowledge, as is necessary to ensure that the party is not unfairly prejudiced. 125. All facts, except the contents of documents, may be proved by oral evidence. 126. Subject to the provisions of Part III, oral evidence shall, in all cases whatever, be direct if it refers to:- (a) A fact which could be seen, it must be the evidence of a witness who says he saw that fact. (b) To a fact which could be heard, it must be the evidence of a witness who says he heard that fact; (c) To a fact which could be perceived by any other sense or in any other manner, it must be the evidence of a witness who says he perceived that fact by that sense or in that manner. (d) If it refers to an opinion or to the grounds on which that opinion is held, it must be the evidence of the person who holds that opinion on those ground:- Provided that the opinion of experts expressed in any treaties commonly offered for sale, and the grounds on which such opinions are held, may be proved by the production of such treaties if the author is dead or cannot be found, or has become incapable of giving evidence, or cannot be called as a witness without an amount of delay or expense which the Court regards as unreasonable." In *Mrs. Elizabeth Anyaebosi* v. *R.T. Briscoe (Nig.) Ltd.* (1987) 6 SC 15 the Supreme Court recognized the essence of computer-generated information which records information supplied by a customer to a supplier which is stored in a computer or computers in the word of

Uwais, JSC (as he then was) observed at page 33 lines 5 to 22 as follows: "At the hearing before the trial Judge (Williams, J.), the plaintiff called only one witness - Mr. Edward Oladipo Aina, who was its Spare Parts Manager. The witness after testifying that the plaintiff's accounts were kept by computer, tendered a statement of account which the plaintiff kept in respect of its transactions with the deceased. The statement was admitted, without objection by the deceased's Counsel, as Exhibit "P4". This exhibit which is in a computer printed form was certified to be a true copy by one Chief T. Ola Odukoya, employed as Senior Accountant in the plaintiff's Motor Account Department. The exhibit was dated 31st December, 1980 and it showed a balance of ₦60,535.10 as outstanding against the deceased." Information from a customer is usually made available to a bank that is stored by officers of the bank in their computer. The information stored in a computer by the officers of the bank becomes a fact that is peculiarly within the knowledge of the bank and in a situation where there is a dispute of a controversy as to the amount in the customer account including the payment of interest to the customer, the usual practice is to reproduce the information in the form of documents supported by oral evidence from the officers of the bank at the trial. The computer contains information peculiarly within the knowledge of the computer which is operated by the officers of the bank. Section 145 of the Evidence Act, 2011 provides that: "140. When a fact is especially within the knowledge of any person, the burden of proofing that fact is upon him." The dispute in the Court below is one of facts to be proved or disproved by oral or documentary evidence. Section 258(1) of the Evidence Act, 2011 defines "documents"; "fact"; "fact in issue" and "statement" in the following manner:- "Documents" includes: (a) Books, maps; plans, graphs, drawings, photographs, and also includes any matter expressed or described upon any substance by means of letters, figures or marks or by more than one of these means, intended to be used or which may be used for the purpose of recording that matter. (b) Any disc, tape, sound track or other device in which sounds or other data (not being visual images) are embodied so as to be capable (with or without the aid of some other equipment) of being reproduced from it; and (c) Any film, negative, tape or other device in which one or more visual images are embodied so as to be capable (with or without the aid of some other equipment) of being reproduced from it; and (d) Any device by means of which information, is recorded, stored or retrievable including computer output. "Fact" includes: (a) Anything, state of things, relation of things, capable of being perceived by the senses; and (b) Any mental condition of which any person is conscious. "Fact in issue" includes any fact from which either by itself or in connection with other facts the existence, non-existence, nature or extent of any right, liability or disability asserted or denied in any suit or proceeding necessarily follows: "Statement" includes any representation of fact whether made in words or otherwise." Any device by means of which information is recorded, stored or retrievable including a computer output is evidenced in a "document" which is to be verified on the sworn oral evidence of an officer of the bank.

IF PHOTOGRAPHS ARE TAKEN WITH A DIGITAL CAMERA OR PRODUCED FROM A DIGITAL CAMERA, IT BECOMES A COMPUTER GENERATED DOCUMENT BY VIRTUE OF SECTION 84 (5) (C) OF THE EVIDENCE ACT, 2011

In *Davou* v. *C.O.P Plateau State Command (2019)* LPELR-47040(CA), Onyemenam, J.C.A. at pp. 14-16, Paras. D-D stated thus:

On the Appellant's contention that Exhibits "P6A" and "P6B" admission offends Section 84 of the Evidence Act, 2011 and as such should be expunged. The said Exhibits which are pictures of the deceased were tendered without recourse to the requirements of Section 84 of the Evidence Act, 2011. The Respondent's counsel subtly conceded to this as he did not make submissions on this but rather stemmed his argument on the fact that the referred Exhibits did not influence the trial Court in its decision. The pictures were just tendered without the negatives nor any explanation. Where if the photographs were taken with a digital camera or produced from a digital camera that becomes a computer generated document by virtue of Section 84 (5) (c) of the Evidence Act, 2011 which provides that; "a document shall be taken to have been produced by a computer whether it was produced by it directly or (with or without human intervention) by means of any appropriate equipment." The camera that was used in taking the photographs ought to have been tendered in evidence, but that was not done. Rather the printed photographs were tendered in evidence. Also, the certification which is a pre-requisite for its admissibility in evidence under Section 84 of the Evidence Act, 2011 was not made. Notably, Section 84 of the Evidence Act, 2011 permits the admission of any document generated or produced by a computer. However, the document may only be admissible if, and only if it is shown that the conditions in Subsection (2) therein are duly satisfied in relation to the document sought to be tendered. The conditions precedent to the admissibility of such documents are contained in Subsection (2) (a) - (d) of Section 84 of the Evidence Act, 2011. Categorically, Section 84 (4) (a) and (b) of the Evidence Act, 2011 made it mandatory that, before a computer generated document can be admissible, a certificate identifying the document and describing the manner in which the document was produced as well as the particulars of the device used in producing or generating the document must first be provided. Exhibits "P6A" and "P6B" failed woefully to abide by the requirements of Section 84 of the Evidence Act thereby making the pictures of the deceased Exhibits "P6A" and "P6B" inadmissible. I therefore hold that Exhibits "P6A" and "P6B" were wrongly admitted and are hereby expunged from the record.

CONDITIONS FOR THE ADMISSIBILITY OF A BANK STATEMENT OF ACCOUNT

In *Lufthansa German Airlines* v. *Ballanyne (*2012) LPELR-7977(CA), Saulawa, J.C.A at pp. 28-32, paras. G-C held thus:

...Ironically, however, the purported bank official "that allegedly" prepared the exhibits in question still remains shrouded in mystery. Such a person was never called to testify at the trial of the case. And yet, the position of the law is very clear on that issue! Recently, this court made this point very clear in the case of *Federal Republic of Nigeria* v. *Femi Fani-Kayode* (2010) 14 NWLR (Pt. 1214) 481 at 506 paragraphs E-H thus: "In the instant case, it is rather inarguable, that the certified true copy of the computer generated bank statement of account of the respondent domiciled with the First Inland Bank at Wharf Road meets all the requirements of being admitted as an exhibit at the trial. In my view, that document does not fall within the category of evidence made completely inadmissible by the law. Rather, it certainly falls within the category of evidence admissible upon the fulfilment of the conditions duly prescribed under section 97(1) and (2) of the Evidence Act (*supra*). See *Anyaebosi* v. *R.T. Briscoe Ltd.* (1987) 3 NWLR (Pt. 59) 108, where the apex court, aptly held, inter alia thus: "It is important to state that a computerized account which Exhibit P4 was described to be does not fall into the category of evidence absolutely inadmissible by law. In my opinion, it falls within the category of evidence admissible on the fulfilment of the conditions prescribed in section 96(1) and (2) of the Evidence Act." Per Saulawa, JCA See also *Trade Bank Plc* v. *Chami* (2003) 13 NWLR (Pt. 836) 216 per Salami, JCA (as he then was); *Esso West Africa Inc.* v. *Oyegbola* (1969) NMLR 194 at 198, respectively. I again made it emphatically clear in *FRN* v. *Fani-Kayode's* case (supra) at page 507 paragraphs D - E (supra) that - As alluded to above, the computer printout of the Bank Statement of the respondent sought to be tendered vide the PW1 was duly certified. It was produced by the very person in custody of the document i.e. the PW1 who was the branch Manager of the Bank at the material time in question. That being the therefore, the document in question is absolutely admissible under the Evidence Act. Alas! The same cannot be said of the present exhibits G - G1, H - H1, J - J1 & K - K1 in question. As pointed out above, the said exhibits (with possible exception of exhibit K) were neither signed nor certified. What's more, there were not tendered vide the bank official who prepared them or (was) in custody thereof. Instructively, under section 2(1) of the Evidence Act, the term "Bankers books" has been defined" as - "Legers, day books, cash books, account books and all other books used in ordinary business of a bank." Thus, as aptly held by this court in *FRN* v. *Fani-Kayode* (*supra*) - "... the definition of the term document in section 2(1) of the Evidence Act includes "computerized statement of accounts. Undoubtedly, the provisions of the Evidence Act and, and indeed, most of the Nigerian Statutes, including the Grundnorm itself; the Constitution of the Federal Republic of Nigeria, 1999, need to be generally overhauled to meet the exigencies of the modern computer age. However, the above contention notwithstanding, I would want to believe that by virtue of the provision of section 2(1) of the Evidence Act (*supra*), the definition of the word 'document, undoubtedly encompasses the computerized bank statement of accounts." Per Saulawa, JCA at 506 paragraphs C - D. In the instant, case the Appellant had opted to rely on exhibits G - GL, H - H1, J - J1, & K - K1 knowing fully well that they were neither signed, nor certified. And that the custody thereof could not be ascertained. Most curiously, the lower court obliged him by admitting and relying upon the said exhibits, when it's so obvious that they did not meet the conditions precedent set out under section 97(2)(a) & (e) of the Evidence Act (supra). Most especially, the provision of section 97(2)(e) of the Evidence Act (*supra*), is to the effect thus: (e) in paragraph (h) the copies cannot be received as evidence unless it be first proved that the book in which the copies were made was of the time of making one of the ordinary books of the bank, and that the entry was made in the usual and ordinary course of business, and that the book is in the custody and control of the bank, which proof may be given orally or by affidavit by o partner or officer of the bank, and that the copy has been examined with the original entry and is correct, which proof must be given by some person who has examined the copy of the original entry and may be given orally or by affidavit.' Thus, having failed to comply with the well set out provisions of section 97(2)(a) & (e) of the Evidence Act, there is no doubt that the said exhibits GG1,, H - H1, J -J1, K-K1 & L- L1, are not admissible. That being the case, therefore, the lower court ought not to have admitted them in evidence. The said exhibits ought to thus be expunged from the records even at this stage in time.

ELECTRONIC LEDGER OR STATEMENT OF ACCOUNT DERIVED ELECTRONICALLY ARE NOT EXCLUDED, BEING DOCUMENTS DERIVABLE OR GENERATED FROM A COMPUTER

In the case of *U.B.N. Plc* v. *Agbontaen & Anor* (2018) LPELR-44160(CA), Oseji, J.C.A. at pp. 11-22, Paras. E-B held thus:

> The issue in contention between the parties is whether the 2nd Respondent's statement of account sought to be tendered in evidence by the Appellant but rejected by the trial Court for being inadmissible complied with the relevant provisions of the Evidence Act, 2011. For the Appellant, the relevant provisions of the Evidence Act governing the admissibility of the said document is Sections 51, 89(1) (h) and 90(1)(e). But the Respondents are of a contrary stance by insisting that the governing provision is Section 84 of the Act which the learned trial Judge relied on rejecting the admissibility of the said statement of account. For purposes of clarity, the relevant provisions of the Evidence Act are herein below set out; 51 entries in books of accounts or electronic records regularly kept in the course of business are admissible whenever they refer to the matter into which the Court has to inquire, but such statements shall not alone be sufficient evidence to charge any person with liability. 84 (1) In any proceedings a statement contained in a document produced by a computer shall be admissible as evidence of any fact stated in it of which oral evidence would be admissible, if it is shown that the conditions in Subsection (2) of this section are satisfied in relation to the statement and computer in question. (2) The conditions referred to in Subsection (1) of this section

are - (a) that the document containing the statement was produced by the computer during a period over which the computer was used regularly to store or process information for the purposes of any activities regularly carried on over that period, whether for profit or not, by anybody, whether corporate or not, or by any individual; (b) that over that period there was regularly supplied to the computer in the ordinary course of those activities information of the kind contained in the statement or of the kind from which the information so contained is derived. (c) that throughout the material part of that period the computer was operating properly or if not, that in any respect in which it was not operating properly or was out of operation during that part of that period was not such as to affect the production of the document or the accuracy of its contents; and (d) that the information contained in the statement reproduces or is derived from information supplied to the computer in the ordinary course of those activities. (3) Where over a period the function of storing or processing information for the purpose of any activities regularly carried on over that period as mentioned in Subsection (2) (a) of this section was regularly performed by computers, whether- (a) a combination of computers operating over that period; or (b) by different computers operating in succession over that period; or (c) by different combinations of computers operating in succession over that period; or (d) in any other manner involving the successive operation over that period, in whatever order, of one or more computers and one or more combinations of computers used for that purpose during that period shall be treated for the purposes of this section as constituting a single computer; and references in this section to a computer shall be construed accordingly. (4) In any proceedings where it is desired to give a statement in evidence by virtue of this section, a certificate doing any of the following things, that is to say - (a) identifying the document containing the statement and describing the manner in which it was produced; (b) giving such particulars of any device involved in the production of that document as may be appropriate for the purpose of showing that the document was produced by a computer; (c) dealing with any of the matters to which the conditions mentioned in Subsection (2) above relate, and purporting to be signed by a person occupying a responsible position in relation to the operation of the relevant device or the management of the relevant activities, as the case may be, shall be evidence of the matter stated in the certificate; and for the purpose of this subsection it shall be sufficient for a matter to be stated to the best of the knowledge and belief of the person stating it. (5) For the purpose of this section-: (a) information shall be taken to be supplied to a computer if it is supplied to it in any appropriate form and whether it is supplied directly or (with or without human intervention) by means of any appropriate equipment; (b) where, in the course of activities carried on by any individual or body, information is supplied with a view to its being stored or processed for the purposes of those activities by a computer operated otherwise than in the course of those activities, that information, if duly supplied to that computer, shall be taken to be supplied to it in the course of those activities; (c) a document shall be taken to have been produced by a computer whether it was produced by it directly or (with or without human intervention) by means of any appropriate equipment." Section 89(1) Secondary evidence may be given of the existence, condition or contents of a document in the following cases:...(h) when the document is an entry in a banker's book." 90(1) "The secondary evidence admissible in respect of the original documents referred to in the several paragraphs of Section 89 is as follows: ... (e) in paragraph (h), the copies cannot be received as evidence unless it is first be proved that - (i) the book in which the entries copied were made was at the time of making one of the ordinary books of the bank; (ii) the entry was made in the usual and ordinary course of business. (iii) the book is in the control and custody of the bank, which proof may be given orally or by a affidavit by an officer of the bank; and (iv) the copy has been examined with the original entry and is correct, which proof must be given by some person who has examined the copy with the original entry and may be given orally or by affidavit." It is however worthy of note that while the learned counsel for the Appellant insists that the provisions of Section 84 of the Evidence Act, 2011 is of general application and

Sections 89(1) (h) and 90 (1) (e) of the specific application in which case they take priority over the former. I do not however see it that way. It is therefore in my humble view, the other way round. What is more, while Section 84 prescribed the conditions for the admissibility of statements in documents produced by computers, Sections 89(1) (h) and (90) (1) (e) deal with admissibility of secondary evidence generally, and the conditions for their admissibility. This reality can be gleaned from the marginal notes of the relevant sections. In Section 84, the marginal note read thus: "Admissibility of statement in document produced by computers." While in Sections 89 and 90 respectively they read thus: "Cases in which secondary evidence relating to document are admissible." and "Nature of secondary evidence admissible under Section 89." It thus emphasise the imperative nature of the provisions of Section 84 of the Act with regard to admissibility of document produced by computer whether being tendered in evidence as a primary (original) or secondary evidence. While on the other hand Sections 89 (1) (h) and 90(1) (e) deals with the admissibility of secondary evidence generally, including banker's books and not limited to electronic or computer derived documents. In the instant case, I believe that there is no disputing the fact that the statement of account sought to be tendered had its origin from a computer whether or not it is asserted to be extracted from an electronic ledger which to all intents and purposes the information therein was imputed through a computer and the print out also derived therefrom. The point that I am trying to make here is that, whether the statement of account or electronic ledger is to be tendered either in its original form or as a secondary evidence it is required that it must satisfy the conditions prescribed by Section 84 of the Act. In this regard, I am inclined to accept the fact that the case of *Kubor* v. *Dickson* cited as (2012) LPELR 15364 (CA) is applicable. Therein this Court while analysing the requirements for the admissibility of documents produced by a computer as provided for under the Section 84 (1) and (2) of the Evidence Act 2011 held, *inter alia*, at pages 3 to 4 as follows: "Section 84(2) provides for the conditions to be satisfied in relation to the statement and computer from which the documents sought to be tendered and admitted were produced. A party who seeks to tender in evidence a computer generated document needs to do more than just tendering same from the bar. Evidence in relation to the use of computer must be called to establish the conditions set out under Section 84(2) of the Evidence Act." The above decision of this Court was given a stamp of approval by the Supreme Court in *Omisore* V. *Aregbesola* (2015) LPELR 24803 (SC). Therein, the issue was whether only internet generated documents are caught by the admissibility requirements of Section 84 of the Evidence Act 2011. It was held per Nweze JSC at pages 97 to 98 of the Report that: "As noted above, the main plank of the argument of the first and second cross-respondents, with regard to the second issue above, was that only internet-generated documents are caught by the admissibility requirements of Section 84 of the 2011 Evidence Act. With profound respect, this argument is untenable, S. Mason (ed) *Electronic Evidence: Disclosure, discovery and Admissibilty*, (London: LexisNezis, Buttersworths, 2007) Passion; HM. Malek (ed), *Phipson on Evidence* (London: Sweet and Maxwell, 2010) Seventeenth Edition) Passion; *R* v. *Shepherd* (1993) 1 All ER 225, 231 (a decision of the defunct House of Lords). *Kubor* v. *Dickson* (2013) 4 NWLR (PT. 1345) 534; 577 - 578. Even the very chapeau or opening statement in Section 84(1) contradicts this submission. The relevant phrase here is 'a statement contained in a document produced by the computer...". Interestingly, the drafts person did not leave the meaning of the word "computer" to conjecture. In Section 258(1), the Act defines "computer" to mean "any device for storing and processing information, and any reference to information being derived from other information is a reference to its being derived from it by calculating; comparison or any other process." Furthermore, in *Dickson* v. *Sylva* (2016) LPELR 41257 (SC) the apex Court also citing *Kubor* v. *Dickson* (*supra*) concluded wholesomely that the correct interpretation to be given to Section 84 of the Evidence Act where electronically generated document is sought to be demonstrated is that such electronic generated evidence must be certified and must comply with the pre-conditions laid down in Section 84(2). From the above cited authorities of this Court and the Supreme Court, the inevitable conclusion reachable in the circumstance is that any computer/electronically generated document, whether tendered as original or secondary evidence is required to comply with Section 84(2) of the Evidence Act, 2011. The electronic ledger or statement of account derived therefrom are not excluded, being documents derivable or generated from a computer. The sound arguments canvassed by learned counsel for the Appellant are quite commendable but unfortunately the requirements of the law are clear to the letter and should be accordingly complied with. In the final result, the sole issue raised for determination is hereby resolved against the Appellant.

JUDICIAL NOTICE MAY BE TAKEN OF THE FACT THAT MANY BANKS NOW OPERATE THEIR BANKING BUSINESSES THROUGH COMPUTER-GENERATED DOCUMENTARY EVIDENCE

In *Uli Microfinance Bank (Nig) Ltd* v. *Okwuchukwu* (2018) LPELR-44956(CA), Tur, J.C.A. at pp. 29-36, Paras. A-D posited as follows:

Judicial notice may be taken of the fact that many banks now operate their banking businesses through computer-generated documentary evidence. The computers are not in the custody of the customers but the bank. The customer supplies information to the banks which are fed into the computers in the custody of the bank. The customer's account are kept and maintained by the bank. I can take judicial notice of these facts under the provisions of Sections 84(1)-(5), 124(1)-(3), 125, 126(a)-(d) of the Evidence Act, 2011 which are couched as follows: "84(1) In any proceedings, a statement contained in a document produced by a computer shall be admissible as evidence of any fact stated in it of which direct oral evidence would be admissible, if it is shown that the conditions in Subsection (2) of this Section are satisfied in relation to the statement and computer in question. (2) The conditions referred to in Subsection (1) of this section are: (a) That the document containing the statement was produced by the computer during a period over which the computer was used regularly to store or process information for the purposes of any activities regularly carried on over that period, whether for profit or not, by anybody, whether corporate or not, or by any individual; (b) That over that period there was regularly supplied to the computer in the ordinary course of those activities or of the kind from which the information so contained is derived; (c) That throughout the material part of that period the computer was operating properly or, if not, that in any respect in which it was not operating properly or was out of operation during that part of that period was not such as to affect the production of the document or the accuracy of it contents; and (d) That the information contained in the statement reproduces or is derived from information supplied to the computer in the ordinary course of those activities. (3) Where over a period the function of storing or processing information for the purposes of any activities regularly carried on over that period as mentioned in Subsection (2): (a) of this section was regularly performed by computers, whether (b) by a combination of computers operating over that period; or (c) by different computers operating in succession over that period, or (d) by different combinations of computers operating in succession over that period; or (e) in any other manner involving the successive operation over that period, in whatever order, of one or more computers and one or more combinations of computers, all the computers used for that purpose during that period shall be treated for the purposes of this section as constituting a single computer; and references in accordingly." (4) In any proceedings where it is desired to give a statement in evidence by virtue of this section...: (a) Identifying the document containing the statement and describing the manner in which it was produced; (b) Giving such particulars of any device involved in the production of that document as may be appropriate for the purpose of showing that the document was produced by a computer; (c)

Dealing with any of the matters to which the conditions mentioned in Subsection (2) above relate, and purporting to be signed by a person occupying a responsible position in relation to the operation of the relevant device or the management of the relevant activities, as the case may be, shall be evidence of the matter stated in the certificate, and for the purpose of this subsection it shall be sufficient for a matter to be stated to the best of the knowledge and belief of the person stating it. (5) For the purposes of this section: (a) Information shall be taken to be supplied to a computer if it is supplied to it in any appropriate form and whether it is supplied directly or (with or without human intervention) by means of any appropriate equipment; (b) Where, in the course of activities carried on by any individual or body, information is supplied with a view to its being stored or processed for the purposes of those activities by a computer operated otherwise than in the course of those activities, that information, if duly supplied to that computer, shall be taken to be supplied to it in the course of those activities. (c) A document shall be taken to have been produced by a computer whether it was produced by it directly or (with or without human intervention) by means of any appropriate equipment. xxx 124(1) Proof shall not be required of a fact the knowledge of which is not reasonably open to question and which is:- (a) Common knowledge in the locality in which the proceeding is being held, or generally; or (b) Capable of verification by reference to a document the authority of which cannot reasonably be questioned. (2) The Court may acquire, in any manner it deems fit, knowledge of a fact to which Subsection (1) of this section refers, and shall take such knowledge into account. (3) The Court shall give to a party to any proceeding such opportunity to make submission, and to refer to a relevant information, in relation to the acquiring or taking into account of such knowledge, as is necessary to ensure that the party is not unfairly prejudiced. 125. All facts, except the contents of documents, may be proved by oral evidence. 126. Subject to the provisions of Part III, oral evidence shall, in all cases whatever, be direct if it refers to: (a) A fact which could be seen, it must be the evidence of a witness who says he saw that fact. (b) To a fact which could be heard, it must be the evidence of a witness who says he heard that fact; (c) To a fact which could be perceived by any other sense or in any other manner, it must be the evidence of a witness who says he perceived that fact by that sense or in that manner. (d) If it refers to an opinion or to the grounds on which that opinion is held, it must be the evidence of the person who holds that opinion on those ground:- Provided that the opinion of experts expressed in any treaties commonly offered for sale, and the grounds on which such opinions are held, may be proved by the production of such treaties if the author is dead or cannot be found, or has become incapable of giving evidence, or cannot be called as a witness without an amount of delay or expense which the Court regards as unreasonable." Where a dispute has arisen between a customer and the bank that is said to be in the custody of the customer's money and would not release same on demand as per the terms of the documents governing their relationship, there is the presumption in law that the bank is under an obligation to produce computer-generated evidence in respect of the customer's account in her possession to prove or disprove the facts in dispute. In *Mrs. Elizabeth Anyaebosi* v. R.*T. Briscoe (Nig.) Ltd.* (1987) 6 SC 15 the Supreme Court recognized the essence of computer-generated information which records information supplied by a customer to a supplier which is stored in a computer or computers in the word of Uwais, JSC (as he then was) observed at page 33 lines 5 to 22 as follows: "At the hearing before the trial Judge (Williams, J.), the plaintiff called only one witness - Mr. Edward Oladipo Aina, who was its Spare Parts Manager. The witness after testifying that the plaintiff's accounts were kept by computer, tendered a statement of account which the plaintiff kept in respect of its transactions with the deceased. The statement was admitted, without objection by the deceased's Counsel, as Exhibit "P4". This exhibit which is in a computer printed form was certified to be a true copy by one Chief T. Ola Odukoya, employed as Senior Accountant in the plaintiff's Motor Account Department. The exhibit was dated 31st December, 1980 and it showed a balance of ₦60, 535.10 as outstanding against the deceased." Section 258(1) of the Evidence Act, 2011 defines a "computer" to mean "any device for storing and processing information and any reference to information being derived from other information is a reference to its being derived from its calculation, comparison or any other process". The information generated in a computer that is in the custody of a bank is a fact peculiarly within the knowledge of the bank that stored the information which was derived from the customer under Section 140 of the Evidence Act, 2011 as follows: "140. When a fact is especially within the knowledge of any person, the burden of proving that fact is upon him.

A STATEMENT OF ACCOUNT, ALONE AND WITHOUT OTHER OR FURTHER EVIDENCE, ORAL OR DOCUMENTARY, IS NOT SUFFICIENT EVIDENCE TO FORM OR WARRANT A CHARGE OF LIABILITY OF A PERSON

Garba, J.C.A. at pp. 18-21, Paras. F-A in the case of *Lumatron (Nig) Ltd & Anor* v. *FCMB* (2016) LPELR-41409*(CA)* remarked as follows:

> Section 51 of the Evidence Act, 2011 provides that: "Entries in books of accounts or electronic records regularly kept in the course of business are admissible whenever they refer to a matter into which the Court has to inquire, but such *statements shall not alone be sufficient evidence to charge any person with liability.*" (Italics provided) For being in plain, ordinary, simple and clear language, the above provisions are entitled to be ascribed the express purport contained therein. By their tenor, statements of entries in books of accounts or electronic records kept or maintained in the ordinary and usual course of business, are admissible whenever they refer to a matter which a Court has to determine in case, but alone, without more, "shall" not be sufficient evidence which can be used or relied upon by a Court to charge any person with liability. It simply means that such statements are not sufficient to prove, on their own, and without other or further evidence, the liability of person for which he can be charged by

a Court. Exhibit CW25 is undoubtedly, a statement of entries in books of accounts kept by the Respondent in the course of its usual business of banking in the relationship between it and the Appellants; its customers. It therefore comes without in the provisions of the Section above, by which the statement alone, shall not be sufficient evidence to charge the Appellants with liability. See *Anyaebasi* v. *RT-Briscoe Nigeria Limited* (1987) 6 SCNJ. 9. It may be noticed that the use of the word "shall" in the provisions does not admit of a discretion on whether the statement mentioned therein alone, could be considered as sufficient evidence upon which the liability of a person can be charged by a Court. The context in which the word was employed by the legislature, eliminates situations when or where the word "shall" may be interpreted to just be permissible or "may" instead of being directory of a command to be complied with in the application of the provisions. The provisions do not deal with procedure but rather, is the law on the requirement of proof of a fact assertion or allegation of liability by the party who alleges or asserts such liability against another person. In the case of *Odogwu* v. *Odogwu* (2006) 2 SCNJ. 96 @ 114, it was held that the word "shall" is used to express a command or exhortation, or what is legally mandatory. See also *Bamayi* v. *A.G.F.* (2001) 468 @ 480; *Agip Nigeria Limited* v. *Agip Pet. Int'l* (2010) 5 NWLR (1187) 348 @ 419. In the above premises, a statement of account, alone and without other or further evidence, oral or documentary, is not sufficient evidence to form or warrant a charge of liability of a person.

DISTINCTION BETWEEN A "COPY OF A DOCUMENT" AND A "DOCUMENT"

In the case of *P. D. Hallmark Contractors Nigeria Ltd & Anor* v. *Gomwalk (*2015) LPELR-24462(CA), Tur, J.C.A. at pp. 58-69, paras. F-B stated the position thus:

Section 258(1) of the Evidence Act, 2011 provides that: "In this Act, unless where the context otherwise requires... "Copy of a document includes:- (a) in the case of a document falling within paragraph (b) but not (c) of the definition of "document" in this subsection, a transcript of the sounds or other data embodied in it; (c) in the case of a document falling within paragraph (b) but not (c) of that definition, a reproduction or still reproduction of the image or images embodied in it whether enlarged or not; (d) in the case of a document falling within both those paragraphs, such a transcript together with such a still reproduction; and (e) in the case of a document not falling within the said paragraph (c) of which a visual image is embodied in a document falling within that paragraph, a reproduction of that image, whether enlarged or not, and any reference to a copy of the material part of a document shall be construed accordingly; "Computer" means any device for storing and processing information, and any reference to information being derived from other information is a reference to its being derived from it by calculation, comparison or any other process; xxxxxxxxxxxxxxxxx "Document" includes:- (a) books, maps, plans, graphs, drawings, photographs, and also includes any matter expressed or described upon any substance by means of letters, figures or marks or by more than one of these means, intended to be used or which may be used for the purpose of recording that matter; (b) any disc, tape, sound track or other device in which sounds or other data (not being visual images) are embodied so as to be capable (with or without the aid of some other equipment) of being reproduced from it, and (c) any film, negative, tape or other device in which one or more visual images are embodied so as to be capable (with or without the aid of some other equipment) of being reproduced from it; (d) in the case of a document not falling within the said paragraph (c) of which the visual image is embodied in a document falling within that paragraph, a reproduction of that image, whether enlarged or not, and any reference to a copy of the material part of a document shall be construed accordingly." The Evidence Act, 2011 distinguishes between a "copy of a document" and a "document". Photographs and films are classified as "documents" under Section 258(1)(a) of the Evidence Act (supra). A photograph, a film and a master card do not come under the tag a "copy of a document." In my humble opinion, if there is a "copy of a document", there has to be an "original" document. A "copy of a document" has been defined by the legislature using the word "includes" for a definite purpose, namely, to widen the scope of the concepts covered by the term a "copy of a document" and a "document" in Section 258(1) of the Evidence Act (supra). See *Rabiu Nafiu* v. *Kano State* (1980) FNLR 509 at 524 and *Okesuji* v. *Lawal* (1991) 2 SCNJ 1 at 13. A "film" also includes "a microfilm". The legislature has therefore distinguished between a "document" and a "copy of a document". In *Udoh & Ors.* v. *Orthopaedic Hospitals Management Board & Anor.* (1993) 7 SCNJ (Pt.2) 436, Karibi-Whyte, JSC held at page 443 that: "It is well settled principle of construction of statutes that where a section names specific things among many other possible alternatives, the intention is that those not named are not intended to be included. *Expressio unius est exclusion alterius.* See *A-G. of Bendel State* v. *Aideyan* (1989) 4 NWLR 646. This is that the express mention of one thing in a statutory provision automatically excludes any other which otherwise would have applied by implication, with regard to the same issue - See *Ogbunyiya* v. *Okudo* (1979) 6-9 SC 32; *Military Governor of Ondo State* v. *Adewunmi* (1988) 3 NWLR (Pt.82) 280." On the authority of *Udoh* v. *Orthopaedic Hospital Management & Anor.* (*supra*) at page 443 I hold that photographs and films do not constitute a "copy of a document" but comes within what is a "document" under Section 258(1) of the Evidence Act, 2011. What then is a photograph? A photograph is "a picture obtained by using a camera and film that is sensitive to light" writes the authors of Longman Dictionary of Contemporary English, 2007 edition, page 1231. In Oxford Advanced Learner's Dictionary, 8th edition, page 1100 a "photograph" is defined as "a picture that is made by using a camera that has a film sensitive to light inside it." A camera and a film are needed to produce a photograph. They are bed-fellows. Without a camera and a film there can be no photograph; and where there is no film in a camera no camera will be snapped to produce a photograph. The practice before the enactment of the Evidence Act, 2011 was to tender the film as primary evidence and the printed photograph as secondary evidence. What then is "photography"? Photography is "the art, process or job of taking photographs or filming something", writes the authors of Oxford Advanced Learner's Dictionary (*supra*) page 1100. In *Cambridge Advanced Learner's Dictionary* (*supra*) page 931, it is "(the activity or job of taking) photographs or films." Section 86(1)-(4) of the Evidence Act, 2011 provides as follows: "86(1) Primary evidence means the document itself produced for the inspection of the Court. (2) Where a document has been executed in several parts, each part shall be primary evidence of the document. (3) Where a document has been executed in counterpart, each counterpart being executed by one or some of the parties only, each counterpart shall be primary evidence as against the parties executing it. (4) Where a number of documents have all been made by one uniform process, as in the case of printing lithography, photography, computer or other electronic or mechanical process, each shall be primary evidence of the contents of the rest, but where they are all copies of a common original, they shall not be primary evidence of the contents of the original." Photographs and films are "documents" which have "been made by one uniform process as in the case of... photography, computer or other electronic or mechanical process." Therefore a photograph and the film, "each shall be primary evidence of the contents of the rest..." of one another. See Section 84(4) of the Evidence Act, 2011. Photographs are no longer secondary evidence and films primary evidence. Both constitute primary evidence of the contents of the rest. This is a complete departure from the law before the coming into effect of the Evidence Act, 2011. See Section 258(1) of the Act (*supra*). Secondary evidence is defined under Section 87(a)-(e) of the Evidence Act (supra) as follows: "87. Secondary evidence includes:- (a) Certified copies given under the provisions hereafter contained in this Act; (b) Copies made from the original by mechanical or electronic processes which in themselves ensure the accuracy of the copy, and copies compared with such copies; (c) Copies made from or compared with the original; (d) Counterparts of documents as against the parties who did not execute them; (e) Oral accounts of the contents of a document given by some person who has himself seen it." If it is intended to tender secondary evidence of the condition or contents of a document the party has to comply with the provisions of Section 83(1)-(5) read together with Sections 89(a)-91(a)-(c) of the Act as follows: "Secondary evidence may be given of the existence, condition or contents of a document in the following cases: (a) When the original is shown or appears to be in the possession or power: (i) of the person against whom the document is sought to be proved, or (ii) of any person legally bound to produce it, and when after the notice mentioned in section 91 such person does not produce it; (b) When the existence, condition or contents of the original have been proved to be admitted in written by the person against whom it is proved or by his representative in interest; (c) When the original bas been destroyed or lost and in the later case all possible search has been made for it; (d) When the original is of such a nature as not to be easily movable; (e) When the original is a public document within the meaning of section 102; (f) When the original is a document of which a certified copy is permitted by this Act or by any other law in force in Nigeria, to be given in evidence; (g) When the originals consist of numerous accounts or other documents which cannot conveniently be examined in Court, and the fact to be proved is the general result of the whole collection; (h) When the document is an entry in a banker's book. 90(1) The secondary evidence admissible in respect of the original documents referred to in the several paragraphs of Section 89 is as follows: (a) In paragraphs (a), (c) and (d) any secondary evidence of the contents of the document is admissible; (b) In paragraph (b), the written admission is admissible; (c) In paragraph (e) or (f), a certified copy of the document, but no other secondary evidence is admissible; (d) In paragraph (g), evidence may be given as to the general result of the documents by any person who has examined them, and who is skilled in the examination of such documents; (e) In paragraph (h), the copies cannot be received as evidence unless it is first be proved that: (i) The book in which the entries copied were made was at the time of making one of the ordinary books of the bank; (ii) The entry was made in the usual and ordinary course of business, (iii) The book is in the control and custody of the bank, which proof may be given orally or by affidavit by an officer of the bank, and (iv) The copy has been examined with the original entry and is correct, which proof must be given by some person who has examined the copy with the original entry, and may be given orally or by affidavit. (2) When a seaman sues for his wages he may give secondary evidence of the ship's articles and of any agreement supporting his case, without notice to produce the originals. 91. Secondary evidence of the contents of the documents referred to in paragraph (a) of Section 89 shall not be given unless the party proposing to give such secondary evidence has previously given to the party in whose possession or power the document is, or to a legal practitioner employed by such party, such notice to produced it as is prescribed by law, and if no notice to produce is prescribed by law then such notice as the Court considers reasonable in the circumstances of the case: Provided that such notice shall not be required in order to render secondary evidence admissible in any of the following cases, or in any other case in which the Court thinks fit to dispense with it: (a) When the document to be proved is itself a notice; (b) When, from the nature of the case, the adverse party must know that he will be required to produce it; (c) When it appears or is proved that the adverse party has obtained possession of the original by fraud or force." But if the evidence to be adduced was produced by a computer Section 84(1)-(3) of the Act provides as follows: "(1) In any proceedings a statement contained in a document produced by a computer shall be admissible as evidence of any fact stated in it of which direct oral evidence would be admissible, if it is shown that the conditions in subsection (2) of this section are satisfied in relation to the statement and computer in question. (2) The conditions referred to in subsection (1) of this section are: (a) That the document containing the statement was produced by the computer during a period over which the computer was used regularly to store or process information for the purposes of any activities regularly carried on over that period, whether for profit or not, by anybody, whether corporate or not, or by any individual; (b) That over that period there was regularly supplied to the computer in the ordinary course of those activities or of the kind from which the information so contained is derived; (c) That throughout the material part of that period the computer was operating properly or, if not, that in any respect in which it was not operating properly or was out of operation during that part of that period was not such as to affect the production of the document or the accuracy of it contents; and (d) That the information contained in the statement reproduces or is derived from information supplied to the computer in the ordinary course of those activities. (3) Where over a period the function of storing or processing information for the purposes of any activities regularly carried on over that period as mentioned in subsection (2): (a) of this section was regularly performed by computers, whether (b) by a combination of computers operating over that period; or (c) by different computers operating in succession over that period, or (d) by different combinations of computers operating in succession over that period; or (e) in any other manner involving the successive operation over that period, in whatever order, of one or more computers and one or more combinations of computers, all the computers used for that purpose during that period shall be treated for the purposes of this section as constituting a single computer; and references in accordingly.

COMMENTARY

It must be appreciated that the above principles of law already highlighted, simple documents generated from computers require no authentication under Section 84 of the Evidence Act, 2011.[1]

It is, therefore, wrong to assume that a document which was typed using a computer is a computer-generated document. Section 84 of the Evidence Act is inapplicable to a simple document produced from a computer when the

[1] See the case of *Attorney General of the Federation* v. *Princewell Ugonna Anuebunwa (SC).*

computer is merely used as a tool such as a typewriter to produce the document. According to Hon. Justice Omolaye – Ajileye,[2] he posited thus:

> The only function the computer is serving is to store the information input by the author. There is no processing or value added in terms of computer-generated data. Furthermore, the fact that the printout is taken at the time of production takes away any challenge as to storage or metadata of the contents or any manipulation. This will be equivalent to when a person writes a letter with a pen or typewriter and signs the same after verifying the contents. The only difference would be the print style; font and the use of features like spell check, etc.

The authenticity of such a document is invariably established by its originality and the signature or seal it carries. The decision of the Supreme Court in the case of *Attorney General of the Federation* v. *Princewell Ugonna Anuebunwa* (SC) has now invalidated the erroneous position in some quarters that any document produced by a computer must necessarily be treated as a computer-generated to call for the application of Section 84 of the Evidence Act. The Court of Appeal of Nigeria in the case of *IBTC Bank* v. *Long Term Bglobal Capital Ltd & Ors*[3] had hitherto conscripted the application of Section 84 when it held that a party who does not have the device from which a document is produced cannot be required to produce a certificate under section 84 of the Evidence Act, 2011 to authenticate it.

---

[2] *Electronic Evidence,* Revised Edition, Jurist Publication – Lokoja, 2019, Pp. 273 – 274.

[3] (2021) LPELR – 55610 (CA).

Chapter 5

ADMISSIBILITY OF SMS FROM GLOBAL SATELLITE MOBILE (GSM), TELEPHONE CONVERSATIONS, EMAILS, TAPE RECORDINGS AND ELECTRONIC SERVICE OF COURT PROCESSES

A GSM GADGET WITH USEFUL INFORMATION CAN BE TENDERED IN EVIDENCE TOGETHER WITH THE MESSAGE OR INFORMATION STORED BY IT

Commenting on the position of the law in relation to the above, Ikyegh, J.C.A. at pp. 43-46, Paras. F-C in the case of *Orogun & Anor* v. *Fidelity Bank* (2018) LPELR-46601(CA) held thus:

> Exhibit P5 is SMS (GSM) message said to have written off the indebtedness. This is electronic or computer crime generated from Global Satellite Mobile (GSM) system into mobile phones which are also computers. When the message so generated is printed out the printed copies become primary documentary evidence. Section 258(1)(d) of the Evidence Act defines a document to include any device by means of which information is stored, recorded or retrievable including computer output. A GSM gadget with useful information can therefore be tendered in evidence together with the message or information stored by it. Once tendered and admitted in

evidence it becomes documentary evidence. The duty then behoved the party that tendered it in evidence to read the information or message in the open Court as is the case with documentary evidence, or the parties may by consensus take the document as read. And/or the GSM gadget may be admitted in evidence as computer generated evidence under Section 84 of the Evidence Act. ?In this case, the respondent denied/disputed the GSM message in Exhibit P5. At that stage it was incumbent on appellant to call logs/evidence of communication from the central portal of the service delivery company, or identification evidence of the sender/receiver of such message should have been called by the appellant under Sections 94, 125 and 126 of the Evidence Act. Section 94 of the Evidence Act, for example provides - "(1) Evidence that a person exists having the same name, address, business or occupation as the maker of a document purports to have, is admissible to show that such was written or signed by that person. (2) Evidence that a document exists to which the document the making of which is in issue purports to be a reply, together with evidence of the making and delivery to a person of such earlier document, is admissible to show the identity of the maker of the disputed document with the person to whom the earlier document was delivered". Or in a case where written records are kept by a mobile phone user such written records are admissible to prove and/or corroborate the call logs on the said GSM phone vide the apt foreign case of *R.* v. *Singh* (2006) 1 WLR 1564 where the holder of the GSM phone kept a separate notebook in which he recorded numbers he had saved in the memory of the GSM phone, it was held that evidence in the notebooks which the user traced to the defendant, was admissible to show that the number saved belonged to the defendant. None of the options (supra) was adopted by the appellant in the instant case, therefore Exhibit P5 has no weight or probative value and cannot be relied upon as evidence that the respondent wrote off the huge debt of ₦29,257,743.51 by GSM message in Exhibit P5. I believe or think the essence of the law of Evidence is discovery of the truth. Genuineness of any piece of evidence sought to be relied upon by a party in the case unless the document is admitted by the adverse party must of necessity be properly ascertained and verified to weed out or eliminate suspicious or spurious documents.

5.2 POSITION OF THE LAW ON ADMISSIBILITY OF TELEPHONE CONVERSATIONS/MESSAGES

Ikyegh, J.C.A. at pp. 19-20, Paras. D-B in the case of *Ahmed* v. *Nigerian Navy* (2017) LPELR-44025(CA) stated as follows:

> In addition, the phone conversation on the allegation of conspiracy or gang-up between the appellant's superiors and some of his ship's company and members of the court-martial were not properly proved in evidence as its contents were not demonstrated in the court-martial by a witness conversant with it vide S.T. Hon's *Law of Evidence in Nigeria* 2012 in pages 506 - 507 where the learned author aptly wrote - "... a GSM gadget or telephone itself, if it contains valuable information, can be successfully tendered in evidence together with whatever message or information stored therein; as evidence, the only duty of the tendering party being to read it in open Court and to demonstrate its contents in the open Court in the similitude of reading ordinary documentary evidence when admitted in evidence or taking them as read.

ADMISSIBILITY OF RECORDED CONVERSATIONS OF PERSONS WHO ARE DECEASED

In the case *Onwuzulike* v. *State* (2017) LPELR-41889(CA), Tur, J.C.A. at pp. 110-123, paras. A-D remarked thus:

> It is a fact that Chinwuba Ekwenze is not alive to testify. But the computer-generated evidence recorded his conversations with the appellant, Nnamdi Osita, PW1-PW4 between 13th January 2013 to 17th January, 2013. MTN also recorded the statement of each prosecution witness that had conversation with the deceased, the appellant and Nnamdi Osita between 13th January, 2013 up to 17th January, 2013.

Each of the prosecution witnesses Nos. PW5 and PW6 had personal knowledge of the matters dealt with in the computer by MTN. This was tendered at the trial through PW5 and PW6. The fact that PW5 was a "mobile forensic expert" (see page 131 lines 13-19 of the printed record) was not contradicted during cross-examination. The defence Counsel did not challenge the credential or expertise of PW6 through whom the call flash was put in as evidence. PW5 and PW6 gave detailed evidence as to how they were able to link the appellant with the disappearance of the deceased. Section 83 of the Evidence Act, 2011 deals generally with the admissibility of documentary evidence. This is made clear by the heading to the section. Section 84 of the Evidence Act (ante) relates specifically to "admissibility of statement in documents produced by computers". There is no challenge to the fact that the information contained in the statement in the computer which the prosecution derived to prosecute the appellant was "...derived from information supplied to the computer in the ordinary course of those activities" under Section 84(1)(d) in the course of the business carried out by MTN in the telecommunication industry. In *Mrs. Elizabeth Anyaebosi* v. *R.T. Briscoe (Nig.) Ltd.* (1987) 6 SC 15 it was common ground that the appellant had an account with the respondent which recorded their business transactions. The respondent had produced a certified true copy of the statement of account (Exhibit "P4") from its computer generated record which was admitted without objection by the appellant's learned Counsel in the Court below. The learned trial Judge relied on Exhibit "P4" to found for the respondent. The appellant contended in the Supreme Court that Exhibit "P4" was inadmissible. Uwais, JSC (as he then was) observed at page 33 lines 5 to 22 as follows: "At the hearing before the trial Judge (Williams, J.), the plaintiff called only one witness - Mr. Edward Oladipo Aina, who was its Spare Parts Manager. The witness after testifying that the plaintiff's accounts were kept by computer, tendered a statement of account which the plaintiff kept in respect of its transactions with the deceased. The statement was admitted, without objection by the deceased's Counsel, as Exhibit "P4". This exhibit which is in a computer printed form was certified to be a true copy by one Chief T. Ola Odukoya, employed as Senior Accountant in the plaintiff's Motor Account Department. The exhibit was dated 31st December, 1980 and it showed a balance of ₦60,535.10 as outstanding against the deceased." The Supreme Court took into consideration the fact that Exhibit "P4" was admitted without objection to hold at page 43 to 47 as follows: "In general, it is true that where a document, which is inadmissible in evidence, is admitted at trial, such document must be rejected on appeal - *Ajayi* v. *Fisher*, 1 FSC 97, *Esso West African Incorporated* v. *Alli* (1968) NMLR 414 at p.423 and *Jacker* v. *International Cable Co. Ltd.* (1888) L.T.R. 13. However, this rule is not without exception. Certain class of evidence is absolutely inadmissible by virtue of some statutory provisions; while another class is made admissible under certain conditions. In the case of the former class the evidence cannot be acted upon whether it was admitted by consent of the parties or otherwise; and the evidence will be rejected on appeal if it was admitted in the trial Court - See *Owonyin* v. *Omotosho* (1961) 1 All NLR 304 at p.308; Yassin v. *Barclays Bank D.C.O.* (1968) 1 All NLR 171 at p.177 and *Alashe* v. *Ilu* (1964) 1 All NLR 390 at p.397. With regard to the latter class if the conditions laid down for the admission of the evidence are not absolute, as in the former class, then such inadmissible evidence if admitted without objection, the appellant cannot complain against the admission - See *Chukwurah Ekume* v. *Mathias Ekwunno & Ors.* 14 WACA 59; *Yassin* v. *Barclays Bank D.C.O.* (*supra*) at p.179; and *Alade* v. *Olukade* (*supra*) where this Court (per Idigbe, JSC) observed as follows: "Dealing with the latter class of cases, however, this Court in *Cavalotti Govianni* v. *Bonaso Luigi*, SC.402/67 of 31/10/69, held that a document (a photocopy) which did not comply with Section 96(1)(b) of the Evidence Act and which had been admitted without objection by the appellant was legal evidence upon which the Court could properly act. See also *Chukwura Akunne* v. *Mathias Ekwunno and Ors.* (1952) 14 WACA 59. Accordingly, in those cases where the evidence complained of is not, by law, inadmissible in any event a party may, by his own conduct at the trial, be precluded from objecting to such evidence on appeal. See *Gilbert* v. *Endean* (1878) 9 Ch. D. 259 where

Cotton, L.J. made the following observations:- "But I must add this where in the Court below the evidence not being that on which the Court can properly act, if the person against whom it is read does not object, but treats it as admissible, then before the Court of Appeal, in my judgment, he is not at liberty to complain of the order on the ground that the evidence was not admissible. It is very clear that Exhibit "P4", in the present case, was admissible under the provisions of Section 96 Subsections (1) and (2) of the Evidence Act. But the respondent did not lead evidence to show which of the conditions under Section 96(1) applied to the exhibit. Appellant on the other had did not object; he cannot therefore now complain that the exhibit is inadmissible because no evidence was led by the respondent at the trial to show which of the paragraphs in Section 96(2) covered its admission. In *Yassin* v. *Barclays Bank D.C.O. (supra),* Lewis, JSC stated at p.179 as follows: "We do not, in this judgment seek to derogate from what we said in *Alashe* v. *Ilu* in any way. That case was dealing with evidence absolutely inadmissible by virtue of the statutory provisions applicable there, but here the statement of account is expressly declared to be admissible under Section 96 of the Evidence Act, if certain conditions are satisfied. If inadmissible evidence is not objected to and is admitted it must still be rejected on appeal but if the evidence can be interpreted as complying with the appropriate statutory requirement, then it is a matter to be taken into consideration when interpreting the evidence that it went in unchallenged. In other words, if the evidence can be treated as inadmissible because there is a possible other interpretation which would render it inadmissible when that possible other interpretation had not been tested by questions from the party who could have objected to the evidence being admitted." (emphasis mine). Karibi-Whyte, JSC held at pages 60 to 67 as follows: "It is pertinent to observe that Exhibit "P4" alleged to be inadmissible by Counsel to the appellants is the statement of account by the respondents of the transaction between appellant and respondents. In Paragraph 5 of the statement of claim which was admitted in Paragraph 3 of the statement of defence, it was pleaded as follows: "5. That the defendant kept account No.534-121-210 with the plaintiff and the plaintiff shall rely on the defendants' statement of account kept with the plaintiff at the trial of this suit." It is this admitted statement of account that was certified by Chief T. Ola Odukoya, the Senior Accountant of the respondent as Exhibit "P4". Chief Odukoya was described by Counsel to the appellant as a party interested within the meaning of Section 90(3) of the Evidence Act. Mr. Aduroja has in his brief of argument submitted that Exhibit "P4", the statement of Account, was rightly admitted under Section 90(2) of the Evidence Act. It was submitted that Exhibit "P4" was not made by a person interested within Section 90(3) of the Evidence Act since Chief T. Ola Odukoya was Senior Accountant of the respondent's Company and by virtue of his office and in the ordinary course of duty, and had no personal financial interest in the result of the case. Counsel also rejected the contention that Exhibit "P4" was made in articulation of litigation. He referred to Exhibit "P10", "P11", and "P12", letters of demand from Solicitors of the respondent to the appellant, and contended that Exhibit "P4" was made not in anticipation of litigation but in the ordinary course of commercial transactions. Counsel referred to *Beamans Ltd.* v. *Metropolitan Police District Receiver* (1961) 1 WLR 634; *Jarman* v. *Lambert and Cooke (Contractors) Ltd.* (1951) 2 All ER 255 at p.261. Without conceding the fact, but assuming that Exhibit "P4" was wrongfully admitted, in evidence, Counsel submitted that the decision having been upheld by the Court of Appeal, the judgment was saved by the provisions of Section 226(1) of the Evidence Act. The dominant consideration is whether substantial justice has been done taking into account what has been properly proved - Counsel cited and relied on *Alhadi* v. *Allie* (1951) 13 WACA 323; *Owoyin* v. *Omotosho* (1961) 1 All NLR 304; *Okirinta Ugbola & Ors.* v. *Awo Okorie & Ors.* (1972) 12 SC 1 at pp.13-14. It is of primary and critical importance that a document used in litigation must not only be relevant, it should also be admissible. Section 96(1) sets out the circumstances where secondary evidence will be admissible. Counsel to the appellant is contending that Exhibit "P4", being a computer copy of the statement of account, does not fall within any of the conditions (a)-(h) set out in Section 96(2). It is well settled that a Judge is perfectly entitled in his judgment to disregard an evidence erroneously admitted at the trial. See *Alashe* v. *Ilu* (1964) 1 All NLR 390, 397. Similarly where the inadmissibility is raised on appeal, such evidence must be rejected and expunged. - See *Ajayi* v. *Fisher* (1956) 1 FSC 97; *Esso West African Incorporation* v. *Alli* (1968) NMLR 414, 428. For the purposes of admissibility, there is the category of evidence which are absolutely inadmissible on the grounds of statutory exclusionary provisions. This category of evidence remain legally inadmissible and cannot under any circumstance constitute evidence in the case at the trial or on appeal even where admitted by consent. See *Ikenye* v. *Ofunne* (1985) 2 NWLR (Pt.5) 1; *Owoyin* v. *Omotosho* (1961) 1 All NLR 304, 308; *Alashe* v. *Ilu* (1964) 1 All NLR 390, 397; *Yashin* v. *Barclays Bank D.C.O.* (1968) 1 All NLR 171, 177. There is the other category of inadmissible evidence rendered admissible on the fulfilment of certain conditions. This category of evidence are admissible if admitted without objection by the other party, and where the admission of the evidence did not affect the result of the case - See *Okeke* v. *Obidife* (1965) NMLR 113; *Alade* v. *Olukade* (1976) 6 SC 183. In the last mentioned category, the other party is not entitled thereafter to complain where such evidence was admitted at the trial without objection. This principle of English common law was stated in the English case of *Gilbert* v. *Endean* (1878) 9 Ch. D. 259, and applied in this Court in *Alade* v. *Olukade* (1976) 6 SC 183. It is not applied to Section 96 of the Evidence Act. In *Gilbert* v. *Endean* (*supra*) Cotton, L.J. said: "But I must add this where in the Court below the evidence not being that on which the Court can properly act, if the person against whom it is led does not object, but treats it as admissible, then before the Court of Appeal, in any judgment, he is not at liberty to complain of the order on the ground that the evidence was not admissible. In adopting this view Idigbe, JSC in *Alade* v. *Olukade* (*supra*) relying on the unreported decision of this Court in *Cavatotti Govianni* v. *Banaso Luigi* SC.402/67 of 31/10/69, and the West African Court of Appeal case of *Akunne* v. *Ekwuno & Ors.* (1951) 14 WACA 59 on the non-compliance with Section 96(1)(b) of the Evidence Act, Cap. 62, and where evidence was admitted without objection said, "...in those cases where the evidence complained of is not, by law, inadmissible in any event a party may, by his own act at the trial, be precluded from objecting to such evidence on appeal..." The legal effect of the two categories of evidence as I have tried to show was stated lucidly in *Yashin* v. *Barclays Bank D.C.O.* (*supra*) at p.179. It is important to state that a computerized account which Exhibit "P4" was described to be, does not fall into the category of evidence absolutely inadmissible by law. In my opinion it falls within the category of evidence admissible on the fulfilment of the conditions prescribed in Section 96(1) and (2) of the Evidence Act, Cap.62. Admittedly, there was no evidence in the trial Court to explain the conditions under which Exhibit "P4" was being tendered, and admitted, this Court has only recently in *Kate Enterprises Ltd.* v. *Daewoo Nig. Ltd.* (1985) 2 NWLR (Pt.5) 116, held that evidence by any servant or agent of a company is relevant and admissible to establish any transaction entered into by that company. That decision went further to hold that the evidence tendered need not be that of the official who took part in the transaction. I do not think that a computerized account could not be brought within the category of documents, establishing the transaction between appellants and respondents as stated in *Kate Enterprises Ltd.* v. *Daewoo (Nig.) Ltd. (supra)*. The originals of this evidence are described in Section 96(1)(d), (g). These are: "(d) When the original is of such a nature as not to be easily movable. xxxxxx (g) When the original consists of numerous accounts or other documents which cannot conveniently be examined in Court, and the fact to be proved is the general result of the whole collection." However, since the basis of the admission of Exhibit "P4" was not at the trial tested by cross-examination to determine whether it fell within either of these classes the validity of its admissibility is merely a matter to be taken into consideration. In the circumstances where appellant was not at any stage disputing that there was an account with the respondent company, and the proper officers of the company were at no time challenged, it is consistent with the provisions of Section

96(2), that Exhibit "P4" is secondary evidence in respect of the documents stated in Section 96(1)(d) or (g) - See Section 96(2)(a), (d)." Karibi-Whyte, JSC concluded at pages 70 to 71 as follows: "In all commercial transactions litigation is always ultimately likely and a possibility. If all statements and documents prepared in the course of business or other transactions were to be excluded from proceedings in Court on this ground, then a serious clog has been introduced into the wheel of legitimate transactions and the administration of justice. In my opinion and for the reasons given above Exhibit "P4" is admissible for the purpose of this appeal, and the Court of Appeal was right in the view that it was too late to complain.

DISTINCTION BETWEEN AN INSTRUMENT AND A TELEPHONE CONVERSATION

In the case of *Minister of Internal Affairs & Ors* v. *Okoro & Ors* (2003) LPELR-7264 (CA), Ogunbiyi, J.C.A. at P. 23, paras. E-G held thus:

The Black's Law Dictionary, Fifth Edition has defined instrument at page 719 as: "A written document, a formal or legal document in writing, such as a contract, deed, will, bond or lease". The same dictionary also defines legislation at page 809 as: "The act of giving or enacting laws..." While instrument or legislation has a force of law, a telephone conversation is a related message and which falls short of any legal interpretation.

THE TEST OF ADMISSIBILITY OF ELECTRONICALLY GENERATED DOCUMENTS SUCH AS AN EMAIL IS ITS AUTHENTICITY AND TRUSTWORTHINESS AND THE RELEVANCE OF ITS CONTENT TO THE PROCEEDINGS

Commenting on the admissibility of electronically generated documents such as an email, Uwa, J.C.A. at pp. 72-79, Paras.

D-B in the case of *Rowaye* v. *FRN & Ors* (2018) LPELR-45650(CA) posited as follows:

> The learned Senior Counsel faulted the E-mails being computer generated evidence and also faulted the decision of the trial Court admitting same on the grounds that the prosecution failed to satisfy the requirement of Section 84 of the Evidence Act, 2011. The lower court in its judgment thoroughly dealt with the admissibility of E-mail evidence and the authentication of the device used to generate the e-mails and their outputs in resolution of the third issue at the lower Court, pages 60 - 66 of Volume III of the printed records of appeal (the judgment of the lower Court). The prosecution made out that the Lloyd's List Intelligence Report has a world class reputation and is conclusive on the status of the Mother Vessel, MT Kriti Akti. Details of how the report was obtained and authenticated were given details of at pages 61 - 62 of Vol. III of the printed records (the judgment) as well as the working condition of the Mechanical Instrument utilized to obtain the report. There was no evidence to the contrary. For clarity, I will reproduce portions of pages 62 - 64 hereunder of what the learned trial judge had to say thus: "The first computer from Lloyd's List Intelligence has a certificate of compliance in conformity with the requirement of Section 84 of the Evidence Act. ... The prosecution provided evidence of compliance with the provisions of the Evidence Act by ensuring the Certification of these Documents by the maker or extractors of the information contained therein. The evidence on Record further shows that the Report was derived from an E-mail correspondence between the Prosecution and an Official of the Lloyd's List. ... Now, the test of admissibility of this Electronically Generated Documents is in its authenticity and trustworthiness and the relevance of its content to the proceedings. The certificate of Identification from the Director of Operations stated that the contents of the Report was an attachment in his e-mail correspondence with the Lloyd's List and that is as seen in the front page of Exhibit Z4, which displayed a chain of communication between the Director of

Operations and Justin Donald of the Lloyd's List Intelligence. The documents containing e-mail correspondences were produced from the Director of Operation's e-mail inbox through an Apple Desktop computer and he named the serial Number and the model of the Printer and computer, certifying that the computer and printer were used regularly to store, process and print information. During the period of use, there was regularly supplied to the E-mail Address and computer in the ordinary course of those activities, information of the kind contained in the inbox of his e-mail address, from which the information, so contained, was derived through the computer and printer. He further certified that throughout the period, the E-mail Address, computer and printer were operating properly and the information contained in the documents reproduced was derived from the information supplied to the E-mail Address. This piece of evidence provided by the PW11 was not controverted by any evidence adduced by the Defence, challenging the trustworthiness of the process in obtaining the Report. Therefore the process of obtaining this Report is deemed properly derived in compliance with the requirements of the law. As regards the fact that the Report is stated to be Hearsay Evidence, the provisions of Section 84 (5)(a) and (c) of the Evidence Act 2011 has settled the issue of hearsay by providing that, with or without human intervention, both the supply of information to the computer and the production of a Document by a computer are to be taken to be appropriately done. The settled Law in Nigeria, by this provision, therefore, is that Hearsay has little or no role to play in admissibility of computer Evidence. This Section permits without qualification, human intervention in supply of information to the computer and even in the printout coming from a computer. As regards the reliability of the information supplied by Lloyd's List Intelligence, it is seen in Exhibit Z4 that the Lloyd's List is an Informa Business, and one of the world's leading providers of specialist information and services for the academic, scientific, professional and commercial business communities. In their Report submitted to the EFCC, they relied on the vessel AIS Box, satellite Sightings and Conventional Movements (Verified by Agents in Ports), and further claimed to correctly reflect real events. It is their summary that no vessel, whether Kriti Akti or Akti, was reported to have arrived at Amsterdam between the 12th and 15th of June 2011, and it was highly unlikely that Kriti Akti could have been at Cotonou in July 2011, because there is sufficient evidence to support the fact that the vessel was demolished at Gadarni Beach in April 2010." Further, at page 65, the learned trial judge in respect of the evidence of the PW11 the (Investigating Police Officer - IPO). In respect of the representative of the Lloyd's List Intelligence held thus: "This Representative highlighted all the relevant information regarding EFCC's Request, which included the List of scrapped vessels at Gadarni Beach in Pakistan in 2010 and had provided further information on two vessels namely, MT Kriti Akti and MT Althea. This information was sent to the commission through the official Email of the Director of Operations, which was subsequently printed out from the central computer and duly certified by the commission. This Representative also furnished the commission with the physical copy of the certificate of compliance signed by the Director, Commercial of Lloyd's List Intelligence. He testified as to the description, day-to-day use and as to the competency of the computer." As to the probative value of the Report, the learned trial judge did a thorough analysis to show that the prosecution proved that the alleged vessel MT Kriti Akti was not in existence as at the time she was alleged to have moved the PMS from Amsterdam to Cotonou having been declared inactive and decommissioned to be broken up on 17th April, 2010. The trial Court rightly held that there was no contrary evidence on all the above procedure followed, before the Email Reports were admitted and utilized by the trial Court in arriving at its decision. The Court was right to have accepted and utilized the Lloyd's List Intelligence Report as a reliable piece of evidence that was not challenged by the appellant. In a decision of this Court, *Continental Sales Limited* v. *R. SHIPPING INC.* (2012) LPELR - 7905 (CA); (2013) 4 NWLR (PT. 1343) P. 67 his Lordship Ogunwumiju, JCA in respect of a computer generated mail held thus: "Email is a form of communication that is set down in writing. It is not oral. The fact that it is electronic is immaterial. It is not in the air. It can be downloaded and as real as a hard copy of the letter or mail in your hand." I hold that the prosecution in tendering Exhibits Z, Z2, Z3 and Z4 dealing with the Lloyd's List Intelligence Report complied with the requirement of Section 84 of the Evidence Act, 2011, as rightly found by the learned trial judge. The evidence of the PW11 (eleven) is also not hearsay.

ELECTRONIC EVIDENCE AS A MEDIUM OF SERVICE OF COURT PROCESSES IS ADMISSIBLE

In the case of *Continental Sales Ltd* v. *R. Shipping Inc (2012) LPELR-7905 (CA)*, Ogunwumiju, J.C.A. at pp. 23-27, paras. B-C opined thus:

The fact that it is electronic is immaterial. It is not in thin air. It can be downloaded and as real as a hard copy of the letter or mail in your hand. Section 76(4) makes a distinction between personally delivered notices and other forms of communication by stating that where the notice is addressed, prepaid and delivered by land post which is the traditional method, then it must be to the addressee's last known principal residence, etc., or where a body corporate to the body's registered or principal office. In my humble view, section 76 (3) is a general provision under which a party must operate to the extent that there must be proof that the service of notice has been effective. Whereas 76(a) relates only to where there has been service by land post. It is obvious from the record that all communication between the parties including the signing of agreements, etc., were performed electronically. It is in my view unconscionable for the Appellant to turn around to say that that form of communication has not been effective. In *Trade Bank Plc* v. *Chami* (2003) 13 NWLR Pt. 836 Pg. 158 at 216-217 Salami JCA (as he then was) held as follows: "Although the law does not talk of "computer" and "computer prints out" it is not oblivious to or ignorant of modern business world and the technological advancement of the modern jet age. As far back as 1969, the Supreme Court in the case of *Esso West Africa Inc.* v. *T. Oyegbola* (1969) NMLR

194, 198 envisaged the need to extend the horizon of the section to include or cover computer which was virtually not in existence or at a very rudimentary stage at that time when the court said- "The Law cannot be and is not ignorant of modern business methods and must not shut its eyes to the mysteries of the computer." In *Bernuth Lines Ltd* v. *High Seas Shipping Ltd* cited *supra* by both counsels, (it is a Lloyds Report), Clark J, in considering whether notice of arbitration by email was properly served held as follows at page 541: "I do not regard the provisions of CPR part 6 as an appropriate benchmark by which to judge whether or not service by e-mail is effective in the context of an arbitration. The Civil Procedure Rules cater for litigants of all kinds from major corporations represented by the most accomplished firms of solicitors to individuals represented by more modest firms and those who are not represented at all. By contrast arbitrations are usually conducted by businessmen represented by, or with ready access to lawyers. Section 76 (3), when providing that a notice could be served on a person by any effective means was, in my judgment, purposely wide. It contemplates that any means of service will suffice provided that it is a recognized means of communication effective to deliver the document to the party to whom it is sent at his address for the purpose of that means of communication (e.g. post fax or e-mail). There is no reason why, in this context, delivery of a document by e-mail - a method habitually used by businessmen, lawyers and civil servants - should be regarded as essentially different from communication by post, fax or telex." I am entitled to be persuaded by the dictum set out above and I hold myself so persuaded. It only stands to reason that any previous accepted and acceptable means of communication among the parties would remain an effective means of service of any subsequent notice of arbitration proceedings. At page 138 of *Bermith Lines Ltd* v. *High Seas Shipping Ltd* the court held thus: "a. Where a party is to be served by "electronic means" the party who is to be served or his legal representative must previously have expressly indicated in writing to the party serving that he is willing to accept service by electronic means. Where a party seeks to serve a document by electronic means he should first seek to clarify with the party who is to be served whether there are any limitations to the recipient's agreement to accept service by such means including the format in which documents are to be sent and the maximum size of attachments that may be received.

Electronic Service of Hearing Notice is Valid

In the case of *C.M & E.S. Ltd* v. *Pazan Services Nig. Ltd* (2020) 1 NWLR (PT. 1704) P. 70, the Court held thus:

> At this age of information and technology, it will be foolhardy for any litigant to insist on being served with a hard copy of a hearing notice. Once a notice is sent to a telephone number supplied by the litigant, it is sufficient.

TAPE RECORDINGS FALLS UNDER THE CATEGORY OF EVIDENCE THAT IS ADMISSIBLE UPON THE FULFILMENT OF CERTAIN CONDITIONS

In the case of *Federal Polytechnic, Ede & Ors* v. *Oyebanji (2012) LPELR-19696(CA),* IYIZOBA, J.C.A. at pp. 45-46, Paras. B-B held as follows:

> ...The courts made the best of the situation by expanding the definition of "document" to include computer generated information which to my mind includes tape recordings. See definition of "document" in Section 2(1) of the Evidence Act 1945 as amended and the cases of *Yusuf* v. *ACB Ltd* (1976) 1 SC 45: *Anyagbosi* v. *R.T. Briscoe Ltd.* (1987) 3 NWLR (Pt. 59) 108: *Trade Bank PLC* v. *Chami* (2003) 13 NWLR (Pt. 836) 216: *FRN* v. *Fani-Kayode* (2010) 14 NWLR (Pt. 1214) 481 at 506. Those types of evidence do not fall within the category of evidence made completely inadmissible in law. Rather they fall within the category of evidence admissible upon the fulfilment of certain conditions. In the case of a tape recording, as in other types of documentary evidence, it must be tendered by the maker subject to the usual exceptions. Contrary to the view of the learned trial judge, the maker of the tape recording

is DW3. He testified that he recorded his conversation with the lady, Bolaji. But DW3 must lay the necessary foundation that will make the tape recording admissible in evidence. He must lead evidence to show that the tape recording is authentic in the sense that it is the original; that the voice in the recording is indeed that of Bolaji Opeseitan; that the tape was in his custody all the time and that there was no opportunity for anyone to tamper with it. None of these conditions was satisfied. If, for example Bolaji herself had identified the tape recording and admitted the voice therein to be hers, then the tape could possibly be rendered admissible but without such identification and in the absence of the person whose voice was said to have been recorded, the evidence is hearsay. The learned trial judge was therefore right in ruling the tape recording inadmissible.

COMMENTARY

What is currently in vogue is the use of SMS (GSM) messages as well as telephone conversations as a means of communication and transactions in our daily lives. The usage is electronic or computer evidence generated from Global Satellite Mobile (GSM) system into mobile phones which are also computers. When the message so generated is printed out the printed copies become primary documentary evidence. Section 258(1) (d) of the Evidence Act defines a document to include any device by means of which information is stored, recorded or retrievable including computer output. A GSM gadget or mobile phone with useful information can therefore be tendered in evidence together with the message or information stored by it. Once tendered and admitted in evidence it becomes documentary evidence. The duty then behoved the party that tendered it in evidence to read the information or message in the open Court as is the case with documentary evidence, or the parties may by consensus take the document as read. The GSM gadget and or mobile phone may be admitted in evidence as computer generated evidence under Section 84 of the Evidence Act. Where however a party denies and or disputed the GSM message or the conversations contained in a mobile phone, it becomes incumbent on the party who tendered same to call logs/evidence of communication from the central portal of the service delivery company, or identification evidence of the sender/receiver of such message(s) under Sections 94, 125 and 126 of the Evidence Act. Section 94(1) & (2) of the Evidence Act, for example provides:

> (1) Evidence that a person exists having the same name, address, business or occupation as the maker of a document purports to have, is admissible to show that such was written or signed by that person;
>
> (2) Evidence that a document exists to which the document the making of which is in issue purports to be a reply, together with evidence of the making and delivery to a person of such earlier document, is admissible to show the identity of the maker of the disputed document with the person to whom the earlier document was delivered.

In cases where written records are kept by a mobile phone user such written records are admissible to prove and/or corroborate the call logs on the said GSM phone vide the apt foreign case of *R.* v. *Singh*[1] where the holder of the GSM phone kept a separate notebook in which he recorded numbers he had saved in the memory of the GSM phone, it

---

[1] (2006) 1 WLR 1564.

was held that evidence in the notebooks which the user traced to the defendant, was admissible to show that the number saved belonged to the defendant. Where any of the above options are utilised by a party seeking to tender such electronic evidence, no weight or probative value would be placed on the said pieces of evidence by the Court and cannot be relied upon as evidence.

Occasions have arisen where arguments have been canvassed that informations contained in emails, SMS and telephone are hearsay evidence. But the provisions of Section 84 (5) (a) and (c) of the Evidence Act 2011 has settled the issue of hearsay by providing that, 'with or without human intervention, both the supply of information to the computer and the production of a Document by a computer are to be taken to be appropriately done.' The settled Law in Nigeria, by this provision, therefore, is that Hearsay has little or no role to play in admissibility of computer Evidence. This Section permits without qualification, human intervention in supply of information to the computer and even in the printout coming from a computer. Suffices to state that by the decision in *Continental Sales Limited* v. *R. Shipping Inc.*[2] his Lordship Ogunwumiju, JCA in respect of a computer generated mail held thus:

> Email is a form of communication that is set down in writing. It is not oral. The fact that it is electronic is immaterial. It is not in the air. It can be downloaded and as real as a hard copy of the letter or mail in your hand." I hold that the prosecution in tendering Exhibits Z, Z2, Z3 and Z4 dealing with the Lloyd's List Intelligence Report complied with the requirement of Section 84 of the Evidence Act, 2011, as rightly

---

[2] (2012) LPELR - 7905 (CA); (2013) 4 NWLR (PT. 1343) P. 67.

found by the learned trial judge. The evidence of the PW11 (eleven) is also not hearsay.

The trite position of the law is that the failure to give notice of proceedings to the opposing party in a case where service of process is required is a fundamental omission which renders such proceedings void. This is so because the Court would have no jurisdiction to entertain it. Hearing notice is a document or information that emanates from the registry of a Court, giving legal notification to parties in a suit the dates on which the suit would be heard. Once a party or his counsel is served a hearing notice, they are both deemed to have actual knowledge of the date the suit would be heard, and if such a party decides to stay away from Court he does so at his own peril[3]. Service vides SMS is now recognised as an appropriate mode of service. The Evidence Act has now taken notice of the technology age by making electronic evidence admissible. Peter-Odili, JSC in the case of *ENL Consortium Ltd.* v. *Shambilat Shelter (NIG.) Ltd*,[4] pungently held thus:

> The point has to be made that the phone call mode of service would ordinarily be of good service so long as the party is provided the notice at least 48 hours before the scheduled Court date. The regularity of service is no longer jettisoned because it was made electronically as the current rules of Court have ensured. See Order 2 Rule 4(c) of the Court of Appeal, 2013 rules.

Nimpar, JCA, in the case of *Compact Manifold & Energy Services Ltd* v. *Pazan Services (Nig.) Ltd*,[5] laid a solid legal

[3] See Per Rhodes-Vivour, JSC in *Darma* v. *Ecobank* (2017) LPELR-41663 (SC).
[4] (2018) LPELR- 43902 (SC).
[5] (2017) LPELR-41913 (CA).

foundation for electronic service of hearing notice and other legal processes thus:

> The essence of a hearing notice is to bring to the notice of the party that his matter will come on the date named in the notice of hearing. Can the notice be effected by other means of notification? The answer is in the affirmative. When the rules use the words hearing notice, it did not specify that it must be hardcopy. Was the judge wrong to use the electronic method of informing parties about the date of hearing? I pause here to say this is the twenty-first century and technology is ruling every aspect of human endeavour and therefore even Courts must be abreast of these technological advancements and be ready to absorb the aspects that will enhance the quality of justice and aid speedy determination of cases. The Courts have also moved on in that regard. Indeed, electronic service has taken root in the Nigerian legal system and it would be strange for anybody to frown at being served electronically. See *Continental Sales Ltd.* v. *R. Shipping Inc* (2012) LPELR- 7905 (CA). I am of the view that the Court below was in order by directing that the appellant should be informed by text. The Court has a discretion to direct the notification in a particular way. Issuance of a hard copy hearing notice is not a requirement of law and failure to issue and serve same cannot offend the rule of fair hearing. See *Mirchandani* v. *Pinheiro* (2001) 3 NWLR (Pt. 701) 552 at 573. wherein the Court held: "It is not in all cases that the absence of it will automatically vitiate trials in the context of Section 36 of the 1999 Constitution. A hearing Notice is not therefore a mandatory judicial process that must be issued and served in all cases. The requirement is a rule of the Court not a statutory requirement. Rules of Court are to aid the Court in adjudication of cases. It is not to arm-twist the Court into becoming a robot.

Chapter 6

ADMISSIBILITY OF FINGERPRINT EVIDENCE, ONLINE NEWSPAPER AND NEWSPAPER PUBLICATION

WHEN FINGERPRINT EVIDENCE CAN BE ADMISSIBLE

In the case of *Shonubi* v. *People of Lagos State* (2015) LPELR-24807 (CA), Ikyegh, J.C.A. at p. 71, paras. A-B stated as follows:

> For in the apt English case of *R.* v. *Buckley* (1999) 13 JP 561 cited by the learned writer, S.T. Hon, SAN, in S.T. Hon's Law of Evidence in Nigeria (vol. 1) page 570, it was held per Rose, L.J., *inter alia,* that fingerprint evidence, like any other evidence, is admissible as a matter of law if it tends to prove the guilt of the defendant.

AN ONLINE NEWSPAPER PUBLICATION IS A COMPUTER-GENERATED EVIDENCE IS ADMISSIBLE UNDER SECTION 84 OF THE EVIDENCE ACT

In the case of *Inyang* v. *APC & Ors* (2019) LPELR-47538 (CA), Shuaibu, J.C.A. at p. 45, Paras. C-G stated thus:

> Learned counsel for the appellant also faulted the findings of the lower Court in respect of Exhibit INE 15 as well as its reliance on the authority of AGBI v. INEC (supra). The Newspaper and Magazine, though private but they fall within the meaning of public document by virtue of Section 102 (b) of the Evidence Act read together with Section 2 (2) (a) of the

National Library Act Cap N56 Laws of Federation 2004. However, an online newspaper publication such as Exhibit INE 15 are admissible under Section 84 of the Evidence Act and thus the case of *Agbi* v. *INEC* (*supra*) is not an authority in that regards.

AN INTERNET PRINT OUT OF A NEWSPAPER IS ADMISSIBLE AS A SECONDARY EVIDENCE OF SAME BY VIRTUE OF SECTIONS 85 AND 87(A) OF THE EVIDENCE ACT 2011

In the case of *Kubor & Anor* v. *Dickson & Ors* (2012) LPELR-9817(SC), Ogunbiyi, J.S.C. at p. 75, paras. C-F stated the position of the law thus:

> Furthermore and on the document exhibit 'D', which is an internet print out of the *Punch* newspaper, it is by nature a secondary evidence of the original by reason of the provisions of sections 85 and 87(a) of the Evidence Act 2011. The law is trite on the admissibility of such category of secondary evidence. In other words and on the authority of sections 90(1) (c) and 102(b) of the Evidence Act, it is only the certified True Copy of the document as secondary evidence and none other that is admissible. It is my considered view therefore that the absence of certification had rendered Exhibit 'D' a worthless document and inadmissible.

POSITION OF THE LAW ON ADMISSIBILITY OF NEWSPAPER PUBLICATION

In the case of *Re: Glaxosmithkline Consumer Nigeria Plc* (2019) LPELR-47498 (CA), Georgewill, J.C.A. at pp. 57-62, Paras. B-E held as follows:

> Having so held as above, the only question left is whether Exhibits E and F were admissible in evidence and rightly acted upon by the Court below and whether they

constituted enough notice of the said meeting to the Appellant? The issue here is one raising a recondite point of law on which opinions of the Court, from this Court to the Apex Court, is still divided. It has to do with the issue of whether a newspaper publication is a public document or private document and whether it would require certification to be admissible in evidence. These are no doubt weightier matters of the law!? Now, if the position of the law were to be that because copies of newspapers are by law required to be kept with the National Library and therefore, the original copies of newspaper would require certification for the purposes of their admissibility in evidence, then the question would arise as posited so aptly by one writer, Harvey Anyalewechi Esq., in his paper titled "The proprietary or otherwise of certifying a newspaper" as to whether all books published in Nigeria, copies of which are as well required by law to be kept with the National Library, would also require certification to be admissible in evidence even when an original copy of the book is produced in Court? I think the answer to this is a resounding no! ? Simply put, once an original copy of a newspaper is produced in Court and it is relevant and duly pleaded as required by law, in my view, it is admissible in evidence without the need for further certification. However, where what is produced is not the original copy but a photocopy of the newspaper, as in the instant appeal, then of course, for the purposes of its authentication, it would require certification to be admissible in evidence. In my view this position appears to be the only logical legal inference deducible from a proper construction and combined effects of Sections 85, 86, 87, 102 and 103 of the Evidence Act 2011 and Sections 2(2)(a), 4(1) and (7) (c) of the National Library Act, CAP N 56 Laws of the Federation 1990. Now, by Section 4(1) of the National Library Act, it is provided as follows: "the publishers of every book published in Nigeria shall within one month after the publication, deliver at his own expense to the National Library three copies of the book, two of which shall be kept in the National Library for permanent preservation and one of which shall be sent by the Director to the Ibadan University library." However, by Section 4(7)(c) of the National

Library Act a book, three copies of which, is required to be kept with the National Library is defined as follows: "a "book" to include "collective works such as encyclopaedias, dictionaries, year book or similar works, newspaper, magazines and similar periodicals." It does appear to me that the real essence of the provisions of Section 4(1) of the National Library Act is to give impetus to the real objective for the setting up of the National Library as encapsulated in its primary function is as stated in Section 2(2)(a) of the National Library Act, which provides as follows: "for the purpose of carrying out the general functions imposed on the Board... it shall be the duty of the Board, so far as its resources permits to assemble, maintain and extend a collection of books, periodicals, pamphlets, newspaper, maps, musical scores, films and recordings and such other matter as the Board considers appropriate for a library of the highest standing." In the light of the above therefore, it is my view that it is not intended that the National Library shall become the authenticating body for original copies of newspapers and books kept in its custody except in cases of photocopies of original copies of newspapers and books kept with the National Library that would require to be authenticated to confirm it as the true copy of the copies kept with the National Library. Thus, once the copy of a newspaper produced is the original copy of the newspaper, including but not limited to the exact copy purchased from a vendor, it is admissible in evidence without any need for further certification. The above conclusion seems to me to flow directly from the succinct provisions of Section 86 (4) of the Evidence Act 2011, which provides as follows: "Where a number of documents have all been made by one uniform process, as in the case of printing, lithography, photography, computer or other electronic or mechanical process, each shall be primary evidence of the contents of the rest; but where they are all copies of a common original, they shall not be primary evidence of the contents of the original." The above position of the law has received judicial approval in the recent case of *Kassim* v. *State* (2017) LPELR - 42586 (SC), where the Supreme Court per Kekere-Ekun, JSC., had opined and held *inter alia* thus: ?"Now, what really is the essence of the demand for a certified true copy of a public document? I think, and in agreement with Adekeye JSC., in *Goodwill & Trust Investment Limited* v. *Witt & Busch Limited* (2011) LPELR - 1333 (SC), the essence of demanding for a certified copy of a public document is the assurance of the authenticity of the document vis-a-vis the original. And so why go for that assurance in the certified true copy vis-a-vis the original, when the original is available? And so, when the cap is in the market, the head is also in the market; there is no further need to take the cap home from the market in order to test it on the head. I therefore agree with the Court below that where the original copy of a document is available, it is admissible without the requirement of certification." Also in *Uwua Udo* v. *The State* (2016) 2 - 3 SC (Pt. 111) 29, the Supreme Court made it abundantly clear in holding that even a public document tendered in its original form is admissible in evidence by virtue of Sections 85 and 86 of the Evidence Act 2011. It follows therefore, in my view, and I so hold firmly that a newspaper produced in its original form is the primary document produced and thus needs no further certification to be admissible in evidence. In my finding therefore, Exhibits E and F, being mere photocopies of newspaper publications, were inadmissible in evidence and were thus wrongly admitted, relied and acted upon by the Court below.

COMMENTARY

With the enactment of the Evidence Act, 2011, it is now easy to tender and use documents produced by computer in courts across Nigeria. The condition for such use is enshrined in section 84 of the Evidence Act and is a certificate of compliance showing that such document was authentically generated from a reliable computer in the ordinary cause of activities. The Supreme Court of Nigeria in *Dickson* v. *Sylva*[1] has held that such certificate can be written or oral. If written, it is still subject to the powers of court to

[1] (2017) 8 NWLR (PT 1567) 167.

demand for oral evidence. Also, the Supreme Court held in our, per Onnoghen, JSC as he then was, that where there is no certificate of compliance, a document produced by computer will not be admissible.

Generally, computer is defined in section 258 of the Evidence Act to include any device for storing and processing information. Hence, Computer and device are used interchangeably, here. Both primary and secondary documents produced by computer must also fulfil the conditions of section 84 of the Evidence Act aside any other condition ordinarily expected for such.

Below are questions and reasons for such questions, needed to lay proper foundation for oral certification of document produced by computer in any court of law in Nigeria.[2]

1. Question:

Please tell this honourable court what document is referred to as "xxxxxxxxxxxx" [insert title of document] in your witness statement on oath?

Reason: Pursuant to section 84(4)(a) of Evidence Act, a document produced by computer should be identified. Such document should be mentioned giving its title and unique name like; bank statement of Mr. AB between 1 January and 23 February, 2023.

2. Question:

How was the document produced?

Reason: Pursuant to section 84(4) (a) of Evidence Act, there should be a description of the manner a document

[2] Onyekachi Umah, Esq. "How To Avoid Certificate of Compliance for Electronic Evidence", Daily Law Tips (Tip 310).

produced by a computer was produced. This may include explaining and mentioning; typing, scanning, saving, emailing, downloading and sending procedures/ steps/ stages.[3]

3. Question:

What device was used in producing the document?

Reason: Pursuant to section 84(4) (b) of Evidence Act, there should is need for provision of particulars/details of the computer like; name, type, model, year and unique title (if any). By section 84(3) of the Evidence Act, where sets, groups or combination of computers were used whether concurrently or simultaneously, they all will be regarded as constituting a single computer. Hence, in such situation one need not mention all the computers employed in producing a document.

4. Question:

How regular was the device used during the period the document was produced?

Reason: Pursuant to sections 84(2) (a) and 84(4) (c) of Evidence Act, there is need to establish that the computer was regularly used to store/process information by any person/persons for regular activities whether the activities are private or for profit making.

5. Question:

What was the device mainly and regularly used for?

Reason: Pursuant to sections 84(2) (b) and 84(4) (c) of Evidence Act, there is need to establish that the computer was regularly supplied information like the type on the document produced by computer sought to be tendered.

---

[3] See, *Rowaye Jubril* v. *Federal Republic of Nigeria* (2018) LPELR-43993(CA).

6. Question:

What was the condition of the device before the production of the document?

Reason: Pursuant to sections 84(2) (c) and 84(4) (c) of Evidence Act, the device was operating properly during the concerned period and that even if it was out of operation or part of it was not operating properly, that such never affected the document produced by computer or its content.

7. Question:

Where was the information on document produced by computer gotten from?

Reason: Pursuant to sections 84(2) (d) and 84(4) (c) of Evidence Act, there is need to establish that the information in the document produced by computer sought to be tendered was derived from the information supplied to the device in the ordinary and regular course of activities.

8. Question:

What is your relationship with the device?

Reason: Pursuant to section 84(4)(c) of Evidence Act, there is need to establish that the person providing a certification for document produced by computer and the computer used for such production, is a person of responsible position with regards to the operation of the device or the management the relevant activities. Such a person needs not be a computer expert; he may even be a manager of a department/company that owns the concerned device and as such familiar with the computer.

Chapter 7

EXPERT OPINION ON COMPUTER-GENERATED EVIDENCE

WHO IS AN EXPERT?

Galinje, J.S.C. at P. 21, Paras. D-E in the case of *Adeyemo Abiodun* v. *Federal Republic of Nigeria* (2018) LPELR-43838(SC) posited thus:

> An expert is a person who is specially skilled in the field which he is giving evidence, and whether or not a witness can be regarded as an expert is a question of law for the judge to decide.

WHEN IS THE EVIDENCE OF AN EXPERT NECESSARY?

In the case of *Adeyemo Abiodun* v. *Federal Republic Of Nigeria* (2018) LPELR-43838(SC), Galinje, J.S.C. at P. 21, Paras. E-F stated thus:

> Expert opinion is only necessary where the expert can furnish the Court with scientific or other information of a technical nature that is likely to be outside the experience and knowledge of the Judge.

POSITION OF THE LAW WITH REGARD TO OPINION EVIDENCE

In the case of *Berende* v. *FRN* (2019) LPELR-48376 (CA) Agim, J.C.A. at pp. 32-36, Paras. B-C held thus:

PW6, Aliyu Usman, a Certified Forensic Examiner with the Counter Terrorism Investigation Department of the Department of State Services, National Headquarters, Abuja, gave detailed explanation of his forensic investigation of the contents of mobile phones, laptops, digital camera, Internet modem and external storage devices recovered from the appellant and his co-accused and made a written report of his investigation which was tendered in evidence as exhibit H. Clearly, PW6 was an officer of the Department of State Services that investigated this case. He testified about what he did and observed while carrying out the forensic examination of electronic devices recovered from the appellant and his co-accused. His testimony of what he did is direct evidence of the conduct of the forensic investigation. The probative value of this part of his testimony is not in doubt. What is in doubt is the probative value and maybe the admissibility, of his testimony and exhibit H relating to the content of the electronic devices investigated by him. His opinion of the content of the said electronic devices qualify as expert opinion in that it is opinion on a point of science or technology that require specialised knowledge to unravel and interpret is admissible in evidence by virtue of S.68 of the Evidence Act 2011. Be that as it is, it is not the evidence of the person who imputed the data in the electronic devices or made the statements contained therein. The probative value of this opinion is heavily diminished for this reason and the further and more weighty reason that most of the materials upon which the findings contained therein were based, were not tendered in evidence before the Court. The call data record of the telephone conversations which exhibit H analysed, the e-mail accounts listed in exhibit H as allegedly opened by the Appellant and even the extracts of the E-mails that were copiously attached to the proof of evidence served on the Appellant, were not tendered in evidence at the trial. The conclusions of the PW6 had no evidential foundation and were therefore not verifiable. Therefore they had no probative value. In *Idudhe* v. *Eseh* (1996) 5 NWLR pt 451 750, at 758 this Court held that "The duty of the expert is to furnish the Judge or jury with the necessary scientific criteria for testing the accuracy of his conclusions so as to enable the Judge or Jury to form their own independent judgment by the application of the criteria to the facts proved in evidence before them". In *Elukpo* v. *FHA* (1991) 3 NWLR Pt 179 322 this principle was applied thusly- "The mere fact that a document is prepared or tendered by an expert does not mean that the Court must accept and act on any or everything that it contains. The Court has a duty to consider the weight, if any, to be attached to any documentary evidence, even when tendered by an expert, before coming to a conclusion as to whether or not it establishes the fact stated therein. In the present case, there was some sort of confusion in the appellant's case, as presented. The issue of the nature or quantum of the work allegedly done by the appellant was lumped together with the issue of the valuation of the work after its nature or quantum had been determined. Valuation of the work after the nature or quantum had been determined was a matter for an expert, for example, a quantity surveyor like the appellant's only witness. However, the nature or quantum of the work allegedly done by the appellant was a question of fact to be determined by the learned trial Judge on the basis of the evidence, if any, led by the appellant. There was nothing scientific or technical, requiring the evidence of an expert, about it. Those who could testify, on the point, were the persons who actually took part in the execution of the work or those who saw them doing so. They were the ones who could give the best evidence on the issue. There was no evidence that quantity Surveyor was one of such people. What the quantity surveyor did was a valuation of the work which the appellant showed or caused to be shown to him as the work allegedly done by the appellant. In short, that aspect of the matter dealt with in the valuation report, Exhibit P.9, was based on hearsay, which is not admissible. The proper thing, which should have been done, was that whoever gave the information to the quantity Surveyor should have come to the Court to testify so that his evidence might be tested by cross-examination by the learned counsel for the respondent. The legal position is that if what purports to be an expert report is, in fact, hearsay evidence or was, on a particular point, based on hearsay evidence, it can be perfectly rejected. Expert evidence, if admitted and it is unchallenged by way of cross-examination or contradictory evidence, does not become inevitably acceptable merely because it is an expert evidence which has not been contradicted or challenged. It should be accepted only if there is no good reason to reject it, and, in the process of scrutinising it, could be rejected if there is reason so to do.

THE RELIABILITY AND FUNCTIONALITY OF A COMPUTER USED IN GENERATING A DOCUMENT CAN BE MADE BY ORAL EVIDENCE

In the case of *Jubril* v. *FRN* (2018) LPELR-43993(CA), Otisi, J.C.A. at pp. 184-187, Paras. B-B stated thus:

> The burden of proving that there had been no improper use of the computer and that it was operating properly could be discharged without calling a computer expert. It may be discharged by calling someone familiar with its operation in the sense of knowing what the machine was required to do and who could say that it was doing it properly. In other words, oral evidence may be given of the working of the computer in line with the provisions of Section 84(2). See: *R* v. *Shephard* [1991] 93 Cr.App.R.139, in which the provisions of Section 69 of the U.K. Police and Criminal Evidence Act, 1984 (now repealed by Section 60 of the U.K. Youth Justice and Criminal Evidence Act 1999) were considered. Section 84 of the Evidence Act, 2011 is similarly worded with the said Section 69 of the U.K. Police and Criminal Evidence Act. 1984. In *Dickson* v. *Sylva* (*supra*), the Supreme Court, per Nweze, JSC, at pages 23 -24 of the E-Report said: "Interpreting provisions similarly worded like Section 84 (supra), the defunct House of Lords [per Lord Griffiths] had this to say in *R.* v. *Shepherd* [1993] 1 All ER 225, 231, paragraphs A-C, [HL], Documents produced by computers are an increasingly common feature of all businesses and more and more people are becoming familiar with uses and operation. Computers vary immensely in their complexity and in the operations they perform. The nature of the evidence to discharge the burden of showing that there

has been no improper use of the computer and it was operating properly will inevitably vary from case to case. The evidence must be tailored to suit the needs of the case. I suspect that it will very rarely be necessary to call an expert and that in the vast majority of cases *it will be possible to discharge the burden by calling a witness who is familiar with the operation of the computer in the sense of knowing what the computer is required to do and who can say that it is doing it properly.* [Italics supplied for emphasis] In actual fact, Section 84 (*supra*) consecrates two methods of proof, either by oral evidence under Section 84(1) and (2) or by a certificate under Section 84(4). In either case, the conditions stipulated in Section 84(2) must be satisfied. However, this is subject to the power of the Judge to require oral evidence in addition to the certificate. As the eminent Lord Griffith explained in the said case [*R* v. *Shepherd*]: Proof that the computer is reliable can be provided in two ways: either by calling oral evidence or by tendering a written certificate subject to the power of the Judge to require oral evidence. It is understandable that if a certificate is to be relied upon it should show on its face that it is signed by a person who from his job description can confidently be expected to be in a person to give reliable evidence about the operation of the computer. This enables the defendant to decide whether to accept at its face value or to ask the Judge to require oral evidence which can be challenged in cross examination [Italics supplied for emphasis]" Thus, proof that the computer used to generate evidence is reliable can be provided in two ways: either by calling oral evidence, under Section 84(2) or by tendering a written certificate, under Section 84(4). The uncontroverted evidence of PW17 before the trial Court supplied the details required by Section 84(2). The computer generated evidence, Exhibit P7, tendered by PW17 was therefore admissible and rightly relied upon by the learned trial Judge.

COMMENTARY

The question of who is an expert and the imperatives of the provision of the scientific basis of their findings has increasingly be called into question. Although expertise, for evidential purposes, cannot be equiparated with Scholastic knowledge or professorial attainment,[1] an expert is, all the same, a person who is specially skilled in the field he is giving evidence. For this purpose, formal learning on the subject is discounted once affirmative responses are returned to Lord Russell's Trinitarian posers in *R.* v. *Silverlock* (*supra*), namely: "is he *peritus*? Is he skilled? Has he adequate knowledge?[2]

The above notwithstanding, such a person, who is paraded as an expert, must furnish the Court with the necessary scientific criteria for testing the accuracy of their conclusions so as to enable it (the Court) to form its own independent judgment by the application of those criteria to the facts proved in evidence.[3] Put differently, the opinion and conclusions, which such an expert proffered before the trial Court, must be supported by scientific analysis otherwise his evidence would be valueless or worthless.[4] It cannot be otherwise for, as Lawton LJ, observed in Turner[5] thus:

> An observation which I adopt as part of my reasoning in this appeal: An expert's opinion is admissible to furnish the Court with scientific information which is likely to be outside the experience and knowledge of a Jury... If on the proven facts, a Judge... can form (his) own conclusions without help, then the opinion of an expert is unnecessary? See, also, M.

---

[1] See the cases of *R* v. *Silverlock* (1894) 2 Q. B. 766; *AG, Federation* v. *Abubakar* (2007) All FWLR (pt 375) 405, 555; *Azu* v. *State* (1993) 7 SCNJ pt 1 151 and *Sowemimo* v. *State* (2004) All FWLR pt 203 951.

[2] See *Oguonzee* v. *State* (1998) 5 NWLR (Pt 551) 60; I. H. Dennis, *The Law of Evidence* (Second Edition) (London: Maxwell, 2002) 702 -710.

[3] Phipson on *Evidence* (12th Edition), paragraph 1227, p. 497; *David* v. *Edinburgh Magistrates* (1953) SC 34, 40.

[4] See the cases of *SPDC Ltd* v *Farah and Ors* (1995) 3 NWLR (pt 382) 148; *SPDC* v. *Otoko* (1990) 6 NWLR (pt. 159) 693; *Ogiale* v. *SPDC (Nig) Ltd* (1997) 3 NWLR (pt 480) 165.

[5] [1975] Q. B. 834, 841.

> Redmayne, *Expert Evidence and Criminal Justice* (Oxford: O. U. P., 2001) 140 - 149, in I. H. Denis. *The Law of Evidence* (*supra*) 702 (pages 29 -30)."

An expert witness must be versed in a subject in dispute. His dexterity and knowledge in a subject must be special in the sense of being superlative. An expert being a person who is specially skilled in the field which he is giving evidence, whether or not a witness can be regarded as an expert is a question of law for the judge to decide. Expert opinion is only necessary where the expert can furnish the Court with scientific or other information of a technical nature that is likely to be outside the experience and knowledge of the Judge.

While explaining the basis of expert opinion, this Court said in *Owale* v. *Shell Petroleum Development Company Ltd*[6] thus"

> The duty of an expert is to furnish the Judge with necessary scientific criteria for testing the accuracy of the conclusions so as to enable the Judge to form his own independent judgment by the application of those criteria to facts provided in evidence.

This Court went further to state:

> The duty of an expert is to utilize his skill or knowledge to bring out and demonstrate features or characteristics of the subject which the uninitiated or unlearned might not otherwise understand so that such revelation will guide lay men."

---

[6] (1997) NWLR Pt. 480 page 148 at 183.

In *ANPP* v. *Usman*,[7] the Court stipulated the criteria upon which a person may be accepted by the Court as an expert as follows:

> Where the evidence of opinion of an expert is relevant he may be called as a witness and must first of all state his qualification and satisfy the Court that he is an expert on the subject in which he is to give his opinion. He must also state clearly the reason/or his opinion.

It follows therefore that where an expert fails to satisfy the Court before whom he testified as to the following:

(a) his qualification;

(b) that he is an expert on the subject in which he is to give his Opinion; and

(c) to clearly state the reason or scientific basis for his opinion, the Court is at liberty to refuse to accept his testimony or opinion.

The Courts have the powers to jettison all the opinions of the experts because they lack probative and/or evidential value. This is because when the Court of Appeal in ANPP –v. Usman (*supra*) was faced with a similar dilemma on the evidence of experts and Aboki JCA held as follows:

> The court must be wary of admitting a report prepared by an expert, not at the instance of the court but at the behest of any of the parties to the disputes such a report should be taken with a pinch of salt.[8]

[7] (2008) 12 NWLR Pt. (1100) p. 1 at 72 – 73.

[8] See equally the case of *Waziri* v. *The State* (1997) 3 NWLR (Pt. 496) at 689.

Therefore, Certified Forensic Examiners with the Counter-Terrorism Investigation Department of the Department of State Services or the Police, Army or Navy are often treated as experts by the courts with regards to their explanations of forensic investigation of the contents of mobile phones, laptops, digital camera, Internet modem and external storage devices recovered from suspects and the written reports of their investigations are treated as expert Reports. Their evidence are direct evidence of the conduct of the forensic investigations and their opinions of the contents of electronic devices qualify as expert opinions which is based on opinion on a point of science or technology that require specialized knowledge to unravel and interpret is admissible in evidence as encapsulated under Section 68 of the Evidence Act 2011.

Chapter 8

CONDITIONS FOR THE ADMISSIBILITY OF COMPUTER-GENERATED EVIDENCE

EVIDENCE IN RELATION TO THE USE OF A COMPUTER MUST BE CALLED TO ESTABLISH THE CONDITIONS SET OUT UNDER SECTION 84(2) OF THE EVIDENCE ACT, 2011

Mukhtar, J.C.A. at pp.6-11, Paras. A-E in the case of *Emmanuel* v. *FRN* (2018) LPELR-45235 (CA) held thus:

> It is pertinent that exhibit A that was intended to supply the necessary certification to ground the admissibility of computer generated evidence falls far short from satisfying the preconditions under Section 84(4) of the Evidence Act as the Learned Counsel for the Appellant rightly submitted. Thus, exhibit A that was signed as certificate by one Solomon Imolega (reproduced on page 158 of the record) merely reproduced the provisions of Section 82(2) of the Evidence Act, 2011. Section 84(4) of the Evidence Act, 2011, did not make provision for a certificate but rather it provides for the fundamental evidence that must be led in Court before a computer-generated evidence can be admitted and relied upon. See *Kubor* v. *Dickson* (2013) All FWLR (Pt. 676) 392 at 428 para G where the Supreme Court held per Onnoghen JSC (as he then was) thus: "Granted, for the purpose of argument, that exhibits "D" and "L" being computer generated documents or document down loaded from the Internet are not public

documents whose secondary evidence are admissible only by certified true copies then it means that their admissibility is governed by the provisions of Section 84 of the Evidence Act, 2011. Section 84(1) provides thus: '(1) In any proceedings, a statement contained in a document produced by a computer shall be admissible as evidence of any fact stated in it of which direct oral evidence would be admissible, if it is shown that the condition in Sub-section (2) of this section are satisfied in relation to the statement and the computer in question.' The conditions are: (a) that the document containing the statement was produced by the computer during a period over which the computer was used regularly to store or process the information for the purpose of any activities regularly carried on over that period, whether for profit or not, by anybody whether corporate or not or by any individual; (b) that over that period there was regularly supplied to the computer in the ordinary course of those activities information of the kind contained in the statement or of the kind from which the information so contained is derived; (c) that throughout the material part of that period the computer was operating properly or if not that in any respect in which it was not operating properly or was out of operation during that point or that period was not such as to affect the production of the document or the accuracy of its contents; and (d) that the information contained in the statement reproduced or is derived from information supplied to the computer in the ordinary course of those activities. There is no evidence on record to show that appellants in tendering exhibits "D" and "L" satisfied any of the above conditions. In fact they did not as the documents were tendered and admitted from the bar. No witness testified before tendering the documents so there was no opportunity to lay the necessary foundations for their admission as e-documents under Section 84 of the Evidence Act, 2011. No wonder therefore that the lower Court held, at page 838 of the record thus: 'A party that seeks to tender in evidence a computer generated document needs to do more than just tendering same from the bar. Evidence in relation to the use of the computer must be called to establish the conditions set out under Section 84(2) of the Evidence Act,

2011". In the instant case, no evidence was given by the PW 1 to lay the necessary foundation or requirement for admissibility of a computer generated document as provided by Section 84(4)(a) and (b) of the Evidence Act, 2011. The provision is reproduced as follows: "In any proceeding where it is desired to give a statement in evidence by virtue of this section a certificate- (a) identifying the document containing the statement and describing the manner in which it was produced; (b) giving such particulars of any device involved in the production of that document as may be appropriate for the purpose of showing that the document was produced by a computer". The supporting certification required under Section 84(4)(a) and (b) are glaringly absent in exhibit A. Similarly, there are no particulars of any device used in the production of exhibits C1-C50. In the circumstances therefore the Court below ought not to have rejected exhibit C1-C50 as inadmissible pieces of evidence. The lower Court was under a duty, where it admitted inadmissible evidence in the course of the trial proceedings, to expunge such evidence. I therefore have no hesitation in expunging exhibits C1 to C50 as this Court has power to expunge from record any inadmissible evidence wrongly admitted. See *Abubakar* v. *Joseph* (2008) All FWLR (Pt. 432) Pg 1065 where the Supreme Court held at page 1103 paras G -- I as follows: "That exhibit D was admitted in evidence without objection, is/was of no moment. This is because and this is also settled in a line of decided authorities, that where inadmissible evidence has been admitted, it is the duty of the Court, not to act upon it. It is immaterial that its admission, was as a result of consent of the opposite party or that party's default in failing to take an objection at the proper time. An appellate Court, has the power to reject such evidence and decide the case, on legal evidence. See the cases of *Owonyin* v. *Omotosho* (1961) 1 (Pt. 11) ANLR 304 at 305; *Alashe & Ors.* v. *Olori Ilu & Ors.* (1961) NMLR 66 at 67; *Yassin* v. *Barclays Bank DCO* (1968) 1 ANLR 171, 177; *Olukade* v. *Alade* (1976) 2 SC 183 at 188." See also *N. M. A.* v. *M. M. A. Inc* (2008) All FWLR (Pt. 446) Pg 1916 at 1949 para D - G. In the instant case, exhibits C1-C50 which the trial Court relied upon in convicting the Appellant were not shown to be admissible due to the failure of the prosecution to meet the requirement of the law as provided under Section 84 (2) and (4)(a) and (b) of the Evidence Act, 2011. There is no doubt that computer print-outs were not hearsay, and so admissible as good as direct oral evidence, if tendered in compliance with the law to prove the transfers of funds recorded in the system and did not merely assert that such transfers had taken place. That was the necessary foundation, which the prosecution had failed to meet in tendering exhibits C1 to C50 that formed the basis of the Appellant's conviction on counts 1, 3, 5 and 12. In the circumstances, I have no hesitation in expunging exhibits C 1 - C 50 as evidence wrongly admitted contrary to the provision of Section 84 of the Evidence Act 2011.

INTERNET-GENERATED DOCUMENTS ARE NOT THE ONLY FORM OF DOCUMENTS CAUGHT BY THE ADMISSIBILITY REQUIREMENTS OF SECTION 84 OF THE EVIDENCE ACT 2011

In the case of *Omisore & Anor* v. *Aregbesola & Ors* (2015) LPELR-24803 (SC), the Supreme Court of Nigeria Per NWEZE, J.S.C. at pp. 97-98, Paras. E-D posited thus:

As noted above, the main plank of the argument of the first and second cross respondents, with regard to the second issue above, was that only internet-generated documents are caught by the admissibility requirements of Section 84 of the 2011 Evidence Act. With profound respect, this argument is untenable, S. Mason (ed), *Electronic Evidence: Disclosure, Discovery and Admissibility*, (London: LexisNexis, Butterworths, 2007) passim; H. M. Malek (ed), *Phipson on Evidence* (London: Sweet and Maxwell, 2010) (Seventeenth Edition) passim; *R.* v. *Shepherd* (1993) 1 All ER 225, 231 [a decision of the defunct House of Lords]; *Kubor* v. *Dickson* [2013] 4 NWLR (Pt. 1345) 534, 577- 578. Even the very chapeau or opening statement in Section 84(1) contradicts this submission. The relevant phrase here is "a statement contained in a document produced by the computer..." Interestingly, the draftsperson did not leave the meaning of the word "computer" to conjecture. In Section 258(1), the Act defines "computer" to mean "any device for storing and processing information, and any reference to information being derived from other information is a reference to its being derived from it by calculation, comparison or any other process.

PAROLE EVIDENCE OF A PERSON FAMILIAR WITH THE OPERATION OF A COMPUTER CAN BE GIVEN OF ITS RELIABILITY AND FUNCTIONALITY IN THE ABSENCE OF A CERTIFICATE UNDER SECTION 84(4) OF THE EVIDENCE ACT

Sankey, J.C.A. at pp. 62-64, Paras. E-B in the case of *Brila Energy Ltd* v. *FRN* (2018) LPELR-43926(CA) stated thus:

It is also settled law that electronic evidence can be made in the ordinary course of business of establishments like banks and corporate bodies. The condition for the admissibility of this kind of evidence is that the maker must have made the statement contemporaneously with the transaction recorded or so soon thereafter that the Court considers it likely that the transaction was at the time still fresh in his memory. This is also the import of Section 41 of the Evidence Act. The Appellant has also sought to impugn the integrity of Exhibit 7 contending that the Respondent failed to tender the certificate of trustworthiness of the computer used in printing the documents in compliance with Section 84(4) of the Evidence Act. However, where such certificate is not produced, it has been held that oral evidence of a person familiar with the operation of the computer can be given of its reliability and functionality; and that such a person need not be a computer expert. See *R* v. *Shephard* (1993) AC 380, where Lord Griffiths on this issue held - "... therefore answer the certified question by saying that Section 69(1) of the Police Criminal Evidence Act 1984 can be satisfied by the oral evidence of a person familiar with the operation of the computer who can give evidence of its reliability and such person need not be a Computer expert." Section 69(1) of the Police Criminal Evidence Act 1984 in the UK is the equivalent of Section of 84 of the Evidence Act, 2011. This condition was satisfied by the testimony of PW17 on oath when he explained the process of how he scanned the emails forwarding the report to him from Saybolt Concremat Brazil, printed them in colour and sent them to EFCC. I therefore have no reason to interfere with the finding of the trial Court in this regard.

A COMPUTER-GENERATED EVIDENCE IS NOT ADMISSIBLE IN EVIDENCE IN THAT IT IS NOT ACCOMPANIED BY CERTIFICATE OF COMPLIANCE

In the case of *Umar & Anor* v. *Kwari & Ors (*2019) LPELR-49454 (CA), Abundaga, J.C.A. at p. 34, Paras. D-E held thus:

> Exhibit A is a computer generated evidence and by reason of non-compliance with Section 84 of the Evidence Act, 2011, is not admissible in evidence in that it is not accompanied by Certificate of compliance. It therefore lacks probative value.

THE PROVISION OF SECTION 84(2) OF THE EVIDENCE ACT, 2011 IS MANDATORY AND ALLOWS FOR NO DISCRETION.

Obaseki-Adejumo, J.C.A. at pp. 41-42, Paras. B-B in the case of *Oyekanmi* v. *FRN (*2019) LPELR-47323 (CA) stated thus:

> With respect to Exhibit D1, which parties agree is a computer generated evidence, but it is the contention of the Appellant's counsel that since the Exhibit was served on the Appellant as part of proof of evidence from the record of the EFCC, and was certified by the EFCC, it cannot be regarded as a computer generated evidence to warrant compliance with Section 84 of the Evidence Act. With respect, I am unable to

accede to the contention urged on us by the Appellant's counsel on this issue. The provision of Section 84(2) of the Evidence Act, 2011 is mandatory and allows for no discretion. It is mandatory for a party who seeks to tender a computer-generated evidence to comply with the conditions stipulated in Section 84(2) and this was not done in the instant case. It is of no moment that the document is a public document and was certified as such; in so far as it is a computer generated evidence, the provision of the Act must be complied. Granted that the document emanated from the EFCC, it is incumbent on the Appellant who seeks to tender and rely on Exhibit D1, to have requested that the provision of Section 84(2) was complied with by the author, the EFCC. It is my candid view that the learned trial judge rightly rejected Exhibit D1 as evidence in this case.

ELECTRONIC EVIDENCE THAT OFFENDS SECTION 84 OF THE EVIDENCE ACT, 2011 ARE TO BE EXPUNGED

In the case of *Dalyop* v. *C.O.P, Plateau State Command* (2019) LPELR-47031 (CA), Onyemenam, J.C.A. at pp.14-16, Paras. D-D stated as follows:

On the Appellant's contention that the admission of Exhibits "P6A" and "P6B" offends Section 84 of the Evidence Act, 2011 and as such should be expunged. The said exhibits which are pictures of the deceased were tendered without recourse to the requirements of Section 84 of the Evidence Act, 2011. The Respondent's counsel subtly conceded to this as he did not make submissions on this but rather stemmed his argument on the fact that the referred exhibits did not influence the trial Court in its decision. The pictures were tendered without the negatives or any explanation. Where if the photographs were taken with a digital camera or produced from a digital camera, that becomes a computer generated document by virtue of Section 84(5)(c) of the Evidence Act, 2011 which provides that; "a document shall be taken to have

> been produced by a computer whether it was produced by it directly or (with or without human intervention) by means of any appropriate equipment." In that case, the camera that was used in taking the photographs ought to have been tendered in evidence, but that was not done. Rather the printed photographs were tendered in evidence. Also, the certification which is a pre-requisite for its admissibility in evidence under Section 84 of the Evidence Act, 2011 was not made. Notably, Section 84 of the Evidence Act, 2011 permits the admission of any document generated or produced by a computer. However, the document may only be admissible if, and only if it is shown that the conditions in Subsection (2) therein are duly satisfied in relation to the document sought to be tendered. The conditions precedent to the admissibility of such documents are contained in Subsection (2) (a) - (d) of Section 84 of the Evidence Act, 2011. Categorically, Section 84 (4) (a) and (b) of the Evidence Act, 2011 made it mandatory that, before a computer generated document can be admissible, a certificate identifying the document and describing the manner in which the document was produced as well as the particulars of the device used in producing or generating the document must first be provided. Exhibits "P6A" and "P6B" failed woefully to abide the requirements of Section 84 of the Evidence Act thereby making the pictures of the deceased Exhibits "P6A" and "P6B" inadmissible. I therefore hold that Exhibits "P6A" and "P6B" were wrongly admitted in evidence and I hereby expunge them from the record.

SECTION 84 OF THE EVIDENCE ACT 2011 CONSECRATES TWO METHODS OF PROOF, EITHER BY ORAL EVIDENCE UNDER SECTION 84 (1) AND (2) OR BY A CERTIFICATE UNDER SECTION 84(4)

In the case of *Unical & Ors* v. *Effiong & Ors* (2019) LPELR-47976(CA), Ogbuinya, J.C.A. at pp. 36-39, Paras. F-A stated thus:

The appellants' coup de main on the second limb is clear. It decries the lower Court's reliance on Exhibit 11 and its attachment of probative value to it. I had found, while dealing with issue three, that the lower Court, deeply erred in law in re-admitting the rejected document in evidence. In due obeisance to the dictate of the law, I have given a careful look at Exhibit 11. The document, Exhibit 11, is a charting report dated 11th November, 2009. It was issued and signed by Surv. Asuquo Ayaya, Deputy Surveyor-General, to Director of Lands of Cross River State. It is a correspondence exchanged inter parties: the Deputy Surveyor-General and Director of Lands, Cross River State. It falls, squarely, within the wide definition of document as ordained in Section 258 of the Evidence Act, 2011 because its contents are "expressed or described upon any substance by means of letters, figures or marks." It was/were procured from computer which, according to the definition prescription of Section 258 of the Evidence Act, 2011, denotes "any device for storing and processing information, and any reference to information being derived from other information is a reference to its being derived from it by calculation, comparison or any other process," see *Omisore* v. *Aregbesola* (2015) 15 NWLR (Pt. 1482) 205. It stems from these, that the Exhibit 11 is classic exemplification of internet/computer-generated document. The exhibit has certified true copy embossed on it. In the first place, the lawyer, who tendered it, starved the lower Court of any certificate of authentication of it or the device whence it was generated from as decreed by the sacrosanct provision of Section 84 (2) and (4) of the Evidence Act, 2011 displayed above. In *Dickson* v. *Sylva* (2017) NWLR (Pt. 1567) 167 at 203, the oracular jurist, Nweze, JSC, incisively, stated: In actual fact, Section 84 (supra) consecrates two methods of proof, either by oral evidence under Section 84 (1) and (2) or by a certificate under Section 84(4). In either case, the conditions stipulated in Section 84(2) must be satisfied. See also, *Kubor* v. *Dickson* (*supra*); *Omisore* v. *Aregbesola* (*supra*). Curiously, the appellants failed to comply with the mandatory requirements of Section 84 (2) and (4) of the Evidence Act, 2011. The rational for the satisfaction of the requirements of

> the sacred provision is to "ensure the authenticity of the document and the integrity of the procedure used to bring it into being," *Dickson* v. *Sylva* (*supra*), at 233, per Kekere-Ekun, JSC. The appellants' flagrant defilement of this inviolable provision is fraught with far-reaching consequence. It renders the document, wholly, inadmissible. Put simply, its admission by the lower Court is an affront to the adjectival law.

IN CONSTRUING THE PROVISIONS OF SECTIONS 83 AND 84 OF THE EVIDENCE ACT, 2011, ATTENTION HAS TO BE GIVEN TO EACH AND EVERY PUNCTUATION INSERTED BETWEEN ONE SECTION, SUBSECTION OR PARAGRAPH TO ARRIVE AT THE INTENTION OF THE LEGISLATURE

In the case of *Onwuzulike* v. *State* (2017) LPELR-41889(CA), Tur, J.C.A. at pp. 129-138, paras. D-B posited thus:

> In construing the provisions of Sections 83 and 84 of the Evidence Act, 2011, attention has to be given to each and every punctuation inserted between one section, subsection or paragraph to arrive at the intention of the legislature. The draftsman employed punctuations such as coma or semi-colon in drafting the provisions of the said section. In *Maxwell On the Interpretation of Statutes*, 12th Edition by p. St. J. Langan appears the following passage at Pages 13 to 14 under "Punctuations" to wit: "Punctuation is disregarded in the construction of statutes, since there was generally no punctuation in old statutes as engrossed on the Parliament Roll, and not all of the modern vellum prints of statutes are punctuated. "In an Act of Parliament there are no such things as bracket any more than there are such things as stops." "Before 1850 there was no punctuation in the manuscript copy of an Act which received the Royal Assent, and it does not appear that the printers had any statutory authority to insert

punctuation thereafter. So even if punctuation in more modern Acts can be looked at (which is very doubtful), I do not think that one can have any regard to punctuation in older Acts." In the same way, the manner in which a statute has been printed, the indentation of the paragraphs and so on is irrelevant. The irrelevance of punctuation has two consequences. First, a provision in a statute may be read as though the punctuation which appears on the face of the Act were omitted. By Section 113(4) of the Housing Act, 1957, "the local authority shall from time to time review rents and make such changes, either of rents generally or of particular rents, and rebates (if any) as circumstances may require." This is to be read as though there were no comma after "rents" where that word occurs for the third time. "The obligation," said Harman, L.J., "is not to make rebates, as grammatically it should be if the comma were there, but to make changes of rebates (if any)." Secondly, where it is necessary to give a provision a particular construction which is at variance with the way in which the section is punctuated, it may be read as though there were in fact punctuation where none appears on the face of the Act. Section 10 of the Fugitive Offenders Act, 1881 conferred on a Superior Court power to discharge a fugitive where "by reason of the trivial nature of the case, or by reason of the application for the return of a fugitive not being made in good faith in the interests of justice or otherwise... it would be unjust or oppressive or too severe a punishment to return" him. It was held that, apart from cases of a trivial nature, the Court's discretion to discharge a fugitive could be exercised in any case in which the return of the man would be unjust or oppressive or too severe, and was not confined to cases in which the application appeared not to have been made in good faith. In other words, the section was given a wide construction, as though a comma had been inserted before "or otherwise"." I think since punctuations are inserted by the draftsman in modern statutes, I do not see any rational reason why the Courts should disregard them in the interpretation of any section, subsection or paragraphs and sub-paragraphs in a statute or rule of Court. In Maxwell On the Interpretation of Statutes (supra) appears once again at Pages

86 to 87 the following exposition of law as to how to construe words and phrases no matter how wide or restrictive they might be in a statute to wit: "However wide in the abstract, general words and phrases are more or less elastic, and admit of restriction or extension to suit the legislation in question. The object or policy of this legislation often affords the answer to problems arising from ambiguities which it contains. For it is a cannon of interpretation that all words, if they be general and not precise, are to restricted to the fitness of the matter, that is, to be construed as particular if the intention be particular. Thus, an Act which, reciting the inconveniences arising from churchwardens and overseers making clandestine rates, enacted that those officers should permit "every inhabitant" of the parish to inspect the rates, under a penalty for refusal, was held not to apply to a refusal to one of the churchwardens, who was also an inhabitant. As the object of the Act was to protect those inhabitants who had previously no access to the rates (which the churchwardens had), the meaning of the term "inhabitants" was limited to them." See *Oyeyemi* v. *Commissioner for Local Government, Kwara State* (1992) 2 SCNJ (Pt. 2) 266; *NEC* v. *Zuogu* (1993) 2 NWLR (Pt. 275) 270 and Orubu vs. NEC (1988) 5 NWLR (Pt. 94) 323. Indeed in *Mobil Nig. Plc* v. *IAL* 36 Inc. (2000) FWLR (Pt. 10) 1632, Karibi-Whyte, JSC explained at page 1650 Paragraphs "C" to "D" to wit: "It is an elementary principle and fundamental to the construction of the provisions of any statute to read the sections as a whole to enable the interpreter to get the collective sense of the provisions. Where the subject matter construed concerns other sections of the same statute, all the related provisions must be read, considered and construed together as forming a composite whole. It is imperative in the construction of a section to read together all the sections and paragraphs. This is because the sub-sections or sub-paragraphs may be and are necessarily complimentary to and explain the meaning and scope of the main section or paragraph. The meaning of a section may be controlled by other individual sections or sub-sections in the same Act. - See Minister of Housing and Local Government vs. Lambert (1969) 2 WLR 447. Clear and unambiguous words

should be given their ordinary literal meaning. See *Olokologbe* v. *Alami* (1987) 3 NWLR (Pt.61) 377 SC; *African Newspaper* v. *Nigeria* (1985) 2 NWLR (Pt.6) 137." See *Tarka & Ors.* v. *D.*p.p. (1961) NRNLR 63. In construing the provisions of Section 84(1)-(4) of the Evidence Act, 2011 it has to be again borne in mind that information might have been generated from "a statement contained in a document produced by a computer" [See Section 84(1) and (2) to (d)] or from "a combination of computers operating in succession over that period" [See Section 84(3) (a)-(b)] or "by different combination of computers operating in succession over that period" (See Section 84 (3)(c)) or in "any other manner involving the successive operation over that period, in whatever order, of one or more computers and one or more combinations of computers all the computers used for that purpose during that period shall be treated for the purpose of this section as constituting a single computer; and references in this section to a computer shall be construed accordingly." [See Section 84(3) (d)] of the Evidence Act, 2011. Section 84(4) and (5) of the Act further provides as follows: "(4) In any proceedings where it is desired to give a statement in evidence by virtue of this section, a certificate doing any of the following things, that is to say: (a) Identifying the document containing the statement and describing the manner in which it was produced; (b) Giving such particulars of any device involved in the production of that document as may be appropriate for the purpose of showing that the document was produced by a computer; (c) Dealing with any of the matters to which the conditions mentioned in Sub-section (2) above relate, and purporting to be signed by a person occupying a responsible position in relation to the operation of the relevant device or the management of the relevant activities, as the case may be, shall be evidence of the matter stated in the certificate, and for the purpose of this subsection it shall be sufficient for a matter to be stated to the best of the knowledge and belief of the person stating it. (5) For the purposes of this section: (a) Information shall be taken to be supplied to a computer if it is supplied to it in any appropriate form and whether it is supplied directly or (with or without human intervention) by means of any appropriate equipment; (b) Where, in the course of activities carried on by any individual or body, information is supplied with a view to its being stored or processed for the purposes of those activities by a computer operated otherwise than in the course of those activities, that information, if duly supplied to that computer, shall be taken to be supplied to it in the course of those activities. (c) A document shall be taken to have been produced by a computer whether it was produced by it directly or (with or without human intervention) by means of any appropriate equipment." Section 84(4)(a)-(b) (i) and 5(a)-(c) of the Evidence Act, 2011 confers an unfettered discretion on the party seeking to rely on computer-generated information or evidence to produce a certificate (a) identifying the document containing the statement and describing the manner in which it was produced; (b) giving such particulars of any device involved in the production of that document as may be appropriate for the purpose of showing that the document was produced by a computer; (i) dealing with any of the matters to which the conditions mentioned in Sub-section (2) of Section 84 of the Act relates. The certificate has to "...purport to be signed by a person occupying a responsible position in relation to the operation of the relevant device or the management of the relevant activities, as the case may be, shall be given in evidence of the matter stated in the certificate; and for the purpose of this subsection it shall be sufficient for a matter to be stated to the best of the knowledge and belief of the person stating it.

THE PROVISION OF SECTION 84(2) OF THE EVIDENCE ACT, 2011 IS MANDATORY AND ALLOWS FOR NO DISCRETION

In *Loben Investment Co-Operative Multipurpose Society Ltd* v. *FRN* (2019) LPELR-47325 (CA), Obaseki-Adejumo, J.C.A. at pp. 37-38, Paras. A-A state as follows:

With respect to Exhibit D1, which parties agree is a computer generated evidence, but it is the contention of the Appellant's counsel that since the Exhibit was served on the Appellant as part of proof of evidence from the record of the EFCC, and was certified by the EFCC, it cannot be regarded as a computer generated evidence to warrant compliance with Section 84 of the Evidence Act. With respect, I am unable to accede to the contention urged on us by the Appellant's counsel on this issue. The provision of Section 84(2) of the Evidence Act, 2011 is mandatory and allows for no discretion. It is mandatory for a party who seeks to tender a computer generated evidence to comply with the conditions stipulated in Section 84(2) and this was not done in the instant case. It is of no moment that the document is a public document and was certified as such; in so far as it is a computer generated evidence, the provision of the Act must be complied. Granted that the document emanated from the EFCC, it is incumbent on the Appellant who seeks to tender and rely on Exhibit D1, to have requested that the provision of Section 84(2) was complied with by the author, the EFCC. It is my candid view that the learned trial judge rightly rejected Exhibit D1 as evidence in this case.

EVIDENCE IN RELATION TO THE USE OF A COMPUTER MUST BE CALLED TO ESTABLISH THE CONDITIONS SET OUT UNDER SECTION 84(2) OF THE EVIDENCE ACT, 2011

In the case of *Rosehill Ltd* v. *GTB* (2016) LPELR-41665(CA), Bdliya, J.C.A. at pp.12-22, Paras. C-E held as follows:

Are Exhibits 1A, 1B, 26, 27 and 30 computer-generated documents which can be admitted in evidence under Section 84(1) and (2) of the Evidence Act, 2011? What then is a computer-generated document under the aforesaid provisions of the Evidence Act, 2011. Section 84(1) provides thus: "84 (1) In any proceeding, a statement contained in a document produced by a computer shall be admissible as evidence of any fact stated in it of which direct oral evidence would be admissible, if it is shown that the conditions in Subsection (2) of this Section are satisfied in relation to the statement and computer in question." Sub-section 4 of Section 84 of the Evidence Act 2011, provides as follows: "(4) In any proceeding where it is desired to give a statement in evidence by virtue of this section, a certificate - (a) Identifying the document containing the statement and describing the manner in which it was produced: (b) Giving such particulars of any device Involved in the production of that document as may be appropriate for the purpose of showing that the document was produced by a computer; (c) Dealing with any of the matters to which the conditions mentioned in Subsection (2) above related, and purporting to be signed by a person occupying a responsible position in relation to the operation of the relevant device or the management of the relevant activities, as the case may be." Subsection (5) of the said section aforesaid provisions thus: "(5) For the purposes of this section - (a) Information shall be taken to be supplied to a computer if it is supplied to it in any appropriate from and whether it is supplied directly or (with or without intervention) by means of any appropriate equipment; (b) Where, in the course of activities carried on by any individual or body, information is supplied with a view to its being stored or processed for the purposes of those activities by a computer operated otherwise that in the course of those activities, that information, if duly supplied to that computer, shall be taken to be supplied to it in the course of those activities. (c) A document shall be taken to have been produced by a computer whether it was produced by it directly or (with or without human intervention) by means of any appropriate equipment." (Underlining for emphasis) I have had a dispassionate perusal of the entire proceedings of the lower Court, particularly the pages of the record of appeal where the aforementioned documents were admitted in evidence. I have not been able to trace or find any statement of facts or evidence proffered in satisfaction or fulfilment of the provisions of Sub-sections (1), (4) and (5) of Section 84 of the Evidence Act, 2011 which has qualified any of the documents admitted in evidence as Exhibits 1A, 1B, 26, 27 and 30 as computer-generated document. I therefore, hold that the said documents were wrongly admitted in evidence under the provisions of Section 84(1) and (2) of the Evidence Act, 2011, which provides that: "84(1) In any preceding a statement contained in a document produced by a computer shall be admissible as evidence of any fact stated in it of which direct oral evidence would be admissible, if it is shown that the conditions in statement and computer in question. (2) The conditions referred to in Subsection (1) of this section are - (a) That the document containing the statement was produced by the computer during a period over which the computer was used regularly to store or process information for the purposes of any activities regularly carried on over that period, whether for profit or not, by anybody, whether corporate or not, or by any individual; (b) That over that period, there was regularly supplied to the computer in the ordinary course of those activities information of the kind contained in the statement or of the kind from which the information so contained in derived; (c) That throughout the material part of that period the computer was operating properly or, if not, that in any respect in which it was not operating properly or was out of operation during that part of that period was not such as to affect the production of the document or the accuracy of its contents; and (d) That the information contained in the statement reproduces or is derived from information supplied to the computer in the ordinary course of those activities." Therefore, having been wrongly admitted in evidence under Section 84(1) and (2) of the Evidence Act, 2011, the said documents ought to have been expunged as evidence, and the lower Court ought not have relied on them in taking a decision. In the event, I erred in arriving at the conclusion and decision supra. Let me proceed to consider whether or not, the conditions enumerated under Sub-section (2) of Section 84 were satisfied or fulfilled to have warranted the admission of Exhibits 1A, 1B, 26,27 and 30 in evidence at the lower Court. The provisions of Section 84(1) and (2) of the Evidence Act, 2011, are statutory, and unambiguous. The law is trite; a literal or ordinary interpretation should be applied to a statute which is unambiguous by the nature of the words used. See *Obi* v. *INEC* (2007) NWLR (Pt. 1046) p. 565 at 643. I therefore agree with the submission of learned senior counsel to the appellant, on page 7 at the Reply brief that: "It is submitted that by the express provisions of Section 84 of the Evidence Act, computer generated evidence will be admissible only upon the satisfaction of certain conditions. Where not complied with, computer generated evidence will be inadmissible. Therefore where compliance with the express provisions of the law cannot be shown or established, the computer generated evidence is for all intents and purposes inadmissible and admitting such evidence will amount to an infraction of the law." The admissibility of a computer generated document or document downloaded from the internet is governed by the provision of Section 84 of the Evidence Act, 2011. By Section 84 (1) of the Evidence Act, in any proceeding, a statement contained in a document produced by a computer shall be admissible as evidence of any fact stated in it of which direct oral evidence would be admissible if it is shown that the following conditions are satisfied in relation to the statement and the computer in question; that is: (a) That the document containing the statement was produced by the computer during a period over which the computer was used regularly to store or process information for the purposes of any activities regularly carried on over that period, whether for profit or not, by anybody, whether corporate or not or by any individual; and (b) That over that period there was regularly supplied to the computer in the ordinary course of those activities information of the kind contained in the statement or of the kind from which the information so contained is derived; and (c) That throughout the material part of that period, the computer was operating properly or, if not, that in any respect in which it was not operating properly or was out of operation during that part of that period was not such as to affect the production of the document or the accuracy of its content; and (d) That the information contained in the statement reproduces or is derived from information supplied to the computer in the ordinary course of those activities. A party that seeks to tender in evidence a computer-generated document needs to do more than just tendering same from the bar. Evidence in relation to the use of the computer must be called to establish the above conditions. I am not mindful of the opinion expressed by Rhodes-Vivour JCA (as he then was) in the case of *Oghoyone* v. *Oghohone* (2010) All FWLR (Pt. 543) p. 1884 at 1861, that wherein his lordship when dealing admission of document under Section 96(h) of the Evidence Act, 2004, held that where there are condition, laid down for admissibility of evidence especially documents, if no objection is raised to the non-compliance to the conditions, it would be taken as having been waived, and the evidence can properly be admitted, its inadmissibility cannot be raised later on appeal. The learned justice said: "Since Exhibits p.16-23 (Statement of Accounts) are not inadmissible, they are admissible subject to certain conditions earlier explained, and since they were admitted (Exhibit p. 19 - p. 21, p. 22 and p. 23) without objection to their admissibility, any further objection to their admissibility is deemed waived and this Court cannot open the admissibility of the said exhibits; *Ofuma* v. *IBWA* (1988) 1 NWLR PART 73 AT 658." In the recent case of *Kubor* v. *Dickson* (2013) 4 NWLR (Pt. 1345) p. 534 at 579, the Supreme Court had the occasion to pronounce on the provisions of Section 84 of the Evidence Act, 2011 wherein Onnoghen JSC, lucidly expressed the position of the admissibility of computer-generated evidence especially documentary, under Section 84 of the Evidence Act, 2011 which provisions are distinct from the provisions of Section 96 of the Evidence Act, 2004. In the case supra, the Supreme Court was emphatic that the conditions specified for the admissibility of computer-generated documents cannot be waived or can parties consent to the admission of document without complying with Sub-section 2 of Section 84 of the Evidence Act, 2011. Onnoghen JSC said: "Granted, for the purpose of argument that Exhibits "D" and "L" being computer generated documents or e-documents downloaded from the internet are not public documents whose secondary evidence are admissible only by certified true copies then it means that their admissibility is governed by the provisions of Section 84 of the Evidence Act, 2011, Section 84(1) Provides thus: "84(1)

In any proceeding, a statement contained in a document produced by a computer shall be admissible as evidence of any fact stated in it of which direct oral evidence would be admissible, if it is shown that the conditions in Sub-section (2) of this Section are satisfied in relation to the statement and the computer in question." The conditions are: (a) That the documents containing the statement was produced by the computer during a period over which the computer was used regularly to store or process information for the purposes of any activities regularly carried on over that period, whether for profit or not, by anybody, whether corporate or not or by any individual; (b) That over that period there was regularly supplied to the computer in the ordinary course of those activities information of the kind contained in the statement or of the kind from which the information so contained is derived; (c) That throughout the material part of that period, the computer was operating properly, or, if not that in any respect in which it was not operating properly or was out of operation during that part of that period was not such as to affect the production of the document or the accuracy of its contents; and (d) That the information contained in the statement reproduces or is derived from information supplied to the computer in the ordinary course of those activities. There is no evidence on record to show that appellants in tendering Exhibits "D" and "L" satisfied any of the above conditions. In fact, they did not as the documents were tendered and admitted from the bar. No witness testified before tendering the documents so there was no opportunity to lay the necessary foundations for their admission as e-documents under Section 84 of the Evidence Act, 2011. No wonder therefore that the lower Court held, at page 838 of the record thus: "A party that seeks to tender in evidence a computer generated document needs to do more than just tendering same from the bar. Evidence in relation to the use of the computer must be called to establish the conditions set out under Section 84(2) of the Evidence Act, 2011. I agree entirely with the above conclusion. Since appellants never fulfilled the pre-conditions laid down by law, Exhibits "D" and "L" were inadmissible as computer generated evidence documents.

THE EVIDENCE ACT PROVIDES AN ELABORATE PROTOCOL FOR THE RECEIPT OF ELECTRONIC EVIDENCE

Nimpar, J.C.A. at pp. 28-29, Paras. C-B in the case of *SDV (Nig) Ltd* v. *Ojo & Anor (*2016) LPELR-40323(CA) posited as follows:

> The Evidence Act 2004 had a provision for the admissibility of electronic evidence. What the current Act did is to provide an elaborate protocol for the receipt of electronic evidence. Section 37 and 97 of the repealed Act are relevant here. See also the case of *Esso West Africa Inc* v. *T. Oyegbola* (1969) NMLR 19 when the Apex Court pronounced on the said section and opined on the admissibility of electronic evidence as follows: "The law cannot be and is not ignorant of the modern business methods and must not shut its eyes to the mysteries of computer. In modern times reproduction and inscription on ledgers or other documents by mechanical process are common place and Section 37 cannot therefore only apply to books of accounts." Again in the case of *Federal Republic of Nigeria* v. *Femi Fani-Kayode* (2010) 14 NWLR (Pt. 1214) 481, computer generated evidence was held admissible in evidence.

COMMENTARY

Under section 83 of the Evidence Act, 2011, where direct oral evidence of a fact would be admissible, any statement made by a person in a document to establish that fact shall only be admissible as evidence of that fact if the conditions contained in paragraphs (a) to (d) thereof are satisfied. Section 84(1) goes on to be more specific on the nature of evidence when it provides, *inter alia*, as follows:

> 84(1) In any proceeding, a statement contained in a document produced by a computer shall be admissible as

> evidence of any fact stated in it of which direct oral evidence would be admissible, if it is shown that the conditions in Subsection (2) of this section are satisfied in relation to the statement and the computer in question.

By the opening statement of the provision, computer generated documents are caught by the admissibility requirements of this provision. The relevant phrase is "a statement contained in a document produced by a computer." The draftsman where very explicit and did not leave the meaning of the word "computer" to conjecture. In Section 258(1), the Act defines "computer" to mean

> Any device for storing and processing information, and any reference to information being derived from other information is a reference to its being derived from it by calculation, comparison or any other process.

Therefore, and computer-generated documents can only be admissible in evidence upon compliance with the requirements of Section 84 of the Evidence Act and not Section 83. The Latin maxim is *enumeratio unius est exclusio alterius,* which means, the specification of one thing is an exclusion of the other. When it relates to computer-generated documents, the provision of Section 83 has been excluded. By Section 84(2) of the Evidence Act, 2011, there are four conditions which are required to be satisfied in relation to the document and computer in question to wit:

1. that the statement sought to be tendered was produced by the computer during a period when it was in regular use;

2. that during the period of regular use, information of the kind contained in the document or statement was supplied to the computer;
3. that the computer was operating properly during that period of regular use; and
4. that the information contained in the statement was supplied to the computer in the ordinary course of its normal use.

There must be the requisite evidence in relation to the satisfactions of the above conditions. A further condition for the admissibility of electronic evidence can be found under Section 84(4) of the Act which relates to the production of an authentication/trustworthiness certificate of the computer used in producing the documents. There are plethora of authorities which shows that this subsection permits even non-experts to issue such a certificate, especially persons who, though not possessing the required professional qualifications may have acquired some practical knowledge and being in the position described in the subsection to bring him within the definition of an expert by the expanded definition of an expert in the case of *OANDO Nig. Plc* v. *Adijere W/A Ltd.*[1] Under section 84,[2] it does not require a person to show that the statement contained in a document is likely to be true. Whether it is likely to be true or not is a question of weight for the Court to decide. What is required as a condition for the admissibility of a computer-generated statement/document is positive evidence that the computer processed, stored and reproduced whatever information it received. It is majorly concerned with the way in which the computer has dealt with the information to generate the

[1] (2013) 5 NWLR (Pt. 1377) 374.
[2] Similar to Section 69 of UK PACE 1984.

statement which is being tendered as evidence of a fact which it states.[3] If an authentication certificate is relied on, it should show on its face that it is signed by a person who, from his job description, can confidently be expected to be in a position to give reliable evidence about the operation of the computer. The nature of the evidence to discharge the burden of showing that there has been no improper use of the computer and that it was operating properly will inevitably vary from case to case.[4] There is no single approach to authentication applicable across board. Instead, the most appropriate form of authenticating electronic evidence will often depend on the nature of the evidence and the circumstances of each particular case. Preferably, such evidence may be authenticated by direct testimony from a witness with personal knowledge, by comparison with other authenticated evidence or by circumstantial evidence. All that is required is for the certification to be in tandem with the production processes approved by the Supreme Court in the case of *Dickson* v. *Sylva*,[5] wherein Galadima, JSC held, *inter alia*:

> From the above provisions, it is crystal-clear that it is only with respect to the computer that "produces" the document, in this case the DVD (Exhibit P42B) that ought to be certified." In addition, under Section 41 of the Evidence Act, 2011, there is an exception to the hearsay rule that relates to electronic evidence when it is a statement made in the ordinary course of business. Also, under the business record exception to the hearsay rule, Section 51 of the Act provides that electronic records regularly kept in the course of business are admissible whenever they refer to a matter before the Court. For ease of

[3] See *DPP* v. *Mckeown* (1997) 1 All ER 737.
[4] See *R* v. *Shephard* (1993) 2 WLR 102.
[5] (2017) 8 NWLR (Pt. 1567) 167.

> reference, the provisions are set out hereunder - "41. A statement is admissible when made by a person in the ordinary course of business, and in particular when it consists of any entry or memorandum made by him in books, electronic device kept in the ordinary course of business, or in the discharge of a professional duty, or of an acknowledgment written or signed by him of the receipt of money, goods, securities or property of any kind, or of a document used in commerce written or signed-by him, or of the date of a letter or other document usually dated, written or signed by him." "51, Entries in books of accounts or electronic records regularly kept in the course of business are admissible whenever they refer to a matter into which the Court has to inquire, but such statements shall not alone be sufficient evidence to charge any person with liability.

The cases of *Abubakar* v. *Chuks,*[6] *Obembe* v. *Ekene*[7] and *Torti* v. *Ukpabi* [8] held that if a document relates to a business record which is also computer-generated, it is not necessary that it should be tendered through the maker.

---

[6] (2007) 18 NWLR (Pt. 1066) 386.
[7] (2001) 10 NWLR (Pt.722) 677.
[8] (1984) 1 SC 370.

Chapter 9

APPEALS ON COMPUTER-GENERATED EVIDENCE

WRONGFULLY ADMITTED/EXCLUDED EVIDENCE ONLY CANNOT CONSTITUTE A GROUND FOR REVERSING A DECISION ON APPEAL

In the case of *Islam Rafiqul* v. *FRN* (2018) LPELR-44520 (CA), Ogakwu, J.C.A. at pp. 22-23, paras. D-E) held thus:

> Undoubtedly, Exhibit P23 is computer-generated evidence. From the Records the said Exhibit P23 was admitted without an accompanying certificate of identification as stipulated in Section 84(4) of the Evidence Act. (See pages 183-184 of the Records) The said Exhibit P23 was therefore wrongfully admitted in evidence and ought to be expunged. See *Kubor* v. *Dickson* (*supra*) and *Dickson* v. *Sylva* (*supra*). The matter does not end there. Section 251(1) of the Evidence Act provides as follows: "The wrongful admission of evidence shall not of itself be a ground for the reversal of any decision in any case where it appears to the Court on appeal that the evidence so admitted cannot reasonably be held to have affected the decision and that such decision would have been the same if such evidence had not been admitted." So the question is whether on expunging the said Exhibit P23, the judgment of the lower Court will be different. Where it will not make any difference to the decision reached, then the wrongful admission shall not be a basis on which to reverse the decision of the lower Court: *The State* v. *Ogbubunjo*

(2001) LPELR-3223 1 at 40-41 (SC), *Nwaeze* v. *The State* (1996) LPELR (2091) 1 at 33 (SC) and *Archibong* v. *The State* (2006) LPELR (537) 1 at 27 (SC).

WHERE WRONGFUL ADMISSION AND OR REJECTION OF ELECTRONIC EVIDENCE WILL NOT MAKE ANY DIFFERENCE TO THE DECISION REACHED, THE WRONGFUL ADMISSION SHALL NOT BE A BASIS ON WHICH TO REVERSE THE DECISION OF THE LOWER COURT

In *Nomany* v. *FRN* (2018) LPELR-44546 (CA), Ogakwu, J.C.A. at pp. 22-24, Paras. C-E held thus:

> The Appellant in his issue number three makes a kerfuffle of Exhibit P23 having been admitted in evidence without the stipulations of Section 84 of the Evidence Act having been complied with. It was opined that this occasioned a miscarriage of justice since the lower Court relied on the said Exhibit P23 to convict the Appellant. Undoubtedly, Exhibit P23 is computer generated evidence. From the Records the said Exhibit P23 was admitted without an accompanying certificate of identification as stipulated in Section 84(4) of the Evidence Act. (See pages 183-184 of the Records). The said Exhibit P23 was therefore wrongfully admitted in evidence and ought to be expunged. See *Kubor* v. *Dickson* (*supra*) and *Dickson* v. *Sylva* (*supra)*. The matter does not end there. Section 251(1) of the Evidence Act provides as follows: "The wrongful admission of evidence shall not of itself be a ground for the reversal of any decision in any case where it appears to the Court on appeal that the evidence so admitted cannot reasonably be held to have affected the decision and that such decision would have been the same if such evidence had not been admitted." So the question is whether on expunging the said Exhibit P23, the judgment of the lower Court will be different. Where it will not make any difference to the decision reached, then the wrongful admission shall not be a basis on which to reverse the decision of the lower Court: *The State* v. *Ogbubunjo*

(2001) LPELR (3223) 1 at 40-41 (SC), *Nwaeze* v. *The State* (1996) LPELR (2091) 1 at 33 (SC) and *Archibong* v. *The State* (2006) LPELR (537) 1 at 27 (SC). So the question is whether on expunging the said Exhibit P23, the judgment of the lower Court will be different. Exhibit P23 was tendered through PW5, the EFCC operative who was a member of the team that investigated the case against the convicts. Exhibit P23 is the Lloyd's Intelligence Report on the International Maritime Organization (I.M.O.) number of 'MT BRUNO' which the convicts claim was the vessel that gave them the Ship To Ship (STS) Transfer of the Crude Oil stored in the tank of the 1st accused vessel. The exhibit shows that the I.M.O. number claimed by the convicts does not belong to 'MT BRUNO' but to a vessel called 'SETUBA'. Apart from Exhibit P23, there is Exhibit P4, tendered through the PW3, which is the Report of the search of the Lloyds List Intelligence Data Base and which shows the status of 'MT BRUNO' as dead and that there was no issue of movement of the vessel on the data base (see pages 132-134 of the Records). The evidence in Exhibit P4 affords conclusive proof that the dead 'MT BRUNO' could not have done a ship to ship transfer with the 1st accused vessel, 'MT ASTERIS', as claimed by the convicts. It is therefore effulgent that expunging the admitted inadmissible Exhibit P23 will make no difference to the decision of the lower Court and therefore no miscarriage of justice was occasioned by the wrongful admission of the said Exhibit P23.

WHEN A DOCUMENT HAS SUBSTANTIALLY COMPLIED WITH THE PROVISIONS OF SECTION 97 (2) (E) OF THE EVIDENCE ACT AND ADMITTED WITHOUT OBJECTION, A PARTY CANNOT LATER RAISE OBJECTION TO IT ON APPEAL

Rhodes-Vivour, J.C.A at pp. 26-27, paras. E-D in the case of *Oghoyone* v. *Oghoyone* (2010) LPELR-4689(CA) posited thus:

> Once there is substantial compliance with the provisions of Section 97(2)(e) of the Evidence Act Banking documents are

admissible in evidence. The fact that p w 2 said on oath (and he was not challenged) that he made comparison as required, then there is substantial compliance with the provisions of Section 97(2)(e) of Evidence Act. Exhibits P 16 - P 23 are secondary evidence and their admissibility in evidence as Exhibits was correct. Furthermore since Exhibit P 16 - 23 (Statement of Accounts) are not inadmissible, they are admissible subject to certain conditions earlier explained, and since there were admitted (Exhibits P 19, P 21, P 22 and P 23) without any objection to their admissibility, any further objection to their admissibility is deemed waived and this court cannot open the admissibility of the said Exhibits. See *Oguma* v. *I.B.W.A.* (1988) 1 N.W.L.R. Pt. 73 p. 658. Finally and for emphasis, since Exhibits P 16 - P 23 were documents admissible under Section 97 (1) (h) and 2(e) of the Evidence Act provided certain conditions were met and those conditions were met (the testimony of p w 2). There has been substantial conformity with the section supra. Consequently the computer generated Statements of Account (Exhibits P 16 - P 23) tendered by the respondent were admissible in law.

AN OBJECTION CANNOT BE RAISED ON THE ADMISSIBILITY OF EVIDENCE WHICH THE COURT HAD RULED ON

In *Adelodun* v. *FRN* (2017) LPELR-42356 (CA), Barka, J.C.A. at pp. 42-43, Paras. D-C held as follows:

By the provision of Section 286 of the Evidence Act 2011, a document includes any devise by means of which information is recorded, stored or retrievable, including computer output. Section 84 (i-iv) prescribes the means and method by which computer generated documents are to be produced and submitted in evidence, and the weight to be ascribed to such evidence is as stipulated by Section 34 (i) (b) of the Evidence Act 2011. See also Sections 51 and 52 of the Evidence Act and the cases of *Kubor* v. *Dickson* (2013) 4

> NWLR (pt 1345) 534, and *Omisore* v. *Aregbesola* (2015) 15 NWLR (pt 1482) 205. It is my humble but firm view that the trial Court was on a sound footing going by the combined provisions of Sections 51, 52 and Section 84 (1-4) of the Evidence Act, to have admitted exhibits 12 and 13 in evidence. The issue of its admissibility having been resolved by the ruling of the trial Court, an objection to the admissibility of same as counsel had wanted to do, cannot legally be granted, as the Court on the issue was *functus officio*; the decision can only be questioned on appeal.

THE SUPREME COURT CANNOT PRONOUNCE ON AN ISSUE NOT RAISED AT THE COURT OF APPEAL REGARDING THE ADMISSIBILITY OF A DOCUMENT ELECTRONIC OR OTHERWISE

Peter-Odili, J.S.C. at pp. 26-27, Paras. B-B in the case of *Ashakacem PLC* v. *Asharatul Mubashshurun Investment Ltd* (2019) LPELR-46541(SC) stated thus:

> The angle taken by the appellant is that Exhibit L which was tendered and admitted before the trial Court should herein be discountenanced as the Court below ought to have known that the document was computer generated and did not meet the conditions provided for under Section 84 (4) of the Evidence Act. The resistance from the respondent stems from the fact that this contention of the appellant is belatedly brought up at this stage as it was not an issue at the Court of Appeal and so cannot be taken up here since it was not protested against in the Court below and a pronouncement made upon it. Again for full measure is that this Court cannot enter into the determination on the issue, leave of Court having not been sought and obtained in that regard being a fresh issue on appeal since not being raised in the Court of Appeal though presented in the trial Court. The implication is that after the trial Court's pronouncement or use thereof, the matter was abandoned at the stage of the Court below and so

the issue rested for all time as there is no competence for appeal from High Court to the Apex. See *Idufueko* v. *Pfizer Products Ltd* (2014) 12 NWLR (Pt.1420) 96 at 122; *Guobadia* v. *The State* (2004) LPELR - 1344 (SC) page 11; Section 233 (1) of the 1999 Constitution; *Aladejobi* v. *NBA* (2013) 5-7 MJSC (Pt.11) 20 -207.

A DOCUMENT NOT TENDERED AT THE TRIAL COURT DUE TO THE INADVERTENCE OF COUNSEL CAN BE TENDERED ON APPEAL AS FRESH EVIDENCE

In the case of *Odunewu* v. *Agoro* (2022) 7 NWLR (PT 1830) 545 at 573 – 574, Paras F – A, the Court held thus:

> A document not tendered at the trial Court due to inadvertence of counsel can be tendered on appeal as fresh evidence in the interest of Justice, particularly if the document had been referred to in the pleadings or evidence by the party who seeks to tender it.

COMMENTARY

In general, where a document which is inadmissible in evidence is admitted at trial, such document must be rejected on appeal. Consequently where the inadmissibility of a document earlier admitted in the course of the trial is raised and sustained on appeal such document must be rejected and expunged. See the cases of *Ajayi* v. *Fisher*[1] *and Esso West Africa Inc.* v. *All.*[2]

It is of primary and crucial important that any document used in litigation must not only be relevant it should also be admissible. Therefore a trial judge is perfectly

[1] 1 F.S.C. 97.
[2] 196 NMLR 44.

entitled in his judgment to disregard evidence erroneously admitted at trial. For the purpose of admissibility, where a documentary evidence is absolutely inadmissible on the grounds of statutory exclusionary provisions, such documentary evidence remains legally inadmissible and cannot under any circumstance constitute evidence in the case at the trial or on appeal, even where such documentary evidence is admitted by consent. See the cases of *Ikenye* v. *Ofunne*,[3] *Owoyin* v. *Omotosho*,[4] *Alashe* v. *ILU*[5] and *Raimi* v. *Akintoye*.[6]

A documentary evidence is only rendered admissible on the fulfilment of certain conditions, such documentary evidence is admissible if admitted without objection by the other party and where the admission of the evidence does not affect the result of the case. See the cases of *Okeke* v. *Obidife*;[7] *Alade* v. *Olukade*;[8] *Yashin* v. *Barclays Bank Dco*.[9]

Although the general rule for the admissibility of statements under section 83(3) of the Evidence Act is that statements are not admissible if made by persons interested or when proceedings are pending or anticipated, section 90(3) of the Evidence Act must be given a narrow interpretation to ensure its effectiveness and to permit the continuance or ordinary legitimate transactions untrammelled by the exclusionary rules of Evidence.

The word "interested" in section 83(3) of the Evidence Act is incapable of any well-defined meaning and to appropriate its proper meaning one must examine the

[3] (1985)2 NWLR (PT. 501).
[4] (1961) 1 ALL NLR 304.
[5] (1964) 1 ALL NLR 390.
[6] (1986) 3 NWLR (PT. 26) 97.
[7] (1965) NMLR 113.
[8] (1976) SC 183.
[9] (1968) 1 All NLR 171.

context in which it is used. The word "interested" in section 83(3) of the Evidence Act may mean a direct financial interest on the one-hand or, on the other hand, it may mean nothing more than the ordinary human interest which everybody has in the outcome of the proceedings in which he is likely to be a witness.

The mere fact that the maker of a statement tendered in evidence is in the employment of a party does not by itself make him a person interested in proceedings within section 83(3) of the Evidence Act. Thus, the evidence by any servant or agent entered into by that company is relevant and admissible to establish any transaction entered into by that company.

APPENDIX

NIGERIAN EVIDENCE ACT, 2011

EVIDENCE ACT 2011(as amended by the Evidence Amendment Act, 2023)

(Sections 1-3) Part I - GENERAL

1. Evidence may be given of facts in issue and relevant facts.
2. Evidence in accordance with section 1 generally admissible.
3. Admissibility of evidence under other legislation.

(Section 4-13) Part II - RELEVANCY

4. Relevance of facts forming part of same transaction.
5. Facts which are the occasion, cause or effect or facts in issue.
6. Motive, preparation and previous or subsequent conduct.
7. Facts necessary to explain or introduce relevant facts.
8. Things said or done by conspirator in reference to common intention.
9. When facts not otherwise relevant become relevant.
10. Certain facts relevant in proceedings for damages.
11. Facts showing existence of state of mind, body or bodily feeling.

12 Facts bearing on question whether act was accidental or intentional.

13. Existence of course of business when relevant.

(Sections 14-36) Part III - RELEVANCE AND ADMISSIBILITY OF CERTAIN EVIDENCE

14. Discretion to exclude improperly obtained evidence.
15. Matters court to take into account under section 14.
16. What customs admissible.
17. Judicial notice of custom.
18. Evidence of customs.
19. Relevant facts as to how matter alleged to be custom understood.
20. Admission defined.
21. Admission by privies.
22. Admissions by persons whose position must be proved as against party to suit.
23. Admissions by persons expressly referred to by party to suit.

24. Proof of admissions against persons making them, and by or on their behalf
25. When oral admissions as to contents of documents are relevant.
26. Admissions in civil cases, when relevant.
27. Admissions not conclusive proof; but may stop.
28. Confession defined.
29. When confession is relevant.
30. Facts discovered in consequence of information given by defendant.
31. Confession otherwise relevant not to become irrelevant because of promise of secrecy, etc.
32. Evidence in other proceedings amounting to a confession is admissible.
33. What evidence to be given when statement forms part of a conversation, document, book or series of letters or papers.
34. Weight to be attached to admissible statements.
35. Acts of possession and enjoyment of land may be evidence.
36. Evidence of scienter upon charge of receiving stolen property.

(Sections 37-82) Part IV - HEARSAY, OPINION AND CHARACTER EVIDENCE: RELEVANCE AND ADMISSIBILITY

37. Hearsay defined.
38. Hearsay rule.
39. Statements by persons who cannot be called as witnesses.
40. Statements relating to cause of death.
41. Statements made in the course of business.
42. Statement against interest of maker with special knowledge.
43. Statements of opinions as to public right or custom and matters of general interest.
44. Statements relating to rile existence of a relationship.
45. Declarations by testators.
46. Admissibility of certain evidence for proving, in subsequent proceeding, the truth of facts stated in it.

47. When statement made under any criminal procedure legislation may be used in evidence.
48. Statement of defendant at preliminary investigation or coroner's inquest.
49. Admission of written statements of investigating police officers in certain cases.
50. Absence of public officers.
51. Statements made in special circumstances entries in books of account.
52. Entry in public records made in performance of duty.
53. Statements in maps, charts and plans.
54. Statement as to fact of public nature contained in certain acts or notifications.
55. Certificates of specified government officers to be sufficient evidence in all criminal cases.
56. Certificates of Central Bank officers as evidence in criminal cases.
57. Service of certificates on other party before hearing,
58. Genuineness of certificates to be presumed,
59. Previous judgments admissible to bar a second suit or trial.
60. Admissibility of certain Judgments in certain jurisdictions,
61. Admissibility and effect of judgments other than those mentioned in section 60,
62. Judgment, etc., other than those mentioned in sections 59 to 61, when admissible
63. Conviction as evidence in civil proceedings
64. Fraud or collusion in obtaining judgment, or non-jurisdiction of court, may be proved,
65. Judgment conclusive in favour of judge,
66. Family or communal tradition admissible in land cases
67. Opinion inadmissible except as provided in this Act.
68. Opinions of experts, when admissible
69. Opinions as to foreign law,
70. Opinions as to customary law and custom
71. Facts bearing upon opinions of experts

72. Opinion as to handwriting, when admissible,
73. Opinion as to existence of "general custom or right" when admissible
74. Opinions as to usages and tenets, when admissible
75. Opinion on relationship, when admissible
76. Grounds of opinion when admissible
77. Character defined
78. In civil cases, evidence of character generally inadmissible
79. Character as affecting damages
80. In libel and slander, notice must be given of evidence of character
81. In criminal cases evidence of good character admissible
82. Evidence of character of the accused in criminal proceedings

(Sections 83-120) Part V - DOCUMENTARY EVIDENCE

83. Admissibility of documentary evidence as to facts in issue
84. Admissibility of statement in document produced by computers
85. Proof of contents of documents
86. Primary evidence.
87. Secondary evidence
88. Proof of documents by primary evidence
89. Cases in which secondary evidence relating to document
90. Nature of secondary evidence admissible under section 89
91. Rules as to notice to produce
92. Proof that bank has made returns or been duly licensed
93. Proof of signature and handwriting and electronic signature
94. Identification of person signing a document
95. Evidence of sealing and delivery of a document
96. Proof of instrument to the validity of which attestation is necessary
97. Admission of execution by part to attested document
98. Cases in which proof of execution or of handwriting unnecessary
99. Proof when attesting witness denies the execution
100. Proof of document not required by law to be attested

101. Comparison of signature, writing, seal or finger impressions with others admitted or proved
102. Public documents
103. Private documents
104. Certified copies of public documents
105. Proof of documents by production of certified copies
106. Proof of other official documents
107. Court may order proof by affidavit
108. Affidavit to be filled
109. Affidavit sworn in Nigeria
110. Proof of document not required by law to be attested
111. Proof of seal and signature
112. Affidavit not to be sworn before certain persons
113. Affidavit defective in form
114. Amendment and re-swearing of affidavit
115. Contents of affidavits
116. Conflicting affidavits
117. Form of affidavits
118. Provisions as to altered affidavit
119. Jurat
120. Declaration without oath may be taken
(Sections 121-124) Part VI - PROOF
121. Proof of facts.
122. Facts of which court must take judicial notice need not to be proved.
123. Facts admitted need to be proved.
124. Facts of common knowledge need not be proved.
(Section 125-127) Part VII - ORAL EVIDENCE AND THE INSPECTION OF REAL EVIDENCE
125. Proof of facts by oral evidence
126. Oral evidence must be direct
127. Inspection when oral evidence refers to real evidence
(Section 128-130) Part VIII - Exclusion of Oral by Documentary Evidence Return to Main Menu

128. Evidence of terms of judgments, contracts, grants and other dispositions of property reduced to a documentary form.
129. Evidence as to interpretation of documents
130. Application of this Part
(Section 131-144) Part IX - Production and Effect of Evidence Return to Main Menu
131. Burden of proof
132. On whom burden of proof lies
133. Burden of proof in civil cases
134. Standard of proof in civil cases
135. Standard of proof where commission of crime in issue and burden where guilt of crime, etc. asserted.
136. Burden of proof as to particular fact.
137. Standard of proof where burden of proving fact, etc. placed on defendant by law.
138. Burden of proving fact necessary to be proved to make evidence admissible.
139. Burden of proof in criminal cases.
140. Proof of facts especially within knowledge.
141. Exceptions need not be proved by prosecution.
142. Burden of proof as to relationship in the case of partners, landlord and tenant, principal and agent.
143. Burden of proof as to ownership.
144. Proof of good faith in transactions where one party is in relation of active confidence.
(Sections 145-174) Part X - PRESUMPTIONS AND ESTOPPEL
145. Rules as to presumptions by the court
146. Presumption as to genuineness of certified copies
147. Presumption as to documents produced as record of evidence
148. Presumption as to gazettes, newspapers, Acts of the National Assembly and other documents.
149. Presumption as to document admissible in other countries without proof or seal or signature.
150. Presumption as to powers of attorney.
151. Presumption as to public maps and charts.

152. Presumption as to books.
153. Presumption as to telegraphic and electronic messages.
154. Presumption as to due execution of documents not produced.
155. Presumption as to handwriting, etc. in documents twenty years old.
156. Proper custody defined.
157. Presumption as to date of documents.
158. Presumption as to stamp of a document.
159. Presumption as to sealing and delivery.
160. Presumption as to alternative.
161. Presumption as to age of parties to a conveyance or instrument.
162. Presumption as to statements in documents twenty years old.
163. Presumption as to deeds of corporation.
164. Presumption of death from seven years absence and other facts.
165. Presumption of legitimacy.
166. Presumption of marriage.
167. Court may presume existence of certain facts.
168. Presumptions of regularity and of deeds to complete title.
169. Estoppel.
170. Estoppel of tenant; and of licensee of person in possession.
171. Estoppel of bailee, agent and licensee
172. Estoppel of person signing Act of lading
173. Judgment conclusive of facts forming ground of judgment
174. Effect of judgment not pleaded as estoppel.
(Sections 175-204) Part XI - WITNESSES
175. Who may testify
176. Dumb witnesses
177. Cases in which banker or officers representing other financial institutions not compellable to produce books
178. Parties to civil suits and their wives or husbands
179. Competence in criminal cases
180. Competence of person charged to give evidence
181. Comment on failure by defendant to give evidence

182. Evidence by husband or wife, when compellable
183. Witness not to be compellable to incriminate himself
184. Production of title deeds or other documents of witness not a party
185. Production of documents which another person could refuse to produce
186. Evidence by spouse as to adultery
187. Communications during marriage
188. Compellability, of justices etc. or the persons before whom the proceeding is being held
189. Restriction on disclosure as to source of information in respect of commission of offences
190. Evidence as to affairs of State
191. Official communication
192. Professional communication between client and legal practitioner
193. Section 192 to apply to interpreters and clerks
194. Privilege not waived by volunteering evidence
195. Confidential communication with legal advisers
196. Statements in documents marked "without prejudice"
197. Corroboration in actions for breach of promise of marriage
198. Accomplice
199. Co-defendant not an accomplice
200. Number of witnesses
201. Treason and treasonable offences
202. Evidence on charge of perjury
203. Exceeding speed limit
204. Sedition

(Section 205-247) Part XII - TAKING OF ORAL EVIDENCE AND EXAMINATION OF WITNESSES

205. Oral evidence to be on oath or affirmation
206. Witness to be cautioned before giving oral evidence
207. Absence of religious belief does not invalidate oath
208. Cases in which evidence not given upon oath may be received
209. Unsworn evidence of child

210. Order of production and examination of witnesses
211. Court to decide as to admission of evidence \
212. Ordering witnesses out of court
213. Preventing communication with witnesses
214. Examination- in-chief, cross-examination and re-examination
215. Order and direction of examination
216. Cross-examination by co-defendant of prosecution witness.
217. Cross-examination by co-defendant of witness called by a defendant
218. Production of documents without giving evidence
219. Cross-examination of person called to produce a document.
220. Witnesses to character
221. Leading question
222. Evidence as to matters in writing
223. Question lawful in cross-examination
224. Court to decide whether question shall be asked and when witness compelled to answer
225. Question not to be asked without reasonable grounds
226. Procedure of court in case of question being asked without reasonable grounds
227. Indecent and scandalous questions
228. Questions intended to insult or annoy
229. Exclusion of evidence to contradict answers to questions testing veracity
230. How far a party may discredit his own witness
231. Proof of contradictory statement of hostile witness
232. Cross-examination as to previous statements in writing
233. Impeaching credit of witness
234. Special restrictions respecting permissible evidence in trial for sexual offences
235. Evidence of witness impeaching credit
236. Questions tending to render evidence of relevant fact more probable, admissible
237. Former statements of witness may be proved to show consistency

238. What matters may be proved in connection with proved statement relevant under sections 40 to 50
239. Refreshing memory
240. Testimony to facts stated in document mentioned in section 239
241. Right of adverse party as to writing used to refresh memory
242. Production of documents
243. Exclusion of evidence on grounds of public interest
244. Giving as evidence document called for and produced on notice
245. Using, as evidence, of document production of which was refused on notice
246. Judge's power to put questions or order production of documents, etc.
247. Power of assessors to put questions
(Section 248-250) Part XIII - EVIDENCE OF PREVIOUS CONVICTION
248. Proof of previous conviction
249. Proof of previous conviction outside Nigeria
250. Additional mode of proof in criminal proceedings of a previous conviction
(Section 251) Part XIV – WRONGFUL ADMISSION AND REJECTION OF EVIDENCE
251. Wrongful admission or exclusion of evidence.
(Sections 252-254) Part XV - SERVICE AND EXECUTION THROUGHOUT NIGERIA OF PROCESS TO COMPEL THE ATTENDANCE OF WITNESSES BEFORE APPLIED TO ALL JUDICIAL PROCEEDINGS IN OR BEFORE COURTS IN NIGERIA
252. Interpretation of "court" in this part.
253. Subpoena or witness summons may be served in another State
254. Orders for production of prisoners
(Sections 255-259) Part XVI - MISCELLANEOUS AND SUPPLEMENTAL
255. Regulations

256. Application
257. Repeal and savings
258. Interpretation
259. Citation

SECTIONS/ PROVISIONS

1. Evidence may be given of facts in issue and relevant facts.

Evidence may be given in any suit or proceeding of the existence or non - existence of every fact in issue and of such other facts as are hereafter declared to be relevant, and of no others: Provided that:-

a. the court may exclude evidence of facts which though relevant or deemed to be relevant to the issue, appears to it to be too remote to be material in all the circumstances of the case; and
b. this section shall not enable any person to give evidence of a fact which he is disentitled to prove by any provision of the law for the time being in force.

2. Evidence in accordance with section 1 generally admissible.

For the avoidance of doubt, all evidence given in accordance with section 1 shall, unless excluded in accordance with this or any other Act, or any other legislation validly in force in Nigeria, be admissible in judicial proceedings to which this Act applies: Provided that admissibility of such evidence shall be subject to all such conditions as may be specified in each case by or under this Act.

3. Admissibility of evidence under other legislation.

Nothing in this Act shall prejudice the admissibility of any evidence that is made admissible by any other legislation validly in force in Nigeria.

4. Relevance of facts forming part of same transaction.

Facts which, though not in issue, are so connected with a fact in issue as to form part of the same transaction, are relevant, whether they occurred at the same time and place or at different times and places.

5. Facts which are the occasion, cause or effect or facts in issue.

Facts which are the occasion, cause or effect, immediate or otherwise, of relevant facts, or facts in issue, or which constitute the state of things under which they happened, or which afforded an opportunity for their occurrence or transaction, are relevant.

6. Motive, preparation and previous or subsequent conduct.

(1) Any fact is relevant which shows or constitutes a motive or preparation for any fact in issue or relevant fact.

(2) The conduct, whether previous or subsequent to any proceedings:-

a. of any party to any proceedings, or an agent to such party, in reference to such suit or proceeding or in reference to any fact in issue in it or a fact relevant to it; and

b. of any person an offence against whom is the subject of any proceedings, is relevant in such proceedings if such conduct influences or is influenced by any fact in issue or relevant fact.

(3) The word "conduct" in this section does not include statements, unless those statements accompany and explain acts other than statements, but this provision shall not affect the relevance of statements under any other section.

(4) When the conduct of any person is relevant, any statement made to him or in his presence and hearing which affects such conduct is relevant.

7. Facts necessary to explain or introduce relevant facts:-

a. necessary to explain or introduce a fact in issue or relevant fact; or

b. which support or rebut an inference suggested by a fact in issue or relevant fact; or

c. which establish the identity of anything or person whose identity is relevant; or

d. which fix the time or place at which any fact in issue or relevant fact happened; or

e. which show the relation of parties by whom any such fact was transacted, are relevant in so far as they are necessary for that purpose.

8. Things said or done by conspirator in reference to common intention.

(1) Where there is reasonable ground to believe that two or more persons have conspired together to commit an offence or an actionable wrong, anything said, done or written by any one of such persons in execution or furtherance of their common intention, after the time when such intention was first

entertained by one of them, is a relevant fact as against each of the persons believed to be so conspiring, for the purpose of proving the existence of the conspiracy as well as for the purpose of showing that any such person was a party to it.

(2) Notwithstanding subsection (1) of this section, statements made by individual conspirators as to measures taken in the execution or furtherance of such common intention are not deemed to be relevant as such as against any conspirators, except those by whom or in whose presence such statements are made.

(3) Evidence of acts or statements deemed to be relevant under this section may not be given until the court is satisfied that, apart from them, there are *prima facie* grounds for believing the existence of the conspiracy to which they relate.

9. When facts not otherwise relevant become relevant.

Facts not otherwise relevant are relevant:

a. if they are inconsistent with any fact in issue or relevant fact;

b. if by themselves or in connection with other facts they make the existence or non - existence of any fact in issue or relevant fact probable or improbable.

10. Certain facts relevant in proceedings for damages.

In proceedings in which damages are claimed any fact which will enable the court to determine the amount of damages which ought to be awarded is relevant.

11. Facts showing existence of state of mind, or body, or bodily feeling.

(1) Facts showing the existence of - (a) any state of mind such as intention, knowledge, good faith, negligence, rashness, ill - will or goodwill towards any particular person; or (b) any state of body or bodily feeling, are relevant when the existence of any such state of mind or body or bodily feeling is in issue or relevant.

(2) A fact relevant as showing the existence of a relevant state of mind must show that the state of mind exists, not generally, but in reference to the particular matter in question.

12. Facts bearing on question whether act was accidental or intentional.

When there is a question whether an act was accidental or intentional, or done with a particular knowledge or intention or to rebut any defence that may otherwise be open to the defendant, the fact that such act formed part of a series of similar occurrences, in each of which the person doing the act was concerned, is relevant.

13. Existence of course of business, when relevant.

When there is a question whether a particular act was done, the existence of any course of business, according to which it naturally would have been done, is a relevant fact.

14. Discretion to exclude improperly obtained evidence

Evidence obtained:

(a) improperly or in contravention of a law; or

(b) in consequence of an impropriety or of a contravention of a law, shall be admissible unless the court is of the opinion that the desirability of admitting the evidence is out - weighed by the undesirability of admitting evidence that has been obtained in the manner in which the evidence was obtained.

15. Matters a court shall take into account under section 14.

For the purposes of section 14, the matters that the court shall take into account include:

a. the probative value of the evidence;

b. the importance of the evidence in the proceeding;

c. the nature of the relevant offence, cause of action or defence and the nature of the subject - matter of the proceeding;

d. the gravity of the impropriety or contravention;

e. whether the impropriety or contravention was deliberate or reckless;

f. whether any other proceeding (whether or not in a court) has been or is likely to be taken in relation to the impropriety or contravention;

g. the difficulty, if any, of obtaining the evidence without impropriety or contravention of law.

16. What customs admissible.

(1) A custom may be adopted as part of the law governing a particular set of circumstances if it can be judicially noticed or can be proved to exist by evidence.

(2) The burden of proving a custom shall lie upon the person alleging its existence.

17. Judicial notice of custom

A custom may be judicially noticed when it has been adjudicated upon once by a superior court of record.

18. Evidence of customs.

(1) Where a custom cannot be established as one judicially noticed, it shall be proved as a fact.

(2) Where the existence or the nature of a custom applicable to a given case is in issue, there may be given in evidence the opinions of persons who would be likely to know of its existence in accordance with section 73. (3) In any judicial proceeding where any custom is relied upon, it shall not be enforced as law if it is contrary to public policy, or is not in accordance with natural justice, equity and good conscience.

19. Relevant facts as to how a matter alleged to be a custom is understood.

Every fact is deemed to be relevant which tends to show how in particular instances a matter alleged to be a custom was understood and acted upon by persons then interested.

20. Admission defined.

An admission is a statement, oral or documentary, or conduct which suggests any inference as to any fact in issue or relevant fact, and which is made by any of the persons, and in the circumstances, hereafter mentioned in this Act.

21. Admission by privies.

(1) Statements made by a party to the proceeding, or by an agent to any such party, whom the court regards, in the circumstances of the case, as expressly or impliedly authorised by him to make them, are admissions. (2) Statements made by parties to suits, suing or sued in a representative character, are not admissions unless they were made while the party making them held that character.

(3) Statements made by –

a. persons who have any proprietary or pecuniary interest in the subject matter of the proceedings, and who made the statements in their character of persons so interested; or

b. persons from whom the parties to the suit have derived their interest in the subject matter of the suit, are admissions, if they are made during the continuance of the interest of the person making the statements.

22. Admissions by persons whose position must be proved as against a party to suit.

Statements made by persons whose position or liability it is necessary to prove as against any party to the suit are admissions if such statements would be relevant as against such persons in relation to such position or liability in a suit brought by or against them, and if they are made whilst the person making them occupies such position or is subject to such liability.

23. Admissions by persons expressly referred to by a party to a suit.

Statements made by persons to whom a party to the suit has expressly referred for information in reference to a matter in dispute are admissions.

24. Proof of admissions against persons making them, and by or on their behalf.

Admissions are relevant and may be proved as against the person who makes them or his representative in interest, but they cannot be proved by or on behalf of the person who makes them or by his representative in interest, except in the following cases:

a. an admission may be proved by or on behalf of the person making it when it is of such a nature that, if the person making it cannot be called as a witness, it would be relevant as between third parties under sections 39 to 45;

b. an admission may be proved by or on behalf of the person making it, when it consists of a statement of the existence of any state of mind or body, relevant or in issue, made at or about the time when such state of mind or body existed, and is accompanied by conduct rendering its falsehood improbable; and

c. an admission may be proved by or on behalf of the person making it, if it is relevant otherwise than as an admission.

25. When oral admissions as to contents of documents are relevant.

Oral admissions as to the contents of a document are not relevant, unless and until the party proposing to prove them shows that he is entitled to give secondary evidence of the contents of such document under Part V or unless the genuineness of a document produced is in question.

26. Admissions in civil cases, when relevant.

In civil cases no admission is relevant, if it is made either upon an express condition that evidence of it is not to be given, or in circumstances from which the court can infer that the parties agreed together that evidence of it should not be given: Provided that nothing in this section shall be taken to exempt any legal practitioner from giving evidence of any matter of which he may be compelled to give evidence under section 192.

27. Admissions not conclusive proof, but may be estopped.

Admissions are not conclusive proof of the matters admitted but they may operate as estoppel under Part X.

28. "Confession" defined.

A confession is an admission made at any time by a person charged with a crime, stating or suggesting the inference that he committed that crime.

29. When confession is relevant.

(1) In any proceedings a confession made by a defendant may be given in evidence against him in so far as it is relevant to any matter in issue in the proceedings and is not excluded by the court in pursuance of this section.

(2) If, in any proceedings where the prosecution proposes to give in evidence a confession made by a defendant, it is represented to the court that the confession was or may have been obtained:

a. by oppression of the person who made it; or

b. in consequence of anything said or done which was likely, in the circumstances existing at the time, to render unreliable any confession which might be made by him in such consequence, the court shall not allow the confession to be given in evidence against him except in so far as the prosecution proves to the court beyond reasonable doubt that the confession (notwithstanding that it may be true) was not obtained in a manner contrary to the provisions of this section.

(3) In any proceedings where the prosecution proposes to give in evidence a confession made by a defendant, the court may of its own motion require the prosecution, as a condition of allowing it to do so, to prove that the confession was not obtained as mentioned in either paragraph (a) or (b) of subsection (2) of this section.

(4) Where more persons than one are charged jointly with an offence and a confession made by one of such persons in the presence of one or more of the other persons so charged is given in evidence, the court shall not take such statement into consideration as against any of such other persons in whose presence it was made unless he adopted the said statement by words or conduct.

(5) In this section "oppression" includes torture, inhuman or degrading treatment, and the use or threat of violence whether or not amounting to torture.

30. Facts discovered in consequence of information given by a defendant.

Where information is received from a person who is accused of an offence, whether such person is in custody or not, and as a consequence of such information any fact is discovered, the discovery of that fact, together with evidence that such discovery was made in consequence of the information received from the defendant, may be given in evidence where such information itself would not be admissible in evidence.

31. Confession otherwise relevant not to become irrelevant because of promise of secrecy, etc.

If a confession is otherwise relevant, it does not become irrelevant merely because it was made under a promise of secrecy, or in consequence of a deception practiced on the defendant for the purpose of obtaining it, or when he was drunk, or because it was made in answer to questions which he need not have answered, whatever may have been the form of these questions, or because he was not warned that he was not bound to make such statement and that evidence of it might be given.

32. Evidence in other proceedings amounting to a confession is admissible.

Evidence amounting to a confession may be used as such against the person who gives it, although it was given upon oath, and although the proceeding in which it was given had reference to the same subject - matter as the proceeding in which it is to be proved, and although the witness might have refused to answer the question put to him; but if, after refusing to answer any such question the witness is improperly compelled to answer it, his answer is not admissible as a confession.

33. What evidence is to be given when statement forms part of a conversation, document, book or series of letters or papers.

When any statement of which evidence is given forms part of a longer statement, or of a conversation or part of an isolated document or is contained in a document which forms part of a book, or of a connected series of letters or papers, evidence shall be given of so much and no more of the statement, conversation, document, book or series of letters or papers as the court considers necessary in that particular case to the full understanding of the nature and effect of the statement, and of the circumstances in which it was made.

34. Weight to be attached to admissible statements

(1) In estimating the weight, if any, to be attached to a statement rendered admissible as evidence by this Act, regard shall be had to all the circumstances from which any inference can reasonably be drawn as to the accuracy or otherwise of the statement, and in particular:

a. To the question whether or not the statement was made contemporaneously with the occurrence or existence of the facts stated, and to the question whether or not the maker of the statement had any incentive to conceal or misrepresent facts; and

b. In the case of a statement contained in a document produced by a computer:-

(i) the question whether or not the information which the statement contained, reproduces or is derived from, was supplied to the relevant computer, or recorded for the purpose of being supplied to it, contemporaneously with the occurrence or existence of the facts dealt with in that information; and

(ii) to the question whether or not any person concerned with the supply of information to that computer or with the operation of that computer or any equipment by means of which the document containing the statement was produced by it, had any incentive to conceal or misrepresent facts.

(2) For the purpose of any rule of law or practice requiring evidence to be corroborated or regulating the manner in which uncorroborated evidence is to be treated, a statement rendered admissible as evidence by this Act shall not be treated as corroboration of evidence given by the maker of the statement.

35. Acts of possession and enjoyment of land may be evidence.

Acts of possession and enjoyment of land may be evidence of ownership or of a right of occupancy not only of the particular piece or quantity of land with reference to which such acts are done, but also of other land so situated or connected with it by locality or similarity that what is true as to the one piece of land is likely to be true of the other piece of land.

36. Evidence of scienter upon charge of receiving stolen property.

(1) Whenever any person is being proceeded against for receiving any property, knowing it to have been stolen or for having in his possession stolen property, for the purpose of proving guilty knowledge there may be given in evidence at any stage of the proceeding:

a. the fact that other property stolen within the period of twelve months preceding the date of the offence charged was found or had been in his possession;

b. the fact that within the five years preceding the date of the offence charged he was convicted of any offence involving fraud or dishonesty.

(2) The fact mentioned in paragraph (b) of subsection (1) of this section may not be proved unless:-

a. seven days' notice in writing has been given to the offender that proof of such previous conviction is intended to be given; and

b. evidence has been given that the property in respect of which the offender is being tried was found or had been in his possession.

37. "Hearsay" defined.

Hearsay means a statement –

a. oral or written made otherwise than by a witness in a proceeding; or

b. contained or recorded in a book, document or any record whatever, proof of which is not admissible under any provision of this Act, which is tendered in evidence for the purpose of proving the truth of the matter stated in it.

38. Hearsay rule.

Hearsay evidence is not admissible except as provided in this Part or by or under any other provision of this or any other Act.

39. Statements by persons who cannot be called as witnesses.

Statements, whether written or oral of facts in issue or relevant facts made by a person:-

a. who is dead;
b. who cannot be found;
c. who has become incapable of giving evidence; or
d. whose attendance cannot be procured without an amount of delay or expense which under the circumstances of the case appears to the court unreasonable, are admissible under section 40 to 50.

40. Statements relating to cause of death

(1) A statement made by a person as to the cause of his death, or as to any of the circumstances of the events which resulted in his death in cases in which the cause of that person's death comes into question is admissible where the person who made it believed himself to be in danger of approaching death although he may have entertained at the time of making it hopes of recovery.

(2) A statement referred to in subsection (1) of this section shall be admissible whatever may be the nature of the proceedings in which the cause of death comes into question.

41. Statements made in the course of business.

A statement is admissible when made by a person in the ordinary course of business, and in particular when it consists of any entry or memorandum made by him in books, electronic device or record kept in the ordinary course of business, or in the discharge of a professional duty; or of an acknowledgment written or signed by him of the receipt of money, goods, securities or property of any kind; or of a document used in commerce written or signed by him; or of the date of a letter or other document usually dated, written or signed by him: Provided that the maker made the statement contemporaneously with the transaction recorded or so soon thereafter that the court considers it likely that the transaction was at that time still fresh in his memory.

42. Statements against interest of maker with special knowledge

A statement is admissible where the maker had peculiar means of knowing the matter stated and such statement is against his pecuniary or proprietary interest; and

a. he had no interest to misrepresent the matter; or
b. the statement, if true, would expose him to either criminal or civil liability.

43. Statements of opinions as to public right or custom and matters of general interest.

(1) A statement is admissible when such statement gives the opinion of a person as to the existence of any public right or custom or matter of general interest, the existence of which, if it existed, the maker would have been likely to be aware.

(2) A statement referred to in subsection (1) of this section shall not be admissible unless it was made before any controversy as to such right, custom or matter, had arisen.

44. Statements relating to the existence of a relationship.

(1) Subject to subsection (2) of this section, a statement is admissible when it relates to the existence of relationship by blood, marriage or adoption between persons as to whose relationship by blood, marriage or adoption the person making the statement had special means of knowledge.

(2) A statement referred to in subsection (1) of this section shall be admissible under the following conditions;

a. that it is deemed to be relevant only in a case in which the pedigree to which it relates is in issue, and not to a case in which it is only relevant to the issue;

b. that it must be made by a declarant shown to be related by blood to the person to whom it relates, or by the husband or wife of such a person:

Provided that:

a. a declaration by a deceased parent, that he or she did not marry the other parent until after the birth of the child is relevant to the question of the paternity of such child upon any question arising as to the right of the child to inherit real or personal property under any legislation, and

b. in proceedings for the determination of the paternity of any person, a declaration made by a person who, if an order were granted, would stand towards the petitioner in any of the relationships mentioned in paragraph (b) of this subsection, is deemed relevant to the question of the identity of the parents of the petitioner; c. that the statement must be made before the question in relation to which it is to be proved had arisen, but it does not cease to be admissible because it was made for the purpose of preventing the dispute from arising.

45. Declarations by testators.

(1) The declarations of a deceased testator as to his testamentary intentions, and as to the content of his will, are admissible:-

a. when his will has been lost, and when there is question as to what were its contents; or

b. when the question is whether an existing will is genuine or was improperly obtained; or

c. when the question is whether any and which of more existing documents than one constitute his will.

(2) In the cases mentioned in subsection (I) of this section, it is immaterial whether the declarations were made before or after the making or loss of the will.

46. Admissibility of certain evidence for proving, in subsequent proceeding, the truth of facts stated in it.

(1) Evidence given by a witness in a judicial proceeding, or before any person authorized by law to take it, is admissible for the purpose of proving in a subsequent judicial proceeding, or in a later stage of the same judicial proceeding the truth of the facts which it states, when the witness cannot be called for any of the reasons specified in section 39, or is kept out of the way by the adverse party:

Provided that:

a. the proceeding was between the same parties or their representatives in interest;

b. the adverse party in the first proceeding had the right and opportunity to cross - examine; and

c. the questions in issue were substantially the same in the first as in the second proceeding.

(2) A criminal trial or inquiry shall be deemed to be a proceeding between the prosecutor and the defendant within the meaning of this section.

47. When statements made under any Criminal Procedure legislation may be used in evidence.

A statement in accordance with sections 290 and 291 or section 319 of the Criminal Procedure Act, may afterwards be used in evidence on the trial, of any person accused of an offence to which the same relates, if the person who made the statement cannot be called for any of the reasons specified in section 39, and if reasonable notice of the intention to take such statement was served upon the person against whom it is to be read in evidence and he had, or might have had, if he had chosen to be present, full opportunity of cross - examining the person making the statement.

48. Statement of defendant at preliminary investigation or coroner's inquest.

Any statement made by a defendant at a preliminary investigation or at a coroner's inquest may be given in evidence.

49. Admission of written statements of investigating police officers in certain cases.

Notwithstanding anything contained in this Act or any other law but subject to this section, where in the course of any criminal trial, the court is satisfied that for any sufficient reason, the attendance of the investigating police officer cannot be procured; the written and signed statement of such officer may be admitted in evidence by the court if:

a. the defence does not object to the statement being admitted; and
b. the court consents to the admission of the statement.

50. Absence of public officers

In the case of a person employed in the public service of the Federation or of a State who is required to give evidence for any purpose connected with a judicial proceeding, it shall be sufficient to account for his non - attendance at the hearing of the said judicial proceeding if there is produced to the court either a Federal or State Gazette, telegram, an e - mail or letter purporting to emanate from the head of his department, sufficiently explaining to the satisfaction of the court his apparent default.

51. Entries in books of account.

Entries in books of accounts or electronic records regularly kept in the course of business are admissible whenever they refer to a matter into which the court has to inquire, but such statements may not alone be sufficient evidence to charge any person with liability.

52. Entry in public records made in performance of duty.

An entry in any public or other official book, register or record, including electronic record, stating a fact in issue or relevant fact and made by a public servant in the discharge of his official duty, or by any other person in the performance of a duty specially enjoined by the law of the country in which such book, register or record is kept, is itself admissible.

53. Statements in maps charts and plans.

Statements of facts in issue or relevant facts made in published maps or charts generally offered for public sale, or in maps or plans made under the authority of Government, as to matters usually represented or stated in such maps, charts or plans, are themselves admissible.

54. Statements as to fact of public nature contained in certain Acts or notifications.

When the court has to form an opinion as to the existence of any fact of a public nature, any statement of it, made in a recital contained in any enactment or in any proclamation or speech of the President in opening the National Assembly, or in any proclamation or speech, or in any statement made in a Government or public notice appearing in the Federal Gazette or in a State notice or a State public notice appearing in a State Gazette or the Government Gazette of any other country is admissible

55. Certificates of specified Government officers to be sufficient evidence in all criminal cases.

(1) Either party to the proceedings in any criminal case may produce a certificate signed by the Government Pharmacist, the Deputy Government Pharmacist, an Assistant Government Pharmacist, a Government pathologist or entomologist or the Accountant - General, or any other pharmacist so specified by the Government Pharmacist of the Federation or of a State, any pathologist or entomologist specified by the Director of Medical Laboratories of the Federation or of a State, or any accountant specified by the Accountant-General of the Federation or of a State (whether any such officer is by that or any other title in the service of the State or of the Federal Government), and the production of any such certificate may be taken as sufficient evidence of the facts stated in it.

(2) Notwithstanding subsection (1) of this section, any certificate issued and produced by any officer in charge of any laboratory established by the appropriate authority may be taken as sufficient evidence of facts stated in it.

(3) Notwithstanding subsections (1) and (2) of this section, the court shall have the power, on the application of either party or of its own motion, to direct that any such officer as is referred to in the subsections shall be summoned to give evidence before the court if it is of the opinion that, either for the purpose of cross- examination or for any other reason, the interests of justice so requires.

(4) The President may by notice in the Federal Gazette declare that any person named in such notice, being an officer in the public service of the Federation employed in a forensic science laboratory in a rank not below that of Medical Laboratory Technologist, shall for the purposes of subsection (1) of this section be empowered to sign a certificate relating to any subject specified in the notice, and while such declaration remains in force subsection (1) of this section shall apply in relation to such person as they apply in relation to an officer mentioned in that subsection: Provided that a certificate signed by such person shall not be admissible in evidence if, in the opinion of the court, it does not relate wholly or mainly to a subject so specified as in such notice.

(5) In this section, unless the context otherwise requires - "Appropriate authority" means the Inspector - General of Police, the Comptroller-General of Customs or the Minister of Health; "Officer" means any officer-in-charge of any laboratory established pursuant to this Act; "Specified" means specified by notice as may be published in the Federal Gazette.

56. Certificates of Central Bank officers as evidence in criminal cases.

Where in criminal proceedings a certificate purports to be signed by an officer of the Central Bank of Nigeria who himself adds after his signature the words "duly authorized by the Governor of the Central Bank of Nigeria" it shall be accepted by all courts and persons as sufficient evidence of the facts stated in the certificate, and no certificate shall be questioned on the ground only of the authorization; but subject to this, section 55(3) shall have effect with regard to any such certificate.

57. Service of certificates on other party before hearing.

Where any such certificate as is mentioned in section 55 or 56 is intended to be produced by either party to the proceedings, a copy of it shall be served on the other party at least ten clear days before the day appointed for the hearing and if it is not so sent the court may, if it thinks fit, adjourn the hearing on such terms as may seem proper.

58. Genuineness of certificates to be presumed.

The court shall, in the absence of evidence to the contrary, presume that the signature to any such certificate as is mentioned in sections 55 and 56 is genuine and that the person signing it held the office or authority which he professed at the time when he signed it.

59. Previous judgments admissible to bar a second suit or trial.

The existence of any judgment, order or decree which by law prevents any court from taking cognizance of a suit or holding a trial, is a relevant fact, evidence of which is admissible when the question is whether such court ought to take cognizance of such suit or to hold such trial.

60. Admissibility of certain judgments in certain jurisdictions.

(1) A final judgment, order or decree of a competent court, in the exercise of probate, matrimonial, admiralty or insolvency jurisdiction, which confers upon or takes away from any person any legal character, or which declares any person to be entitled to any such character, or to be entitled to any specific thing, not as against any specified person but absolutely, is admissible when the existence of any such legal character, or the title of any such legal persons to any such thing, is relevant.

(2) Such judgment, order or decree is conclusive proof:

a. that any legal character which it confers accrued at the time when such judgment, order or decree came into operation;

b. that any legal character, to which it declares any such person to be entitled, accrued to that person at the time when such judgment, order or decree declares it to have accrued to that person;

c. that any legal character which it takes away from any such person ceased at the time from which such judgment, order or decree declared that it had ceased or should cease; and d. that anything to which it declares any person to be so entitled was the property of that person at the time from which such judgment, order or decree declares that it had been or should be his property.

61. Admissibility and effect of judgments other than those mentioned in section 60.

Judgments, orders or decrees other than those mentioned in section 60 are admissible if they relate to matters of a public nature relevant to the inquiry; but such judgments, orders or decrees are not conclusive proof of that which they state.

62. Judgment, etc., other than those mentioned in sections 59 to 61, when admissible.

Judgments, orders or decrees, other than those mentioned in sections 59,60 and 61 are inadmissible unless existence of such judgment, order or decree is a fact in issue, or is admissible under some other provision of this or any other Act.

63. Conviction as evidence in civil proceedings.

(1) Notwithstanding section 62, in any civil proceedings the fact that a person has been convicted of any offence by a court of competent jurisdiction shall be admissible for the purpose of proving, where to do so is relevant to any issue in those proceedings that he committed that offence, but no conviction that has been quashed on appeal by a court of competent jurisdiction or in respect of which an appeal is pending shall be admissible in evidence by virtue of this section.

(2) If in any civil proceedings it is proved in accordance with subsection (1) of this section that any person has been convicted of an offence by a court of competent jurisdiction:

a. that person shall be presumed to have committed the offence unless he proves to the contrary; and

b. without prejudice to the admission of any other evidence for the purpose of determining the facts upon which the conviction is based, the contents of any information, complaint or, charge sheet, according to which that person has been convicted shall also be admissible in evidence for this purpose.

64. Fraud or collusion in obtaining judgment, or non - jurisdiction of court, may be proved.

Any party to a suit or other proceeding may show that any judgment, order or decree which is admissible under sections 59, 60 or 61 and which has been proved by the adverse party, was delivered by a court without jurisdiction, or was obtained by fraud or collusion.

65. Judgment conclusive in favour of judge

When any action is brought against any person for anything done by him in a judicial capacity, the judgment delivered, and the proceedings antecedent to it, are conclusive proof of the facts stated in such judgment, whether they are or are not necessary to give the defendant jurisdiction, if assuming them to be true, they show that he had jurisdiction.

66. Family or communal tradition admissible in land cases.

Where the title to or interest in family or communal land is in issue, oral evidence of family or communal tradition concerning such title or interest is admissible.

67. Opinion inadmissible except as provided in this Act.

The opinion of any person as to the existence or non - existence of a fact in issue or relevant to the fact in issue is inadmissible except as provided in sections 68 to 76 of this Act.

68. Opinions of experts, when admissible.

When the court has to form an opinion upon a point of foreign law, customary law or custom, or of science or art, or as to identity of handwriting or finger impressions, the opinions upon that point of persons specially skilled in such foreign law, customary law or custom, or science or art, or in questions as to identity of handwriting or finger impressions, are admissible. (2) Persons so specially skilled as mentioned in sub - section (1) of this section are called experts.

69. Opinions as to foreign law.

Where there is a question as to foreign law the opinions of experts who in their profession are acquainted with such law are admissible evidence of it, though such experts may produce to the court books which they declare to be works of authority upon the foreign law in question, which books the court, having received all necessary explanations from the expert, may construe for itself.

70. Opinions as to customary law and custom.

In deciding questions of customary law and custom the opinions of traditional rulers or chiefs or other persons having special knowledge of the customary law and custom and any book or manuscript recognized as legal authority by people indigenous to the locality in which such law or custom applies, are admissible.

71. Facts bearing upon opinions of experts.

Facts not otherwise relevant are relevant if they support or are inconsistent with the opinions of experts, when such opinions are admissible.

72. Opinion as to handwriting, when admissible.

(1) When the court has to form an opinion as to the person by whom any document was written or signed, the opinion of any person acquainted with the handwriting of the person by whom it is supposed to be written or signed, that it was or was not written or signed by that person, is admissible.

(2) A person is said to be acquainted with the handwriting of another person when he has seen that person write, or when he has received documents purporting to be written by that person in answer to documents written by himself or under his authority and addressed to that person, or when in the ordinary course of business, documents purporting to be written by that person have been habitually submitted to him.

73. Opinion as to existence of "general custom or right" when admissible.

(1) When the court has to form an opinion as to the existence of any general custom or right, the opinions, as to the existence of such custom or right, of persons who would be likely to know of its existence if it existed are admissible.

(2) The expression "general custom or right" includes customs or rights common to any considerable class of persons.

74. Opinions as to usages, tenets, when admissible.

When the court has to form an opinion as to:-

a. the usages and tenets of any body of men or family; or

b. the constitution and government of any religious or charitable foundation; or

c. the meaning of words or terms used in particular districts or by particular classes of people, the opinions of persons having special means of knowledge on the matters specified in this section, are admissible.

75. Opinion on relationship, when admissible.

When the court has to form an opinion as to the relationship of one person to another, the opinion expressed by conduct, as to the existence of such relationship of any person who, as a member of the family or otherwise, has special means of knowledge on the subject, is admissible:

Provided that; such opinion shall not be sufficient to prove a marriage in proceedings for a divorce or in a petition for damages against an adulterer or in a prosecution for bigamy.

76. Grounds of opinion when admissible

Whenever the opinion of any living person is admissible, the grounds on which such opinion is based are also admissible.

77. "Character" defined.

In sections 78 to 82, the expression "character" means reputation as distinguished from disposition, and except as mentioned in those sections, evidence may be given only of general reputation, and not of particular acts by which reputation or disposition is shown.

78. In civil cases, evidence of character generally inadmissible.

In civil cases evidence of the fact that the character of any person concerned is such as to render probable or improbable any conduct imputed to him is inadmissible except in so far as such

79. Character as affecting damages

Notwithstanding section 78, in civil cases the fact that the character of any person is such as to affect the amount of damages which he ought to receive may be given in evidence.

80. In libel and slander, notice must be given of evidence of character

In actions for libel and slander in which the defendant does not by his defence assert the truth of the statement complained of, the defendant is not entitled on the trial to give evidence in chief with a view to mitigation of damages, as to the circumstances under which the libel or slander was published, or as to the character of the plaintiff, without the leave of the judge, unless seven days at least before the trial he furnishes particulars to the plaintiff of the matters as to which he intends to give evidence.

81. In criminal cases evidence of good character admissible

In criminal proceedings evidence of the fact that a defendant is of good character is admissible.

82. Evidence of character of the accused in criminal proceedings

(1) Except as provided in this section, evidence of the fact that a defendant is of bad character is inadmissible in criminal proceedings.

(2) The fact that a defendant is of bad character is admissible:
a. when the bad character of the defendant is a fact in issue;
b. when the defendant has given evidence of his good character
(3) A defendant may be asked questions to show that he is of bad character in the circumstances mentioned in paragraph (c) of the proviso to section 180.
(4) Whenever evidence of bad character is admissible, evidence of a previous conviction is also admissible.
(5) In cases where subsection (4) of this section applies, the court shall only admit evidence of previous convictions which are related in substance to the offence charged.
(6) Evidence of a previous conviction shall be proved in accordance with Part XIII.

83. Admissibility of documentary evidence as to facts in issue

(1) In any proceedings where direct oral evidence of a fact would be admissible, any statement made by a person in a document which seems to establish that fact shall, on production of the original document, be admissible as evidence of that fact if the following conditions are satisfied –
(a) if the maker of the statement either:
(i) had personal knowledge of the matters dealt with by the statement, or
(ii) where the document in question is or forms part of a record purporting to be a continuous record, made the statement (in so far as the matters dealt with by it are not within his personal knowledge) in the performance of a duty to record information supplied to him by a person who had, or might reasonably be supposed to have, personal knowledge of those matters; and
(b) if the maker of the statement is called as a witness in the proceedings: Provided that the condition that the maker of the statement shall be called as a witness need not be satisfied if he is dead, or unfit by reason of his bodily or mental condition to attend as a witness, or if he is outside Nigeria and it is not reasonably practicable to secure his attendance, or if all reasonable efforts to find him have been made without success.
(2) In any proceedings, the court may at any stage of the proceedings, if having regard to all the circumstances of the case it is satisfied that undue delay or expense would otherwise be caused, order that such a statement as is mentioned in

subsection (1) of this section shall be admissible as evidence or may, without any such order having been made, admit such a statement in evidence notwithstanding that the;

(a) maker of the statement is available but is not called as a witness;

(b) original document is not produced, if in lieu of it there is produced a copy of the original document or of the material part of it certified to be a true copy in such manner as may be specified in the order or as the court may approve, as the case may be.

(3) Nothing in this section shall render admissible as evidence any statement made by a person interested at a time when proceedings were pending or anticipated involving a dispute as to any fact which the statement might tend to establish.

(4) For the purposes of this section, a statement in a document shall not be deemed to have been made by a person unless the document or the material part of it was written, made or produced by him with his own hand, or was signed or initialled by him or otherwise recognized by him in writing as one for the accuracy of which he is responsible.

(5) For the purpose of deciding whether or not a statement is admissible as evidence by virtue of this section, the court may draw any reasonable inference from the form or contents of the document in which the statement is contained, or from any other circumstances, and may, in deciding, whether or not a person is fit to attend as a witness, act on a certificate purporting to be the certificate of a registered medical practitioner.

84. Admissibility of statements in document produced by computers.

(1) In any proceedings, a statement contained in a document produced by a computer shall be admissible as evidence of any fact stated in it of which direct oral evidence would be admissible, if it is shown that the conditions in subsection (2) of this section are satisfied in relation to the statement and the computer in question.

(2) The conditions referred to in subsection (1) of this section are:

(a) that the document containing the statement was produced by the computer during a period over which the computer was used regularly to store or process information for the purposes of any activities regularly carried on over that period, whether for profit or not, by anybody, whether corporate or not, or by any individual;

(b) that over that period there was regularly supplied to the computer in the ordinary course of those activities information of the kind contained in the statement or of the kind from which the information so contained is derived;

(c) that throughout the material part of that period the computer was operating properly or, if not, that in any respect in which it was not operating properly or was out of operation during that part of that period was not such as to affect the production of the document or the accuracy of its contents; and

(d) that the information contained in the statement reproduces or is derived from information supplied to the computer in the ordinary course of those activities.

(3) Where over a period, the function of storing or processing information for the purposes of any activities regularly carried on over that period, as mentioned in subsection (2) (a) of this section was regularly performed by computers, whether –

(a) by a combination of computers operating over that period; or

(b) by different computers operating in succession over that period; or

(c) by different combinations of computers operating in succession over that period; or

(d) in any other manner involving the successive operation over that period, in whatever order, of one or more computers and one or more combinations of computers,

all the computers used for that purpose during that period shall be treated for the purposes of this section as constituting a single computer; and references in this section to a computer shall be construed accordingly.

(4) In any proceedings where it is desired to give a statement in evidence by virtue of this section, a certificate:

a. identifying the document containing the statement and describing the manner in which it was produced; or

b. giving such particulars of any device involved in the production of that document as may be appropriate for the purpose of showing that the document was produced by a computer; or

c. dealing with any of the matters to which the conditions mentioned in subsection (2) above relate, and purporting to be signed by a person occupying a responsible position in relation to the operation of the relevant device or the management of the relevant activities, as the case may be,

shall be evidence of the matter stated in the certificate, and for the purpose of this subsection it shall be sufficient for a matter to be stated to the best of the knowledge and belief of the person stating it.

(5) For the purposes of this section;

a. information shall be taken to be supplied to a computer if it is supplied to it in any appropriate form and whether it is supplied directly or (with or without human intervention) by means of any appropriate equipment;

b. where, in the course of activities carried on by any individual or body, information is supplied with a view to its being stored or processed for the purposes of those activities by a computer operated otherwise than in the course of those activities, that information, if duly supplied to that computer, shall be taken to be supplied to it in the course of those activities;

c. a document shall be taken to have been produced by a computer whether it was produced by it directly or (with or without human intervention) by means of any appropriate equipment.

84A. Information in electronic form

Where any law provides that information or any other matter shall be in writing or in the typewriting or printed from, then, notwithstanding anything contained in such law, such requirement shall be deemed to have been satisfied if such information or matter is:-

(a)rendered or made available in the electronic form; and

(b) accessible so as to be usable for a subsequent reference.

84B Records in a computer to be admissible

Notwithstanding anything contained in this Act, any information contained in an electronic record which is printed on a paper, stored, recorded or copied in optical or magnetic media or cloud computing or database produced by a computer shall be deemed to also be a document, if the conditions mentioned in this section are satisfied in relation to the information and computer in question and shall be admissible in any proceedings, without further proof or production of the original, as evidence or any contents of the original or of any fact stated in it of which direct evidence would be admissible.

84C Authentication of electronic record

(1) Subject to the provisions of this section any person any authenticate an electronic record by affixing his digital signature on it.

(2) A person may authenticate any electronic record by such digital signature or electronic authentication technique which:-

(a) is considered reliable; or

(b) may be specified by this Act.

(3) For the purpose of this subsection (2), any digital signature or electronic authentication technique will be considered reliable if:

(a) the signature creation data or the authentication data are, within the context in which they are used, linked to the signatory or, as the case may be, the authenticator and of no other person;

(b) any alteration to the digital signature made after affixing such signature is detectable;

(c) any alteration to the information made after its authentication by the digital signature is detectable; and

(d) it fulfils such other conditions which may be prescribed.

Proof of Digital Signature

84D(1) Except in the case of a secure digital signature, if the digital signature of any person is alleged to have been affixed on the electronic record, the fact that such digital signature is the digital signature of the person must be proved.

(2) A digital signature shall be deemed to be secure if the signature creation data:-

(a) at the time of affixing the signature, was under the exclusive control of the signatory and no other person; and

(b) was stored and affixed in such exclusive manner as may be prescribed.

85. Proof of contents of documents

The contents of documents may be proved either by primary or by secondary evidence.

86. Primary evidence

(1) Primary evidence means the document itself produced for the inspection of the court.

(2) Where a document has been executed in several parts, each part shall be primary evidence of the document.

(3) Where a document has been executed in counterpart, each counterpart being executed by one or some of the parties only, each counterpart shall be primary evidence as against the parties executing it.

(4) Where a number of documents have all been made by one uniform process, as in the case of printing, lithography, photography, computer or other electronic or mechanical process, each shall be primary evidence of the contents of the rest; but where they are all copies of a common original, they shall not be primary evidence of the contents of the original.

87. Secondary evidence

Secondary evidence includes:

(a) certified copies given under the provisions hereafter contained in this Act;

(b) copies made from the original by mechanical or electronic processes which in themselves ensure the accuracy of the copy, and copies compared with such copies;

(c) copies made from or compared with the original;

(d) counterparts of documents as against the parties who did not execute them;

(e) Oral accounts of the contents of a document given by some person who has himself seen it.

88. Proof of documents by primary evidence

Documents shall be proved by primary evidence except in the cases hereafter mentioned in this Act.

89. Cases in which secondary evidence relating to documents may be given

Secondary evidence may be given of the existence, condition or contents of a document in the following cases:

(a) when the original is shown or appears to be in the possession or power –

(i) of the person against whom the document is sought to be proved, or

(ii) of any person legally bound to produce it, and when after the notice mentioned in section 91 such person does not produce it;

(b) when the existence, condition or contents of the original have been proved to be admitted in writing by the person against whom it is proved or by his representative in interest;

(c) when the original has been destroyed or lost and in the latter case all possible search has been made for it;

(d) when the original is of such a nature as not to be easily movable; (e) when the original is a public document within the meaning of section 102;

(f) when the original is a document of which a certified copy is permitted by this Act or by any other law in force in Nigeria, to be given in evidence;

(g) when the originals consist of numerous accounts or other documents which cannot conveniently be examined in court, and the fact to be proved is the general result of the whole collection;

(h) When the document is an entry in a banker's book.

90. Nature of secondary evidence admissible under section 89

(1) The secondary evidence admissible in respect of the original documents referred to in the several paragraphs of section 89 is as follows:

(a) in paragraphs (a), (c) and (d) any secondary evidence of the contents of the document is admissible;

(b) in paragraph (b), the written admission is admissible;

(c) in paragraph (e) or (f), a certified copy of the document, but no other secondary evidence is admissible;

(d) in paragraph (g), evidence may be given as to the general result of the documents by any person who has examined them, and who is skilled in the examination of such documents;

(e) in paragraph (h), the copies cannot be received as evidence unless it is first proved that –

(i) the book in which the entries copied were made was at the time of making one of the ordinary books of the bank,

(ii) the entry was made in the usual and ordinary course of business,

(iii) the book is in the control and custody of the bank, which proof may be given orally or by affidavit by an officer of the bank, and

(iv) The copy has been examined with the original entry and is correct, which proof must be given by some person who has examined the copy with the original entry, and may be given orally or by affidavit.

(2) When a seaman sues for his wages he may give secondary evidence of the ship's articles and of any agreement supporting his case, without notice to produce the originals.

91. Rules as to notice to produce

Secondary evidence of the contents of the documents referred to in paragraph (a) of section 89 shall not be given unless the party proposing to give such secondary evidence has previously given to the party in whose possession or power the document is, or to a legal practitioner employed by such party, such notice to produce it as is prescribed by law, and if no notice to produce is prescribed by law, then such notice as the court considers reasonable in the circumstances of the case:

Provided that such notice shall not be required in order to render secondary evidence admissible in any of the following cases, or in any other case in which the court thinks fit to dispense with it:

(a) when the document to be proved is itself a notice;
(b) when, from the nature of the case, the adverse party must know that he will be required to produce it;
(c) when it appears or is proved that the adverse party has obtained possession of the original by fraud or force;
(d) when the adverse party or his agent has the original in court;
(e) when the adverse party or his agent has admitted the loss of the document.

92. Proof that bank has made returns, or been duly licensed

(1) The fact of any bank having duly made a return to the Central Bank, the Nigerian Deposit Insurance Corporation or the Federal Inland Revenue Service may be proved in any legal proceedings by the production of a copy of its return verified by the affidavit of an officer of the bank, or by the production of a copy of a newspaper purporting to contain a copy of such return published by the Central Bank, the Nigerian Deposit Insurance Corporation or the Federal Inland Revenue Service, as the case may be.

(2) The fact of any bank having been licensed under the Banks and Other Financial Institutions Act may be proved by the production of a certificate by an officer of the bank that it has been duly licensed under that Act. (3) In this section - "Central Bank" means the Central Bank of

Nigeria established by the Central Bank of Nigeria Act; "Federal Inland Revenue Service" means the Federal Inland Revenue Service established by the Federal Inland Revenue Service Act; and "Nigerian Deposit Insurance Corporation means the Nigerian Deposit Insurance Corporation established by the Nigerian Deposit Insurance Corporation Act.

93. **Proof of signature, handwriting and electronic signature or digital signature**

(1) If a document is alleged to be signed or to have been written wholly or in part by any person, the signature or the handwriting of so much of the document as is alleged to be in that person's handwriting must be proved to be in his handwriting.

(2) Where a rule of evidence requires a signature, or provides for certain consequences if a document is not signed, an electronic signature or digital signature satisfies that rule of law or avoids those consequences.

(3) An electronic signature or digital signature may be proved in any manner, including by showing that a procedure existed by which it is necessary for a person, in order to proceed further with a transaction, to have executed a symbol or security procedure for the purpose of verifying that an electronic record is that of the person.

94. Identification of person signing a document

(1) Evidence that a person exists having the same name, address, business or occupation as the maker of a document purports to have, is admissible to show that such document was written or signed by that person.

(2) Evidence that a document exists to which the document the making of which is in issue purports to be a reply, together with evidence of the making and delivery to a person of such earlier document, is admissible to show the identity of the maker of the disputed document with the person to whom the earlier document was delivered.

95. Evidence of sealing and delivery of a document

(1) Evidence that a person signed a document containing a declaration that a seal was his seal is admissible to prove that he sealed it.

(2) Evidence that the grantor on executing any document requiring delivery expressed an intention that it should operate at once is admissible to prove delivery.

96. **Proof of instrument the validity of which attestation is necessary**

(1) In any proceedings, whether civil or criminal, an instrument the validity of which attestation is required by law may, instead of being proved by an attesting witness, be proved in the manner in which it might be proved if no attesting witness were alive: Provided that nothing in this section shall apply to the proof of wills or other testamentary documents.

(2) If no attesting witness is alive, an instrument the validity of which attestation is required by law is proved by showing that the attestation of one attesting witness at least is in his handwriting, and that the signature of the person executing the documents is in the handwriting of that person.

97. Admission of execution by party to attested document

The admission of a party to an attested document of its execution by himself shall be sufficient proof of its execution as against him, though it be a document required by law to be attested.

98. Cases in which proof of execution or of handwriting unnecessary

(1) A person seeking to prove the due execution of a document is not bound to call the party who executed the document or to prove the handwriting of such party or of an attesting witness in any case where the person against whom the document is sought to be proved –

(a) produces such document and claims an interest under it in reference to the subject matter of the suit; or

(b) is a public officer bound by law to procure its due execution, and he has dealt with it as a document duly executed.

(2) Nothing contained in this section shall prejudice the right of a person to put in evidence any document in the manner mentioned in sections 89 and 90, or under section 155 of this Act.

99. Proof when attesting witness denies the execution

If the attesting witness denies or does not recollect the execution of the document, its execution may be proved by other evidence.

100. Proof of document not required by law to be attested

An attested document not required by law to be attested may be proved as if it was unattested.

101. Comparison of signature, writing, seal or finger impressions with others admitted or proved.

(1) In order to ascertain whether a signature, writing, seal or finger impression is that of the person by whom it purports to have been written or made, any signature, writing, seal or finger impression admitted or proved to the satisfaction of the court to have been written or made by that person may be compared with the one which is to be proved although that signature, writing, seal or finger impression has not been produced or proved for any other purpose.

(2) The court may direct any person present in court to write any words or figures or to make finger impressions for the purpose of enabling the court to compare the words, figures or finger impressions so written with any words, figures or finger impressions alleged to have been written or made by such person: Provided that where a defendant does not give evidence he may not be so directed to write any words or figures or to make finger impressions.

(3) After the final termination of the proceedings in which the court required any person to make his finger impressions, such impressions shall be destroyed.

102. Public documents

The following documents are public documents –

(a) documents forming the official acts or records of the official acts –

(i) of the sovereign authority; (ii) of official bodies and tribunals;

(iii) of public officers, legislative, judicial and executive, whether of Nigeria or elsewhere;

(b) Public records kept in Nigeria of private documents

103. Private documents

All documents other than public documents are private documents.

104. Certified copies of public documents

(1) Every public officer having the custody of a public document which any person has a right to inspect shall give that person on demand a copy of it on payment of the legal fees prescribed in that respect, together with a certificate written at the foot of such copy that it is a true copy of such document or part of it as the case may be.

(2) Such certificate as is mentioned in subsection (1) of this section shall be dated and subscribed by such officer with his name and his official title, and shall be sealed, whenever such officer is authorized by law to make use of a seal, and such copies so certified shall be called certified copies.

(3) Any officer who, by the ordinary course of official duty, is authorized to deliver such copies, shall be deemed to have the custody of such documents within the meaning of this section.

105. Proof of documents by production of certified copies

Copies of documents certified in accordance with section 104 may be produced in proof of the contents of the public documents or parts of the public documents of which they purport to be copies.

106. Proof of other official documents

The following public documents may be proved as follows –

(a) Acts of the National Assembly, Laws of the House of Assembly of a State or bye - laws of a Local Government Council, proclamations, treaties or other acts of State, orders, notifications, nominations, appointments and other official communications of the Government of the Federation or of any State Government or Local Government in Nigeria –

(i) which appear in the Federal Gazette or the Gazette of a state, by the production of such Gazette, and shall be prima facie proof of any fact of a public nature which they were intended to notify,

(ii) by a copy of the document certified by the officer who authorized or made such order or issued such official communication,

(iii) by the records of the government departments concerned certified by the heads of those departments respectively or by the Minister, or in respect of matters to which the executive authority of a State or Local Government extends by the Governor or the Chairman of the Local Government Council, or any person nominated by such Governor or Chairman, or

(iv) by any document purporting to be printed by order of Government;

(b) the proceedings of the Senate or of the House of Representatives, by the minutes of that body or by published Acts or abstracts, or by copies purporting to be printed by order of Government;

(c) the proceedings of a State House Assembly, by the minutes of that body or by published Laws, or by copies purporting to be printed by order of Government;

(d) the proceedings of a Local Government Council, by the minutes of that body or by published bye - laws, or by copies purporting to be printed by order of the Local Government;

(e) the Acts or Ordinances of any part of the Commonwealth, and the subsidiary legislation made under their authority, by a copy purporting to be printed by the Government Printer of any such country;

(f) proclamations, treaties or acts of State of any other country, by journals published by their authority or commonly received in that country as such, or by a copy certified under the seal of the country or sovereign;

(g) books printed or published under the authority of the Government of a foreign country, and purporting to contain the statutes, code or other written law of such country, and also printed and published books of reports of decisions of the courts of such country, and books proved to be commonly admitted in such courts as evidence of the law of such country, shall be admissible as evidence of the law of such foreign country;

(h) any judgment, order or other judicial proceedings outside Nigeria, or any legal document, filed or deposited in any court –

(i) by a copy sealed with the seal of a foreign or other court to which the original document belongs or, in the event of such court having no seal, to be signed by the judge, or, if there be more than one judge, by anyone of the judges of the said court, and such judge must attach to his signature a statement in writing on the said copy that the court of which he is judge has no seal, or

(ii) by a copy which purports to be certified in any manner which is certified by any representative of Nigeria to be the manner commonly in use in that country for the certification of copies of judicial records;

(i) public documents of any other class elsewhere than in Nigeria, by the original, or by a copy certified by the legal keeper of such documents, with a certificate under the seal of a notary public, or of a (ii) consul or diplomatic agent that the copy is duly certified by the officer having the legal custody of the original, and upon proof of the character of the document according to the law of the foreign country.

107. Court may order proof by affidavit

A court may in any civil proceeding make an order at any stage of such proceeding directing that specified facts may be proved at the trial by affidavit with or without the attendance of the deponent for cross examination: Provided that where a party desires the attendance of such deponent for cross - examination the court shall require his attendance for that purpose where this would not result in unjustifiable delay or expense.

108. Affidavits to be filled

(1) Before an affidavit is used in the court for any purpose, the original shall be filed in the court, and the original or an office copy shall alone be recognized for any purpose in the court.

(2) Notwithstanding subsection (1), where the affidavit is deposed to electronically before any person duly authorised to take affidavits, a copy shall be filed at the court registry and may be recognized for any purpose in the court.

109. Affidavit sworn in Nigeria

Any affidavit sworn before any judge, officer or other person duly authorized to take affidavits in Nigeria whether in person or through audio visual means, may be used in the court in all cases where affidavits are admissible.

110. **Affidavit sworn in country other than Nigeria**

Any affidavit sworn in any country other than Nigeria whether in person or through audio-visual means before:

(a) a judge or magistrate, being authenticated by the official seal of the court to which he is attached, or by a notary public; or

(b) The duly authorized officer in the Nigerian Embassy, High Commission or Consulate, in that country, may be used in the court in all cases where affidavits are admissible.

111. Proof of seal and signature

The fact that an affidavit purports to have been sworn in the manner prescribed in the preceding sections shall be prima facie evidence –

(a) of the seal, or signature as the case may be, of any such court, judge, magistrate or other officer or person mentioned in, or appended or subscribed to, any such affidavit; and

(b) Of the authority of such court, judge, magistrate or other officer or person to administer oaths.

112. Affidavit not to be sworn before certain persons

An affidavit shall not be admitted which is proved to have been sworn before a person on whose behalf the same is offered, or before his legal practitioner, or before a partner or clerk of his legal practitioner.

113. Affidavit defective in form

The court may permit an affidavit to be used, notwithstanding that it is defective in form according to this Act, if the court is satisfied that it has been sworn before a person duly authorized.

114. Amendment and re-swearing of affidavit

A defective or erroneous affidavit may be amended and re - sworn by leave of the court, on such terms as to time, costs or otherwise as seem reasonable.

115. Contents of affidavits

(1) Every affidavit used in the court shall contain only a statement of facts and circumstances to which the witness

deposes, either of his own personal knowledge or from information which he believes to be true.

(2) An affidavit shall not contain extraneous matter, by way of objection, or prayer, or legal argument or conclusion.

(3) When a person deposes to his belief in any matter of fact, and his belief is derived from any source other than his own personal knowledge, he shall set forth explicitly the facts and circumstances forming the ground of his belief.

(4) When such belief is derived from information received from another person, the name of his informant shall be stated, and reasonable particulars shall be given respecting the informant, and the time, place and circumstance of the information.

116. Conflicting affidavits

When there are before a court affidavits that are irreconcilably in conflict on crucial facts, the court shall for the purpose of' resolving the conflict arising from the affidavit evidence, ask the parties to proffer oral evidence as to such facts, and shall hear any such oral evidence of the deponents of the affidavits and such other witnesses as may be called by the parties.

117. Form of affidavits

(1) Every affidavit taken in a cause or matter shall –

(a) be headed in the court and in the cause or matter;

(b) state the full name, trade or profession, residence, and nationality of the deponent; and

(c) Be in the first person, and divided into convenient paragraphs numbered consecutively.

(2) Any erasure, interlineation or alteration made before the affidavit is sworn, shall be attested by the person before whom it is taken, who shall affix his signature or initial in the margin immediately opposite to the interlineation, alteration or erasure.

(3) Where an affidavit proposed to be sworn is illegible or difficult to read, or is in the judgment of the person before

whom it is taken so written as to facilitate fraudulent alteration, he may refuse to swear the deponent, and require the affidavit to be re - written in an unobjectionable manner.

(4) An affidavit when sworn shall be signed by the deponent or if he cannot write or is blind, marked by him personally with his mark in the presence of the person before whom it is taken.

118. Provisions as to altered affidavit

The person before whom an affidavit is taken shall not allow it, when sworn, to be altered in any manner without being re - sworn; and may refuse to allow an altered affidavit to be re - sworn and require instead a fresh affidavit.

119. Jurat

(1) Where the deponent is illiterate or blind the affidavit shall state that fact, and shall be accompanied with a jurat.

(2) The jurat shall:

(a) be written without interlineation, alteration or erasure immediately at the foot of the affidavit, and towards the left side of the paper, and shall be signed by the person before whom it is taken;

(b) state the date of the swearing and the place where it is sworn;

(bA) if the affidavit is taken via audio – visual means, then the electronic record shall state which audio – visual method was used and the date on which it was used;

(c) state that the affidavit was sworn before the person taking the same; and

(d) where the deponent is illiterate or blind it shall state such fact and shall state that the affidavit was read over to such illiterate or blind deponent or translated into his own language (in the case of a deponent not having sufficient knowledge of English), and that he appeared to understand it.

(3) Where the deponent makes a mark instead of signing, the jurat shall state that fact, and that the mark was made in the presence of the person before whom it is taken.

(4) Where two or more persons join in making an affidavit their several names shall be written in the jurat and it shall appear by the jurat that each of them has been sworn to the truth of the several matters stated by him in the affidavit.

(5) If the jurat has been added and signed on an altered affidavit, the person before whom it is taken shall add a new jurat on the affidavit being re sworn and in the new jurat he shall mention the alteration.

120. Declarations without oath may be taken

(1) The person before whom an affidavit may be taken may take without oath the declaration of any person –

(a) who affirms that the taking of any oath whatsoever is, according to his religious belief, unlawful, or

(b) Who by reason of immature age or want of religious belief, ought not, in the opinion of the person taking the declaration to be admitted to make a sworn affidavit.

(2) The person taking the declaration shall record in the attestation the reason of such declaration being taken without oath.

121. Proof of facts.

A fact is said to be –

(a) "proved" when, after considering the matters before it, the court either believes it to exist or considers its existence so probable that a prudent man ought, in the circumstances of the particular case, to act upon the supposition that it does exist;

(b) "disproved' when after considering the matters before it, the court either believes that it does not exist or considers its non - existence so probable that a prudent man ought, in the circumstances of the particular case, to act upon the supposition that it does not exist;

(c) "Not proved" when it is neither proved nor disproved.

122. Facts of which court must take judicial notice need not be proved

(1) No fact of which the court must take judicial notice under this section need be proved.

(2) The court shall take judicial notice of the following facts –

(a) all laws or enactments and any subsidiary legislation made under them having the force of law now or previously in force, in any part of Nigeria;

(b) all public Acts or Laws passed or hereafter to be passed by the National Assembly or a State House of Assembly, as the case may be, and all subsidiary legislation made under them and all local and personal Acts or Laws directed by the National Assembly or a State House of Assembly to be judicially noticed;

(c) the course of proceedings of the National Assembly and of the Houses of Assembly of the States of Nigeria;

(d) the assumption of office of the President, a State Governor or the Chairman of a Local Government Council, and of any seal used by any such public officer;

(e) the seals of all the courts of Nigeria; the seals of notaries public, and all seals which any person is authorized to use by any Act of the National Assembly or other enactment having the force of law in Nigeria;

(f) the existence, title and national flag of every State or Sovereign recognized by Nigeria;

(g) the divisions of time, the geographical divisions of the world, the public festivals, fasts and holidays notified in the Federal Gazette or fixed by an Act;

(h) the territories within the Commonwealth;

(i) the commencement, continuance and termination of hostilities between the Federal Republic of Nigeria and any other State or body of persons;

(j) the names of the members and officers of the court and of their deputies and subordinate officers and assistants, and also of all officers acting in execution of its process, and of all legal practitioners and other persons authorized by law to appear or act before it;

(k) the rule of the road on land or at sea;

(l) all general customs, rules and principles which have been held to have the force of law in any court established by or under the Constitution and all customs which have been duly certified to and recorded in any such court;

(m) The course of proceeding and all rules of practice in force in any court established by or under the Constitution.

(3) In all cases in subsection (2) of this section and also on all matters of public history, literature, science or art, the court may resort for its aid to appropriate books or documents of reference.

(4) If the court is called upon by any person to take judicial notice of any fact, it may refuse to do so unless and until such person produces any such book or document, as it may consider necessary to enable it to do so.

123. Facts admitted need not be proved

No fact need be proved in any civil proceedings which the parties to the proceedings or their agents agree to admit at the hearing, or which, before the hearing, they agree to admit by any writing under their hands, or which by any rule or pleading in force at the time they are deemed to have admitted by their pleadings: Provided that the court may, in its discretion, require the facts admitted to be proved otherwise than by such admissions.

124. Facts of common knowledge need not be proved

(1) Proof shall not be required of a fact the knowledge of which is not reasonably open to question and which is –

(a) common knowledge in the locality in which the proceeding is being held, or generally; or

(b) Capable of verification by reference to a document the authority of which cannot reasonably be questioned.

(2) The court may acquire in any manner it thinks fit knowledge of a fact to which subsection (1) of this section refers, and shall take such knowledge into account.

(3) The court shall give to a party to any proceedings such opportunity to make submission, and to refer to relevant information, in relation to the acquiring or taking into account of such knowledge, as is necessary to ensure that the party is not unfairly prejudiced.

125. Proof of fact by oral evidence

All facts, except the contents of documents, may be proved by oral evidence.

126. Oral evidence must by direct

Subject to the provisions of Part III of this Act, oral evidence must, in all cases whatever, be direct –

(a) if it refers to a fact which could be seen, it must be the evidence of a witness who says he saw that fact;

(b) if it refers to a fact which could be heard, it must be the evidence of a witness who says he heard that fact;

(c) if it refers to a fact which could be perceived by any other sense or in any other manner, it must be the evidence of a witness who says he perceived that fact by that sense or in that manner;

(d) if it refers to an opinion or to the grounds on which that opinion is held, it must be the evidence of the person who holds that opinion on those grounds:

Provided that the opinions of experts expressed in any treatise commonly offered for sale, and the grounds on which such opinions are held, may be proved by the production of such treatise if the author is dead or cannot be found, or has become incapable of giving evidence, or cannot be called as a witness without an amount of delay or expense which the court regards as unreasonable.

127. Inspection when oral evidence refers to real evidence

(1) If oral evidence refers to the existence or condition of any material thing other than a document, the court may, if it thinks fit –

(a) require the production of such material thing for its inspection, or

(b) Inspect any moveable or immovable property the inspection of which may be material to the proper determination of the question in dispute.

(2) When an inspection of property under this section is required to be held at a place outside the courtroom, the court shall either –

(a) be adjourned to the place where the subject - matter of the said inspection may be and the proceedings shall continue at that place until the court further adjourns back to its original place of sitting, or to some other place of sitting; or

(b) attend and make an inspection of the subject - matter only, evidence, if any, of what transpired there being given in court afterwards, and in either case the defendant, if any, shall be present.

128. **Evidence of terms of judgments, contracts, grants and other dispositions of property reduced to a documentary form**

(1) When any judgment of any court or any other judicial or official proceedings, or any contract, or any grant or other disposition of property has been reduced to the form of a document or series of documents, no evidence may be given of such judgment or proceedings or of the terms of such contract, grant or disposition of property except the document itself, or secondary evidence of its contents in cases in which secondary evidence is admissible under this Act; nor may the contents of any such document be contradicted, altered, added to or varied by oral evidence:

Provided that any of the following matters may be proved –

(a) fraud, intimidation, illegality; want of due execution; the fact that it is wrongly dated; existence or want or failure, of consideration; mistake in fact or law; want of capacity in any contracting party, or the capacity in which a contracting party acted when it is not inconsistent with the terms of the contract; or any other matter which, if proved, would produce any effect upon the validity of any document, or of any part of it, or which would entitle any person to any judgment, decree, or order relating to it;

(b) the existence of any separate oral agreement as to any matter on which a document is silent, and which is not inconsistent with its terms, if from the circumstances of the case the court infers that the parties did not intend the document to be a complete and final statement of the whole of the transaction between them;

(c) the existence of any separate oral agreement, constituting a condition precedent to the attaching of any obligation under any such contract, grant or disposition of property;

(d) the existence of any distinct subsequent oral agreement to rescind or modify any such contract, grant or disposition of property;

(e) Any usage or custom by which incidents not expressly mentioned in any contract are annexed to contracts of that description; unless the annexing of such incident to such contract would be repugnant to or inconsistent with the express terms of the contract.

(2) Oral evidence of a transaction is not excluded by the fact that a documentary memorandum of it was made, if such memorandum was not intended to have legal effect as a contract, grant or disposition of property. (3) Oral evidence of the existence of a legal relationship is not excluded by the fact that it has been created by a document, when the fact to be proved is the existence of the relationship itself, and not the terms on which it was established or is carried on.

129. **Evidence as to the interpretation of documents**

(1) Evidence may be given to show the meaning of illegible or not commonly intelligible characters of foreign, obsolete, technical, local and provincial expressions, of abbreviations and words used in a peculiar sense.

(2) Evidence may not be given to show that common words, the meaning of which is plain, and which do not appear from the context to have been used in a peculiar sense, were in fact so used.

(3) If the words of a document are so defective or ambiguous as to be unmeaning, no evidence can be given to show what the author of the document intended to say.

(4) In order to ascertain the relationship of the words of a document to facts, every fact may be proved to which it refers, or may probably have been intended to refer, or which identifies any person or thing mentioned in it; and such facts are hereafter in this section called the circumstances of the case.

(5) If the words of a document have a proper legal meaning, and also a less proper meaning, they must be deemed to have their proper legal meaning, unless such a construction would be unmeaning in reference to the circumstances of the case, in which case they may be interpreted according to their less proper meaning.

(6) If the document has one distinct meaning in reference to the circumstances of the case, it must be construed accordingly, and evidence to show that the author intended to express some other meaning is not admissible.

(7) If the document applies in part but not with accuracy or not completely to the circumstances of the case, the court may draw inferences from those circumstances as to the meaning of the document whether there are more than one or only one thing or person to whom or to which the inaccurate description may equally well apply; and in such cases no evidence can be given of statements made by the

author of the document as to his intentions in reference to the matter to which the document relates, though evidence may be given as to his circumstances, and as to his habitual use of language or names for particular persons or things.

(8) If the language of the document, though plain in itself, applies equally well to more objects than one, evidence may be given both of the circumstances of the case and of statements made by any party to the document as to his intentions in reference to the matter to which the document relates.

(9) If the document is of such a nature that the court will presume that it was executed with any other than its apparent intention, evidence may be given to show that it was in fact executed with its apparent intention.

130. **Application of this Part**

(1) Sections 128 and 129 apply only to parties to documents, and their representatives in interest, and only to cases in which some civil right or civil liability is dependent upon the terms of a document in question.

(2) Any person other than a party to a document or his representative in interest may, notwithstanding the existence of any document, prove any fact which he is otherwise entitled to prove.

(3) Any party to any document or any representative in interest of any such party may prove any such fact for any purpose other than that of varying or altering any right or liability depending upon the terms of the document.

(4) Nothing contained in this Part shall be taken to affect any of the provisions of any enactment as to the construction of wills.

131. **Burden of proof**

(1) Whoever desires any court to give judgment as to any legal right or liability dependent on the existence of facts which he asserts must prove that those facts exist.

(2) When a person is bound to prove the existence of any fact it is said that the burden of proof lies on that person.

132. On whom burden of proof lies.

The burden of proof in a suit or proceeding lies on that person who would fail if no evidence at all were given on either side.

133. **Burden of proof in civil cases**

(1) In civil cases the burden of first proving existence or non - existence of a fact lies on the party against whom the judgment of the court would be given if no evidence were produced on either side, regard being had to any presumption that may arise on the pleadings.

(2) If the party referred to in subsection (1) of this section adduces evidence which ought reasonably to satisfy the court that the fact sought to be proved is established, the burden lies on the party against whom judgment would be given if no more evidence were adduced, and so on successively, until all the issues in the pleadings have been dealt with.

(3) Where there are conflicting presumptions, the case is the same as if there were conflicting evidence.

134. **Standard of proof in civil cases**

The burden of proof shall be discharged on the balance of probabilities in all civil proceedings.

135. **Standard of proof where commission of crime in issue; and burden where guilt of crime etc. asserted**

(1) If the commission of a crime by a party to any proceeding is directly in issue in any proceeding civil or criminal, it must be proved beyond reasonable doubt.

(2) The burden of proving that any person has been guilty of a crime or wrongful act is, subject to section 139 of this Act, on the person who asserts it, whether the commission of such act is or is not directly in issue in the action.

(3) In election matters, whether the commission of crime is in issue or not, proof shall be on the preponderance of evidence or balance of probabilities.

136. **Burden of proof as to particular fact**

(1) The burden of proof as to any particular fact lies on that person who wishes the court to believe in its existence unless it is provided by any law that the proof of that fact shall lie on any particular person, but the burden may in the course of a case be shifted from one side to the other.

(2) In considering the amount of evidence necessary to shift the burden of proof regard shall be had by the court to the opportunity of knowledge with respect to the fact to be proved which may be possessed by the parties respectively.

137. **Standard of proof where burden of proving fact, etc. placed on defendant by law**

Where in any criminal proceedings the burden of proving the existence of any fact or matter has been placed upon a defendant by virtue of the provisions of any law, the burden shall be discharged on the balance of probabilities.

138. **Burden of proving fact necessary to be proved to make evidence admissible**

(1) The burden of proving any fact necessary to be proved in order to –

(a) enable a person to adduce evidence of some other fact; or

(b) prevent the opposite party from adducing evidence of some other fact, lies on the person who wishes to adduce, or to prevent the adduction of such evidence, respectively.

(2) The existence or non - existence of facts relating to the admissibility of evidence under this section is to be determined by the court.

139. **Burden of proof in criminal cases**

(1) Where a person is accused of any offence, the burden of proving the existence of circumstances bringing the case within any exception or exemption from, or qualification

to, the operation of the law creating the offence with which he is charged is upon such person.

(2) The burden of proof placed by this Part upon a defendant charged with a criminal offence shall be deemed to be discharged if the court is satisfied by evidence given by the prosecution, whether on cross - examination or otherwise, that such circumstances in fact exist.

(3) Nothing in sections 135 and 140 or in subsection (1) or (2) of this section shall –

(a) prejudice or diminish in any respect the obligation to establish by evidence according to law any acts, omissions or intentions which are legally necessary to constitute the offence with which the person accused is charged; or

(b) impose on the prosecution the burden of proving that the circumstances or facts described in subsection (2) of this section do not exist; or

(c) affect the burden placed on a defendant to prove a defence of intoxication or insanity.

140. **Proof of facts especially within knowledge**

When any fact is especially within the knowledge of any person, the burden of proving that fact is upon him.

141. **Exceptions need not be proved by prosecution**

Any exception, exemption, proviso, excuse, qualification, whether it does or does not accompany in the same section the description of the offence in the legislation creating the offence, may be proved by the defendant, provided that the prosecution is not required to specify or refute any of the exceptions mentioned in this section and if specified or denied, no proof in relation to the matter so specified or denied shall be required on the part of the prosecution.

142. **Burden of proof as to relationship in the cases of partners, landlord and tenant, principal and agent**

When the question is whether persons are partners, landlord and tenant, or principal and agent, and it has been shown that they have been acting as such, the burden of proving that they do not stand, or have ceased to stand to each other in those relationships respectively, is on the person who affirms it.

143. **Burden of proof as to ownership**

When the question is whether any person is the owner of anything of which he is shown to be in possession, the burden of proving that he is not the owner is on the person who affirms that he is not the owner.

144. **Proof of good faith in transactions where one party is in relation of active confidence**

Where there is a question as to the good faith of a transaction between parties, one of whom stands to the other in a position of active confidence, the burden of proving the good faith of the transaction is on the party who is in a position of active confidence.

145. **Rule as to presumptions by the court**

(1) Whenever it is provided by this Act that the court may presume a fact, it may either regard such fact as proved unless and until it is disproved, or may call for proof of it.

(2) Whenever it is directed by this Act that the court shall presume a fact, it shall regard such fact as proved unless and until it is disproved.

(3) When one fact is declared by this Act to be conclusive proof of another, the court shall, on proof of the one fact, regard the other as proved and shall not allow evidence to be given for the purpose of disproving it.

146. **Presumption as to genuineness of certified copies**

(1) The court shall presume every document purporting to be a certificate, certified copy or other document, which is by law declared to be admissible as evidence of any particular fact and which purports to be duly certified by any officer in Nigeria who is duly authorised in that behalf to be genuine, provided that such document is

substantially in the form and purports to be executed in the manner directed by law in that behalf.

(2) The court shall also presume that any officer by whom any such document purports to be signed or certified, held, when he signed it, the official character which he claims in such document.

147. **Presumption as to documents produced as record of evidence**

(1) Whenever any document is produced before any court, purporting to be a record or memorandum of the evidence, or of any part of the evidence, given by a witness in a judicial proceeding or before any officer authorized by law to take such evidence or to be a statement or confession by any prisoner or defendant, taken in accordance with law, and purporting to be signed by any judge or magistrate or by any such officer as mentioned in this section, the court shall presume that –

(a) the document is genuine;

(b) any statements as to the circumstances in which it was taken, purporting to be made by the person signing it, are true; and

(c) Such evidence, statement or confession was duly taken.

(2) In the absence of evidence to the contrary, the integrity of the electronic records system in which an electronic record is recorded or stored is presumed in any legal proceedings:

(a) Where evidence is adduced that supports a finding that at all material times the computer system or other similar device was operating properly, or if not, that in any respect in which it was not operating properly or out of operation, the integrity of the record was not affected by such circumstances, and there are no reasonable grounds to doubt the integrity of the record.

(b) Where it is established that the electronic record was recorded or stored by a party to the proceedings who is adverse in interest to the party seeking to introduce it; or

(c) Where it is established that the electronic record was recorded or stored in the usual and ordinary course of business by a person who is not a party to the proceedings and who did not record or store it under the control of the party seeking to introduce the record.

148. **Presumption as to Gazettes, newspapers, Acts of the National Assembly, and other documents**

The court shall presume the genuineness of every document purporting to be –

(a) the official Gazette of Nigeria or of a State,

(b) the official Gazette of any country other than Nigeria,

(c) a newspaper or journal,

(d) a copy of the resolutions of the National Assembly or of the House of Assembly of a State, printed by the Government Printer, or

(e) a copy of a document directed by any law to be kept by any person, if such document is kept substantially in the form required by law and is produced from proper custody.

149. **Presumption as to document admissible in other countries without proof of seal or signature**

When any document is produced before any court, purporting to be a document which by the law in force for the time being in any country other than Nigeria would be admissible in proof of any particular in any court of justice in that country, without proof of the seal or stamp or signature authenticating it, or of the judicial or official character claimed by the person by whom it purports to be signed, the court shall presume that –

(a) such seal, stamp or signature, is genuine; and

(b) the person signing it held, at the time when he signed it, the judicial or official character which he claims, and the document shall be admissible for the same purpose for which it would be admissible in the country where the document is produced.

150. **Presumption as to powers of attorney**

The court shall presume that every document purporting to be a power of attorney, and to have been executed before and authenticated by a notary public or any court, judge, magistrate, consul or representative of Nigeria or, as the case may be, of the President, was so executed and authenticated.

151. **Presumption as to public maps and charts**

(1) All maps or charts made under the authority of any Government, or of any public municipal body, and not made for the purpose of any proceedings, shall be presumed to be correct, and shall be admitted in evidence without further proof.

(2) Where maps or charts so made are reproduced by printing, lithography, or other mechanical or electronic process, all such reproductions purporting to be reproduced under the authority which made the originals shall be admissible in evidence without further proof.

152. **Presumption as to books**

The court may presume that any book to which it may refer for information on matters of public or general interest, the statements of which are relevant facts and which is produced for its inspection was written and published by the person, and at the time and place by whom or at which it purports to have been written or published.

153. **Presumption as to telegraphic and electronic messages**

(1) The court may presume that a message forwarded from a telegraph office to the person to whom such message purports to be addressed corresponds with a message delivered for transmission at the office from which the message purports to be sent; but the court shall not make

any presumption as to the person by whom such message was delivered for transmission

(2) The court may presume that on electronic message forwarded by the originator through an electronic mail server to the addressee to whom the message purports to be addressed corresponds with the message as fed into his computer for transmission; but the court shall not make any presumption as to the person to whom such message was sent.

154. **Presumption as to due execution of documents not produced**

The court shall presume that every document called for and not produced after notice to produce given under section 91, was attested, stamped and executed in the manner required by law.

155. **Presumption as to handwriting etc in documents twenty years old**

Where any document purporting or proved to be twenty years old or more is produced from any custody which the court in the particular case considers proper, the court may presume that the signature and every other part of such document which purports to be in the handwriting of any particular person is in that person's handwriting, and in the case of a document executed or attested, that it was duly executed and attested by the person by whom it purports to be executed and attested.

156. **"Proper custody" defined**

Documents are said to be in proper custody within the meaning of sections 148 to 155 if they are in the place in which, and under the care of the person with whom, they would naturally be; but no custody is improper if it is proved to have had a legitimate origin, or if the circumstances of the particular case are such as to render such an origin probable.

157. **Presumption as to date of document**

When any document bearing a date has been proved, it is presumed to have been made on the date on it bears and if more documents than one bear the same date, they are presumed to have been executed in the order necessary to effect the object for which they were executed, but independent proof of the correctness of the date will be required if the circumstances are such that there may have been collusion as to the date which may injure any person or defeat the objects of any law.

158. **Presumption as to stamp of a document**

When any document is not produced after due notice to produce, and after being called for, it is presumed to have been duly stamped unless it is shown to have remained unstamped for some time after its execution.

159. **Presumption as to sealing and delivery**

When any document purporting to be, and stamped as, a deed, appears or is proved to be or to have been signed and duly attested, it is presumed to have been sealed and delivered although no impression of a seal appears on it.

160. **Presumption as to alterations**

(1) No person producing any document which upon its face appears to have been altered in a material part can claim under it the enforcement of any right created by it, unless the alteration was made before the completion of the document or with the consent of the party to be charged under it or his representative in interest.

(2) Subsection (1) of this section shall extend to cases in which the alteration was made by a stranger, whilst the document was in the custody of the person producing it, but without his knowledge or leave.

(3) Alterations and interlineations appearing on the face of a deed, are in the absence of all evidence relating to them, presumed to have been made before the deed was completed.

(4) Alterations and interlineations appearing on the face of a will are, in the absence of all evidence relating to them, presumed to have been made after the execution of the will.

(5) There is no presumption as to the time when alterations and interlineations appearing on the face of writings not under seal were made except that it is presumed that they were so made that the making would not constitute an offence.

(6) An alteration is said to be material when, if it had been made with the consent of the party charged, it would have affected his interest or varied his obligations in any manner whatsoever.

(7) An alteration which in no way affects the rights of the parties or the legal effect of the instrument is immaterial.

161. **Presumption as to age of parties to a conveyance or instrument**

The persons expressed to be parties to any conveyance or instrument relating to an interest in land shall, until the contrary is proved, be presumed to be of full age at the date of the conveyance or instrument.

162. **Presumption as to statements in documents twenty years old.**

Recitals, statements, and descriptions of facts, matters, and parties contained in deeds, instruments, Acts of the National Assembly, or statutory declarations twenty years old or more at the date of the contract in which such deed, instrument or other document is sought to be relied upon shall, unless and except so far as they may be proved to be inaccurate, be taken to be sufficient evidence of such facts, matters and descriptions.

163. **Presumption as to deeds of corporations**

(1) In favour of a purchaser, a deed shall be deemed to have been duly executed by a body corporate if its seal is affixed to the deed in the presence of and attested by its clerk,

secretary or other permanent officer or his deputy, and a member of the board of directors, council or other governing body of the corporation.

(2) Where a seal purporting to be the seal of a corporation has been affixed to a deed, attested by persons purporting to be persons holding such offices as are mentioned in subsection (1) of this section, the deed shall be deemed to have been executed in accordance with the requirements of this section, and to have taken effect accordingly.

164. **Presumption of death from seven years absence and other facts**

(1) A person shown not to have been heard of for seven years by those, if any, who if he had been alive would naturally have heard of him, is presumed to be dead unless the circumstances of the case are such as to account for his not being heard of without assuming his death; but there is no presumption as to the time when he died, and the burden of proving his death at any particular time is upon the person who asserts it.

(2) For the purpose of determining title to property where two or more persons have died in circumstances in which it is uncertain which survived the other they are presumed to have died in order of seniority.

(3) There is no presumption as to the age at which a person died who is shown to have been alive at a given time.

165. **Presumption of paternity**

Without prejudice to section 84 of the Matrimonial Causes Act, where a person was born during the continuance of a valid marriage between his mother and any man, or within 280 days after dissolution of the marriage, the mother remaining unmarried, the court shall presume that the person in question is the child of that man.

166. **Presumption of marriage**

When in any proceedings whether civil or criminal there is a question as to whether a man or woman is the husband or wife under Islamic or Customary law, of a party to the proceedings the court shall, unless the contrary is proved, presume the existence of a valid and subsisting marriage between the two persons where evidence is given to the satisfaction of the court, of cohabitation as husband and wife by such man and woman.

167. **Court may presume existence of certain fact**

The court may presume the existence of any fact which it thinks likely to have happened, regard being had to the common course of natural events, human conduct and public and private business, in their relationship to the facts of the particular case, and in particular the court may presume that –

(a) a man who is in possession of stolen goods soon after the theft is either the thief or has received the goods knowing them to be stolen, unless he can account for his possession;

(b) a thing or state of things which has been shown to be in existence within a period shorter than that within which such things or state of things usually cease to exist, is still in existence;

(c) the common course of business has been followed in particular cases;

(d) evidence which could be and is not produced would, if produced, be unfavourable to the person who withholds it;

(e) when a document creating an obligation is in the hands of the obligor, the obligation has been discharged.

168. **Presumptions of regularity and of deeds to complete title**

(1) When any judicial or official act is shown to have been done in a manner substantially regular, it is presumed that formal requisites for its validity were complied with.

(2) When it is shown that any person acted in a public capacity, it is presumed that he had been duly appointed and was entitled so to act.

(3) When a person in possession of any property is shown to be entitled to the beneficial ownership of it, there is a presumption that every instrument has been executed which it was the legal duty of his trustees to execute in order to perfect his title.

(4) When a minute is produced purporting to be signed by the chairman of a company incorporated under the Companies and Allied Matters Act and purporting to be a record of proceedings at a meeting of the company or of its directors it is presumed, until the contrary is shown, that such meeting was duly held and convened and that all proceedings at the meeting have been duly had, and that all appointments of directors, managers and liquidators are valid.

169. **Estoppel**

When one person has either by virtue of an existing court judgment, deed or agreement, or by his declaration, act or omission, intentionally caused or permitted another person to believe a thing to be true and to act upon such belief, neither he nor his representative in interest shall be allowed, in any proceedings between himself and such person or such person's representative in interest, to deny the truth of that thing.

170. **Estoppel of tenant, and of licensee of person in possession**

No tenant of immovable property or person claiming through such tenant, shall during the continuance of the tenancy, be permitted to deny that the landlord of such tenant had at the beginning of the tenancy a title to such immovable property and no person who came upon any immovable property by the licence of the person in possession of it shall be permitted to deny that such person had a title to such possession at the time when such licence was given.

171. **Estoppel of bailee, agent and licensee**

No bailee, agent or licensee is permitted to deny that the bailor, principal or licensor, by whom any goods were entrusted to any of them respectively, was entitled to those goods at the time when they were so entrusted: Provided that any such bailee, agent or licensee may show that he was compelled to deliver up any such goods to some person who had a right to them as against his bailor, principal or licensor, or that his bailor, principal or licensor wrongfully and without notice to the bailee, agent or licensee, obtained the goods from a third person who has claimed them from such bailee, agent or licensee.

172. **Estoppel of person signing bill of lading**

Every bill of lading in the hands of a consignee or endorsee for valuable consideration, representing goods to have been shipped on board a vessel, is conclusive proof of that shipment as against the master or other person signing the same, notwithstanding that some goods or some part of them may not have been so shipped, unless such holder of the bill of lading had actual notice at the time of receiving the same that the goods had not been in fact laden on board: Provided that the master or other person so signing may exonerate himself in respect of such misrepresentation by showing that it was caused without any default on his part, and wholly by the fraud of the shipper or of .the holder or some person under whom the holder holds.

173. **Judgment conclusive of facts forming ground of judgment**

Every judgment is conclusive proof, as against parties and privies, of facts directly in issue in the case, actually decided by the court, and appearing from the judgment itself to be the ground on which it was based; unless evidence was admitted in the action in which the judgment was delivered which is excluded in the action in which that judgment is intended to be proved.

174. **Effect of judgment not pleaded as estoppel**

(1) If a judgment is not pleaded by way of estoppel it is as between parties and privies deemed to be a relevant fact, whenever any matter, which was or might have been decided in the action in which it was given, is in issue, or is deemed to be relevant to the issue in any subsequent proceeding.

(2) Such judgment is conclusive proof of the facts which it decides, or might have decided, if the party who gives evidence of it had no opportunity of pleading it as an estoppel.

175. **Who may testify**

(1) All persons shall be competent to testify, unless the court considers that they are prevented from understanding the questions put to them, or from giving rational answers to those questions, by reason of tender years, extreme old age, disease, whether of body or mind, or any other cause of the same kind.

(2) A person of unsound mind is not incompetent to testify unless he is prevented by his mental infirmity from understanding the questions put to him and giving rational answers to them.

176. **Dumb witnesses**

(1) A witness who is unable to speak may give his evidence in any other manner in which he can make it intelligible, as by writing or by signs, but such writing must be written and the signs made in open court.

(2) Evidence so given shall be deemed to be oral evidence.

177. **Cases in which banker or officers representing other financial institutions not compellable to produce books**

A banker or an officer of a bank or of other financial institution shall not, in any legal proceeding to which the bank or financial institution is not a party, be compellable to produce any banker's book or financial book, the contents of which can be proved in the manner provided in sections 89 and 90 of this Act or to appear as a witness to prove the matters, transactions and accounts recorded in such book, unless by order of the court made for special cause.

178. **Parties to civil suit and their wives or husbands**

Subject to the exception applicable by virtue of section 165 of this Act in all civil proceedings the parties to the suit, and the husband or wife of any party to the suit, shall be competent witnesses.

179. **Competence in criminal cases**

Subject to this Part, in criminal cases the defendant, his wife or her husband, as the case may be, or any person jointly charged with such defendant and tried at the same time, and the wife or husband of the person so jointly charged, is competent to testify.

180. **Competence of person charged to give evidence**

Every person charged with an offence shall be a competent witness for the defence at every stage of the proceedings whether the person so charged is charged solely or jointly with any other person:

Provided that: –

(a) a person so charged shall not be called as a witness in pursuance of this section except upon his own application;

(b) a person charged and being a witness in pursuance of this section may be asked any question in cross - examination notwithstanding that it would tend to incriminate him as to the offence charged;

(c) when the only witness to the facts of the case called by the defence is the person charged he shall be called as a witness immediately after the close of the evidence for the prosecution;

(d) every defendant called as witness in pursuance of this section shall, unless otherwise ordered by the court, give his evidence from the witness box or other place from which the other witnesses give their evidence; (e) nothing in this section shall affect the right of the person charged to make a statement without being sworn;

(f) in cases where the right of reply depends upon the question, whether evidence has been called for the defence, the fact that the person charged has been called as a witness shall not of itself confer on the prosecution the right of reply.

(g) A person charged and called as a witness in pursuance of this section shall not be asked, and if asked, shall not be required to answer, any question tending to show that he has committed or been convicted of or been charged with any offence other than that with which he is then charged, or is of bad character unless –

(i) the proof that he has committed or been convicted of such other offence is admissible evidence to show that he is guilty of the offence with which he is then charged, or

(ii) he has personally or by his legal practitioner asked questions of the witnesses for the prosecution with a view to establish his own good character or has given evidence of his good character, or the nature or conduct of the defence is such as to involve imputations on the prosecutor or the witnesses for the prosecution, or

(iii) he has given evidence against any other person charged with the same offence;

181. **Comment on failure by defendant to give evidence**

In any criminal proceedings, where a defendant has not given evidence, the court, the prosecution or any other party to the proceedings may comment on the failure of the defendant to give evidence but the comment shall not suggest that the defendant failed to do so because he was, or that he is, guilty of the offence charged.

182. **Evidence by husband or wife: when compellable**

(1) When a person is charged –

(a) with an offence under sections 217, 218, 219, 221, 222, 223, 224, 225, 226, 231, 300, 301, 340, 341, 357 to 362, 369, 370, or 371 of the Criminal Code;

(b) subject to section 36 of the Criminal Code with an offence against the property of his wife or her husband; or

(c) with inflicting violence on his wife or her husband, the wife or husband of the person charged shall be a competent and compellable witness for the prosecution or defence without the consent of the person charged.

(2) When a person is charged with an offence other than one of those mentioned in subsection (1) of this section the husband or wife of such person is a competent and compellable witness but only upon the application of the person charged.

(3) Nothing in this section shall make a husband compellable to disclose any communication made to him by his wife during the marriage or a wife compellable to disclose any communication made to her by her husband during the marriage.

(4) The failure of the wife or husband of any person charged with an offence to give evidence shall not be made the subject of any comment by the prosecution.

183. **Witness not to be compellable to incriminate self**

No one is bound to answer any question if the answer to it would, in the opinion of the court, have a tendency to expose the witness or the wife or husband of the witness to any criminal charge, or to any penalty or forfeiture which the judge regards as reasonably likely to be preferred or sued for:

Provided that: –

(a) a person charged with an offence, and being a witness in pursuance of section 180 of this Act may be asked and is bound to answer any question in cross - examination notwithstanding that it would tend to incriminate him as to the offence charged;

(b) no one is excused from answering any question only because the answer may establish, or tend to establish that he owes a debt or is otherwise liable to any civil suit either at the instance of the Federal, State, or Local Government or any other person;

(c) Nothing contained in this section shall excuse a witness at any inquiry by the direction of the Attorney - General of the Federation or of a State, under Part 49 of the Criminal Procedure Act from answering any question required to be answered under section 458 of that Act.

184. **Production of title deeds or other documents of witness not a party**

No witness who is not a party to a suit shall be compelled to produce his title - deeds to any property or any document by virtue of which he holds any property as pledgee or mortgagee or any document the production of which might tend to incriminate him, unless he has agreed in writing to produce them with the person seeking the production of such deeds or some person through whom he claims.

185. **Production of documents which another person could refuse to produce**

No one shall be compelled to produce documents in his possession which any other person would be entitled to refuse to produce if they were in his possession, unless such last mentioned person consents to their production.

186. **Evidence by spouse as to adultery**

The parties to any proceedings instituted in consequence of adultery and the husbands and wives of the parties shall be competent to give evidence in the proceedings, but no witness in any such proceedings whether a party to them or not, shall be liable to be asked or bound to answer any question tending to show that he or she has been guilty of adultery, unless he or she has already given evidence in the same proceeding in disproof of the alleged adultery.

187. **Communications during marriage**

No husband or wife shall be compelled to disclose any communication made to him or her during marriage by any person to whom he or she is or has been married nor shall he or she be permitted to disclose any such communication, unless the person who made it, or that person's representative in interest, consents, except in suits between married persons, or proceedings in which one married person is prosecuted for an offence specified in section 182(1) of this Act.

188. **Compellability of justices, etc. or the persons before whom the proceeding is being held**

No Justice, Judge, Grand Kadi or President of a Customary Court of Appeal and, except upon the special order of the High Court of the State, or of the Federal Capital Territory, Abuja or the Federal High Court, no magistrate, or other persons before whom a proceeding is being held shall be compelled to answer any questions as to his own conduct in court in any of the capacities specified in this section, or as to anything which came to his knowledge in court in such capacity but he may be examined as to other matters which occurred in his presence whilst he was so acting.

189. **Restriction on disclosure as to source of information in respect of commission of offences**

No magistrate, police officer or any other public officer authorized to investigate or prosecute offences under any written law shall be compelled to disclose the source of any information as to the commission of an offence which he is so authorized to investigate or prosecute and no public officer employed in or about the business of any branch of the public revenue, shall be compelled to disclose the source of any information as to the commission of any offence against the public revenue.

190. **Evidence as to affairs of State**

(1) Subject to any directions of the President in any particular case, or of the Governor of a State where the records are in the custody of a State, no one shall be permitted to produce any unpublished official records relating to affairs of State, or to give any evidence derived from such record except with the permission of the officer at the head of the Ministry, Department or Agency concerned who shall give or withhold such permission as he thinks fit:

Provided that the Ministry, Department or Agency concerned shall, on the order of the court, produce to the judge the official record in question or, as the case may be, permit evidence derived from it to be given to the judge alone in chambers and if the judge after careful consideration shall decide that the record or the oral evidence, as the case may be, should be received as evidence in the proceedings, he shall order this to be done in private as provided in section 36(4) of the Constitution.

(2) Any order made under the proviso to subsection (1) of this section may be appealed against by the department concerned or by a party to the case.

191. **Official communication**

No public officer shall be compelled to disclose communications made to him in official confidence, when he considers that the public interests would suffer by the disclosure: Provided that the public officer concerned shall on the order of the court, disclose to the judge alone in chambers the substance of the communication in question and if the judge is satisfied that the communication should be received in evidence this shall be done in private in accordance with section 36 (4) of the Constitution.

192. **Professional communication between client and legal practitioner**

(1) No legal practitioner shall at any time be permitted, unless with his client's express consent, to disclose any communication made to him in the course and for the purpose of his employment as such legal practitioner by or on behalf of his client, or to state the contents or condition of any document with which he has become acquainted in the course and for the purpose of his professional employment or to disclose any advice given by him to his client in the course and for the purpose of such employment: Provided that nothing in this section shall protect from disclosure –

(a) any such communication made in furtherance of any illegal purpose;

(b) Any fact observed by any legal practitioner in the course of his employment as such, showing that any crime or fraud has been committed since the commencement of his employment.

(2) It is immaterial whether the attention of such legal practitioner was or was not directed to such fact by or on behalf of his client.

(3) The obligation stated in this section continues after the employment has ceased.

193. **Section 192 to apply to interpreters and clerks**

The provisions of section 192 of this Act shall apply to interpreters and the clerks of legal practitioners.

194. **Privilege not waived by volunteering evidence**

If any party to a suit or proceeding gives evidence in such suit or proceeding, whether at his own instance or otherwise, he shall not be deemed to have by this reason consented to such disclosure as is mentioned in section 192 of this Act and, if any party to a suit or proceedings calls any such legal practitioner as a witness, he shall be deemed to have consented to such disclosure only if he questions such legal practitioner on matters which, but for such question, he would not be at liberty to disclose.

195. **Confidential communication with legal advisers**

No one shall be compelled to disclose to the court any confidential communication which has taken place between him and a legal practitioner consulted by him, unless he offers himself as a witness in which case he may be compelled to disclose any such communications as may appear to the court necessary to be known, in order to explain any evidence which he has given, but no others.

196. **Statements in documents marked "without prejudice"**

A statement in any document marked "without prejudice" made in the course of negotiation for a settlement of a dispute out of court, shall not be given in evidence in any civil proceedings in proof of the matters stated in it.

197. **Corroboration in actions for breach of promise of marriage**

A plaintiff in any action for breach of promise of marriage is not entitled to succeed unless his or her testimony is corroborated by some other material evidence in support of such promise and the fact that the defendant did not answer letters affirming that he had promised to marry the plaintiff is not such corroboration.

198. **Accomplice**

(1) An accomplice shall be a competent witness against a defendant, and a conviction is not illegal merely because it proceeds upon the uncorroborated testimony of an accomplice: Provided that in cases when the only proof against a person charged with a criminal offence is the evidence of an accomplice, uncorroborated in any material particular implicating the defendant, the court shall direct itself that it is unsafe to convict any person upon such evidence.

(2) In this section and in section 199 of this Act, an accomplice is any person who pursuant to section 7 of the

Criminal Code may be deemed to have taken part in committing the offence as the defendant or is an accessory after the fact to the offence, or a receiver of stolen goods.

199. **Co - defendant not an accomplice.**

Where defendants are tried jointly and any of them gives evidence on his own behalf which incriminates a co-defendant the defendant who gives such evidence shall not be considered to be an accomplice.

200. **Number of witnesses**

Except as provided in sections 201 to 204 of this Act no particular number of witnesses shall in any case be required for the proof of any fact.

201. **Treason and treasonable offences**

(1) A person charged with treason or with any of the felonies mentioned in sections 40, 41 and 42 of the Criminal Code Act cannot be convicted, except on his own plea of guilty, or on the evidence in open court of two witnesses at least to one overt act of the kind of treason or felony alleged, or the evidence of one witness to one overt act and one other witness to another overt act of the same kind of treason or felony.

(2) Subsection (1) of this section does not apply to cases in which the overt act of treason alleged is the killing of the President or a direct attempt to endanger the life or injure the person of the President.

202. **Evidence on charge of perjury**

A person shall not be convicted of committing perjury or for counselling or procuring the commission of perjury, upon the uncorroborated testimony of one witness contradicting the oath on which perjury is assigned, unless circumstances are proved which corroborated such witness.

203. **Exceeding speed limit**

(1) A person charged under any road traffic legislation with driving at a speed higher than the allowed maximum shall

not be convicted solely on the evidence of one witness that in the opinion of that witness he was driving at such speed: Provided that the evidence of a duly authorized officer of the relevant authority who was at the time of the commission of the offence operating any mechanical, electronic or other device for the recording of the speed of a moving vehicle, the record of such device being additionally tendered in evidence against the defendant, shall not require further corroboration.

(2) In this section, "relevant authority" means the Nigeria Police Force, the Federal Road Safety Commission, or any other body charged with responsibility for offences of speeding under the road traffic legislation.

204. **Sedition**

A person shall not be convicted of the offence of uttering seditious words under paragraph (b) of subsection (1) of section 51 of the Criminal Code Act upon the uncorroborated testimony of one witness.

205. **Oral evidence to be on oath or affirmation**

Save as otherwise provided in sections 208 and 209 of this Act all oral evidence given in any proceedings must be given upon oath or affirmation administered in accordance with the Oaths Act or Law, as the case may be.

206. **Witness to be cautioned before giving oral evidence**

Any witness summoned to give oral evidence in any proceedings shall before giving such evidence be cautioned by the court, or the registrar upon the court's direction, in the following words - "You (Full name) .... are hereby cautioned that if you tell a lie in your testimony in this proceeding or wilfully mislead this court you are liable to be prosecuted and if found guilty you will be seriously dealt with according to law."

207. **Absence of religious belief does not invalidate oath**

Where an oath has been duly administered and taken, the fact that the person to whom the same was administered had, at the time of taking such oath, no religious belief, does not for any purpose affect the validity of such oath.

208. **Cases in which evidence not given upon oath may be received**

(1) Any court may on any occasion, if it thinks it just and expedient, receive the evidence, though not given upon oath, of any person declaring that the taking of any oath whatsoever is, according to his religious belief, unlawful, or who, by reason of want of religious belief ought not, in the opinion of the court, to be admitted to give evidence upon oath.

(2) The fact that in any case evidence not given upon oath has been received, and the reasons for the reception of such evidence, shall be recorded in the minutes of the proceedings.

209. **Unsworn evidence of a child**

(1) In any proceedings in which a child who has not attained the age of fourteen years is tendered as a witness, such child shall not be sworn and shall give evidence otherwise than on oath or affirmation, if in the opinion of the court, he is possessed of sufficient intelligence to justify the reception of his evidence and understands the duty of speaking the truth.

(2) A child who has attained the age of fourteen years shall, subject to section 175 and 208 of this Act give sworn evidence in all cases.

(3) A person shall not be liable to be convicted for an offence unless the testimony admitted by virtue of subsection (1) of this section and given on behalf of the prosecution is corroborated by some other material evidence in support of such testimony implicating the defendant.

(4) If any child whose evidence is received under this section wilfully gives false evidence in such circumstances that he would, if the evidence had been given on oath have been guilty of perjury, he shall be guilty of an offence under

section 191 of the Criminal Code and on conviction shall be dealt with accordingly.

210. **Order of production and examination of witnesses**

The order in which witnesses are produced and examined shall be regulated by the law and practice for the time being relating to civil and criminal procedure respectively, and, in the absence of any such law, at the discretion of the court.

211. **Court to decide as to admission of evidence**

(1) When either party proposes to give evidence of any fact, the court may ask the party proposing to give the evidence in what manner the alleged fact, if proved, would be relevant; and the court shall admit the evidence if it thinks that the fact, if proved, would be relevant and not otherwise.

(2) If the fact proposed to be proved is one of which evidence is admissible only upon proof of some other fact, such last mentioned fact must be proved before evidence is given of the fact first mentioned, unless the party undertakes to give proof of such fact, and the court is satisfied with such undertaking.

(3) If the relevancy of one alleged fact depends upon another alleged fact being first proved, the court may in its discretion, either permit evidence of the first fact to be given before the second fact is proved, or require evidence to be given of the second fact before evidence is given of the first fact.

212. **Ordering witnesses out of court**

On the application of either party, or of its own motion, the court may order witnesses on both sides to be kept out of court; but this provision does not extend to the parties themselves or to their respective legal advisers, although intended to be called as witnesses.

213. **Preventing communication with witnesses**

The court may during any trial take such means as it considers necessary and proper for preventing communication with witnesses who are within the court house or its precincts awaiting examination.

214. **Examination-in-chief, cross - examination and re - examination**

(1) The examination of a witness by the party who calls him shall be called examination-in-chief.

(2) The examination of a witness by a party other than the party who calls him shall be called cross - examination.

(3) Where a witness has been cross-examined and is then examined by the party who called him, such examination shall be called re-examination.

215. **Order and direction of examination**

1. Witnesses shall be first examined-in-chief, then, if any other party so desires, cross-examined, then, if the party calling him so desires, re-examined.

(2) The examination and cross-examination must relate to relevant facts, but the cross-examination need not be confined to the facts to which the witness testified on his examination-in-chief.

(3) The re - examination shall be directed to the explanation of matters referred to in cross-examination and, if a new matter is, by permission of the court, introduced in re-examination, the adverse party may further cross examine upon that matter.

216. **Cross-examination by co-defendant of prosecution witness**

Where more than one defendant is charged at the same time, each defendant shall be allowed to cross - examine a witness called by the prosecution before the witness is re-examined.

217. **Cross-examination by co-defendant of witness called by a defendant**

Where more than one defendant is charged at the same time, a witness called by one defendant may be cross-examined by the other defendant and if cross-examined by the other defendant such cross-examination shall take place before cross-examination by the prosecution.

218. **Production of documents without giving evidence**

Any person, whether a party or not, in a cause may be summoned to produce a document without being summoned to give evidence, and if he causes such document to be produced in court the court may dispense with his personal attendance.

219. **Cross-examination of person called to produce a document**

A person summoned to produce a document does not become a witness by the mere fact that he produces it and cannot be cross-examined unless and until he is called as a witness.

220. **Witnesses to character**

Witnesses to character may be cross-examined and re-examined.

221. **Leading question**

(1) Any question suggesting the answer which the person putting it wishes or expects to receive is called a leading question.

(2) Leading questions shall not be asked in examination - in - chief, or in re - examination, except with the permission of the court.

(3) The court shall permit leading questions as to matters which are introductory or undisputed, or which have, in its opinion, been already sufficiently proved.

(4) Leading questions may be asked in cross-examination.

222. **Evidence as to matters in writing**

(1) Any witness may be asked, whilst under examination, whether any contract, grant or other disposition of property, as to which he is giving evidence was not

contained in a document, and if he says that it was, or if he is about to make any statement as to the contents of any document, which, in the opinion of the court, ought to be produced, the adverse party may object to such evidence being given until such document is produced, or until facts have been proved which entitle the party who called the witness to give secondary evidence of it.

(2) A witness may however give oral evidence of statements made by other persons about the content of a document if such statements are in themselves relevant facts.

223. **Question lawful in cross-examination**

When a witness is cross-examined, he may in addition to the question referred to in preceding sections of this Part, be asked any questions which tend to –

(a) test his accuracy, veracity or credibility; or

(b) discover who he is and what is his position in life; or

(c) shake his credit, by injuring his character: Provided that a person charged with a criminal offence and being a witness may be cross examined to the effect, and under the circumstances, described in paragraph (c) of the proviso to section 180 of this Act.

224. **Court to decide whether question shall be asked and when a witness may be compelled to answer**

(1) If any question permitted to be asked under section 223 of this Act relates to a matter not relevant to the proceedings, except in so far as it affects the credit of the of the witness by injuring his character, the court shall decide whether or not the witness shall be compelled to answer it, and may, if it thinks fit, warn the witness that he is not obliged to answer it.

(2) In exercising its discretion, the court shall have regard to the following considerations –

(a) such question are proper if they are of such a nature that the truth of the imputation conveyed by them would seriously affect the opinion of the court as to the credibility of the witness on the matter to which he testifies;

(b) such questions are improper if the imputation which they convey relates to matters so remote in time, or of such a character, that the truth of the imputation would not affect, or would affect in a slight degree, the opinion of the court as to the credibility of the witness on the matter to which he testifies;

(c) Such questions are improper if there is a great disproportion between the importance of the imputation made against the witness's character and the importance of his evidence.

(3) The court may, if it sees fit, draw, from the refusal of the witness to answer, the inference that the answer if given would be unfavourable.

225. **Question not to be asked without reasonable grounds**

Any question as referred to in section 224 of this Act may not be asked, unless the person asking it has reasonable grounds for thinking that the imputation which it conveys is well founded.

226. Procedure of court in case of question being asked without reasonable grounds.

If the court is of the opinion that any question referred to in section 224 of this Act was asked without reasonable grounds, it may, if it was asked by any legal practitioner, report the circumstances of the case to the Attorney General of the Federation or other authority to which such legal practitioner is subject in the exercise of his profession.

227. **Indecent and scandalous questions**

The court may forbid any questions or inquiries which it regards as indecent or scandalous although such questions or inquiries may have some bearing on the questions before the court, unless they relate to facts in issue or to matters necessary to be known in order to determine whether or not the facts in issue existed.

228. **Questions intended to insult or annoy**

The court shall forbid any question which appears to it to be intended to insult or annoy, or which, though proper in itself, appears to the court needlessly offensive in form.

229. **Exclusion of evidence to contradict answers to questions testing veracity**

When a witness has been asked and has answered any question which is relevant to the inquiry only in so far as it tends to shake his credit by injuring his character, no evidence shall be given to contradict him; but if he answers falsely, he may afterwards be charged with an offence under section 191 of the Criminal Code and on conviction, shall be dealt with accordingly:

Provided that –

(a) if a witness is asked whether he has been previously convicted of any crime and denies it, evidence may be given of his previous conviction;

(b) If a witness is asked any question tending to impeach his impartiality and answers it by denying the facts suggested, he may be contradicted.

230. **How far a party may discredit his own witness**

The party producing a witness shall not be allowed to impeach his credit by general evidence of bad character, but he may in case the witness shall, in the opinion of the court, prove hostile, contradict him by other evidence, or by leave of court, prove that he has made at other times a statement inconsistent with his present testimony; but before such last mentioned proof can be given, the circumstances or the supposed statement, sufficient to designate the particular occasion, must be mentioned to the witness and he must be asked whether or not be has made such statement.

231. **Proof of contradictory statement of hostile witness**

If a witness upon cross-examination as to a former statement made by him relative to the subject - matter of the trial, and inconsistent with his present testimony, does not distinctly admit that he has made such statement, proof may be given that he did in fact make it; but before such proof can be given the circumstances of the supposed statement sufficient to designate the particular occasion must be mentioned to the witness, and he must be asked whether or not he has made such statement.

232. **Cross-examination as to previous statements in writing**

A witness may be cross-examined as to previous statements made by him in writing or reduced into writing and relative to matters in question in the suit or proceedings in which he is cross-examined without such writing being shown to him or being proved, but if it is intended to contradict such witness by the writing, his attention must, before such writing can be proved, or such contradictory proof given, be called to those parts of the writing which are to be used for the purpose of contradicting him:

Provided always that it shall be competent for the court at any time during the trial to require the production of the writing for its inspection, and the court may thereupon make use of it for the purposes of the trial, as it shall think fit.

233. **Impeaching credit of witness**

The credit of a witness may be impeached in the following ways by any party other than the party calling him or with the consent of the court by the party who calls him by –

(a) the evidence of persons who testify that they, from their knowledge of the witness, believe him to be unworthy of credit;

(b) proof that the witness has been bribed, or has accepted the offer of a bribe, or has received any other corrupt inducement to give his evidence; or

(c) Proof of former statements inconsistent with any part of his evidence which is liable to be contradicted.

234. **Special restrictions in respect of permissible evidence in trial for sexual offences**

Where a person is prosecuted for rape or attempt to commit rape or for indecent assault, except with the leave of the court no evidence shall be adduced, and, except with the like leave, no question in cross-examination shall be asked by or on behalf of the defendant, about any sexual experience of the complainant with any person other than the defendant.

235. **Evidence of witness impeaching credit**

A witness declaring another witness to be unworthy of credit may not, upon his examination-in-chief give reasons for his belief but he may be asked his reasons in cross-examination, and the answers which he gives cannot be contradicted, though, if they are false, he may afterwards be charged with an offence under section 191 of the Criminal Code and on conviction, shall be dealt with accordingly.

236. **Questions tending to render evidence of relevant fact more probable, admissible**

When a witness gives evidence of any relevant fact, he may be questioned as to any other circumstances which he observed at or near to the time or place at which such relevant fact occurred, if the court is of the opinion that such circumstances if proved, would render more probable the testimony of the witness as to the relevant fact which he testifies.

237. **Former statements of witness may be proved to show consistency**

Any former statement made by a witness relating to the same fact at or about the time when the fact took place, or before any authority legally competent to investigate the fact may be proved in order to show consistency in the testimony of the witness or to show that his testimony is not an afterthought.

238. **What matters may be proved in connection with proved statement relevant under sections 40 to 50**

Whenever any statement admissible under sections 40 to 50 of this Act, is proved, all matters may be proved either in order to contradict or to confirm it, or in order to impeach or confirm the credit of the person by whom it was made, which might have been proved if that person had been called as a witness and had denied upon cross-examination the truth of the matters suggested.

239. **Refreshing memory**

(1) A witness may, while under examination, refresh his memory by referring to any writing made by himself at the time of the transaction concerning which he is questioned, or so soon afterwards that the court considers it likely that the transaction was at that time fresh in his memory.

(2) The witness may also refer to any such writing made by any other person, and read by the witness within the time mentioned in subsection (1) of this section, if when he read it he knew it to be correct. (3) An expert may refresh his memory by reference to professional treatises.

240. **Testimony to facts stated in document mentioned in section 239.**

A witness may also testify to facts mentioned in any such document as is mentioned in section 239 of this Act, although he has no specific recollection of the facts themselves, if he is sure that the facts were correctly recorded in the document.

241. **Right of adverse party as to writing used to refresh memory**

Any writing referred to under sections 239 and 240 of this Act must be produced and shown to the adverse party if he requires it, and such party may, if he pleases, cross - examine the witness upon the writing.

242. **Production of documents**

(1) Subject to section 243 of this Act, a witness summoned to produce a document shall, if it is in his possession or power, bring it to court, notwithstanding any objection which there may be to its production or to its admissibility and the validity of any such objection shall be decided by the court.

(2) The court, if it sees fit, may inspect the document or take other evidence to enable it to determine on its admissibility.

(3) If for such a purpose, it is necessary to cause any document to be translated, the court may, if it thinks fit, direct the translator to keep the contents secret, unless the document is to be given in evidence and, if the translator disobeys such direction, he shall be held to have committed an offence under section 97(1) of the Criminal Code.

243. **Exclusion of evidence on grounds of public interest**

(1) A Minister, or in respect of matters to which the executive authority of a State extends, the Governor or any person nominated by him, may in any proceedings object to the production of documents or request the exclusion of oral evidence when after consideration he is satisfied that the production of such document or the giving of such oral evidence is against public interest.

(2) Any such objection as mentioned in subsection (1) of this section shall if taken –

(a) Before trial, be by affidavit, or

(b) At the hearing, be by certificate produced by a public officer.

(3) The court shall have a discretion whether or not to uphold any such

objection, and may in determining how to exercise its discretion, inspect such documents or be informed as to the *nature of the oral evidence to which the objection relates.*

244. **Giving as evidence document called for and produced on notice**

When a party calls for a document which he has given the other party notice to produce, and such document is produced and inspected by the party calling for its production, he is bound to give it as evidence if the party producing it requires him to do so.

245. **Using as evidence a document production of which was refused on notice**

When a party refuses to produce a document which he has had notice to produce, he cannot afterwards use the document as evidence without the consent of the other party or the order of the court.

246. **Judge's power to put questions or order production of documents, etc.**

(1) The court, or any other person empowered by law to take evidence may, in order to clear up ambiguities or to clarify points which have been left obscure in the evidence given by any witness, ask any question he pleases, in any form, at any time, of any witness, or of the parties about any fact relevant or irrelevant; and may order the production of any document or thing; and neither the parties nor their agents shall be entitled to make any objection to any such question or order or, without the leave of the court, to cross - examine any witness upon any answer given in reply to any such question:

(2) The question referred to in subsection 1 must be based upon facts declared by this Act to be relevant, and duly proved;

(3) A judge shall not under this section compel any witness to answer any question or to produce any document

which such witness would be entitled to refuse to answer or produce under this Act, if the question were asked or the documents were called for by the adverse party; nor shall the judge ask any question which it would be improper for any person to ask under section 224 or 225 of this Act nor shall the judge dispense with primary evidence of any document, except in the cases excepted in preceding sections of this Act.

247. **Power of assessors to put questions**

In cases tried with assessors, the assessors may put question to the witnesses, through or by leave of the judge, which the judge himself may put and which he considers proper.

248. **Proof of previous conviction**

(1) Where it is necessary to prove a conviction for a criminal offence the same may be proved –

(a) by the production of a certificate of conviction containing the substance and effect of the conviction only, purporting to be signed by the registrar or other officer of the court in whose custody is the record of such conviction;

(b) if the conviction was before a customary court, by a similar certificate signed by the clerk of court or scribe of the court in whose custody is the record of such conviction; or

(c) by a certificate purporting to be signed by the Director of Prisons or officer in charge of the records of a prison in which the prisoner was confined giving the offence for which the prisoner was convicted, the date and the sentence.

(2) If the person alleged to be the person referred to in the certificate denies that he is such person the certificate shall not be put in evidence unless the court is satisfied by the evidence, that the individual in question and the person named in the certificate are the same.

249. **Proof of previous conviction outside Nigeria**

(1) A previous conviction in a place outside Nigeria may be proved by the production of a certificate purporting to be given under the hand of a police officer in the country where the conviction was had, containing a copy of the sentence or order and the finger prints of the person or photographs of the finger prints of the person so convicted, together with evidence that the finger prints of the person so convicted are those of the defendant.

(2) A certificate given under sub - section (1) of this section shall be prima facie evidence of all facts set out in it, without proof that the officer purporting to sign it did in fact sign it and was empowered to do so.

250. **Additional mode of proof in criminal proceedings of a previous conviction**

(1) A previous conviction may be proved against any person in any criminal proceedings by the production of such evidence of the conviction as is mentioned in this section, and by showing that his fingerprints and those of the person convicted are the finger prints of the same person.

(2) A certificate –

(a) purporting to be signed by or on behalf of the central registrar; and

(b) containing particulars relating to a conviction extracted from the criminal records kept by him or a photographic copy certified as such of particulars relating to a conviction as entered in the said records; and

(c) certifying that the copies of the finger print exhibited to the certificate are copies of the finger prints appearing from the said record to have been taken from the person convicted on the occasion of the conviction, shall be evidence of the conviction and evidence that the copies of the finger prints exhibited to the certificate are copies of the finger prints of the person convicted.

(3) A certificate –

(a) purporting to be signed by or on behalf of the superintendent of a prison in which any person has been detained in connection with any criminal proceedings or by a police officer who has had custody of any person charged with an offence in connection with any such proceedings; and

(b) certifying that the finger prints exhibited to it were taken from such person while he was so detained or was in such custody as mentioned in paragraph (a), shall be evidence in those proceedings that the finger prints exhibited to the certificate are the finger prints of that person.

(4) A certificate –

(a) purporting to be signed by or on behalf of the central registrar; and

(b) certifying that the finger prints –

(i) copies of which are certified as mentioned in this section by or on behalf of the central registrar to be copies of the finger prints of a person previously convicted, and

(ii) certified by or on behalf of the superintendent of the prison or the police officer as mentioned in this section or otherwise shown to be the finger prints of the person against whom the previous conviction is sought to be proved are the finger prints of the same person shall be evidence of the matter so certified.

(5) The method of proving a previous conviction authorized by this section shall be in addition to any other method authorized by law for proving such conviction.

(6) For the purposes of this section, "the central registrar" means the person in charge of the principal registry of criminal records established under the Prevention of Crimes Act.

251. **Wrongful admission or exclusion of evidence**

(1) The wrongful admission of evidence shall not of itself be a ground for the reversal of any decision in any case where it shall appear to the court on appeal that the evidence so

admitted cannot reasonably be held to have affected the decision and that such decision would have been the same if such evidence had not been admitted.

(2) The wrongful exclusion of evidence shall not of itself be a ground for the reversal of any decision in any case if it shall appear to the court on appeal that had the evidence excluded been admitted it may reasonably be held that the decision would have been the same.

(3) In this section the term "decision" includes a judgment, order, finding or verdict.

252. **Interpretation of "court" in this Part**

In this Part - "Court" means a High Court or a magistrate's court and courts of similar jurisdiction.

253. **Subpoena or witness summons may be served in another State**

(1) When a subpoena or summons has been issued by any court in any State or in the Federal Capital Territory, Abuja or by the Federal High Court in the exercise of its civil jurisdiction in accordance with any power conferred by law requiring any person to appear and give evidence or to produce books or documents in any proceeding, such subpoena or summons may upon proof that the testimony of such person or the production of such books or documents is necessary in the interests of justice by leave of such court on such terms as the court may impose be served on such person in any other State or the Federal Capital Territory, Abuja.

(2) If a person upon whom a subpoena or summons has been served in accordance with subsection (1) of this section fails to attend at the time and place mentioned in such subpoena or summons such court may on proof that the subpoena or summons was duly served on such person and that the sum prescribed by law was tendered to him for his expenses, issue such warrant for the apprehension of such person as such court might have issued if the

subpoena or summons had been served in the State or the Federal Capital Territory, Abuja in which it was issued.

(3) Such warrant may be executed in such other State or the Federal Capital Territory, Abuja in the manner provided in Chapter 12 of the Criminal Procedure Act, in the case of warrants issued for the apprehension of persons charged with an offence.

254. **Orders for production of prisoners**

(1) Where it appears to any court of a State or of the Federal Capital Territory, Abuja that the attendance before the court of a person who is undergoing sentence in any State or the Federal Capital Territory, Abuja is necessary for the purpose of obtaining evidence in any proceeding before the court, the court may issue an order directed to the superintendent or officer in charge of the prison or place where the person is undergoing sentence requiring him to produce the person at the time and place specified in the order.

(2) Any order made under this section may be served upon the superintendent or officer to whom it is directed in any State or the Federal Capital Territory, Abuja, he may be and he shall thereupon produce in such custody as the superintendent or officer thinks fit, the person referred to in the order at the time and place specified in it.

(3) The court before which any person is produced in accordance with an order issued under this section may make such order as to the costs of compliance with this order as may seem just to the court.

255. **Regulations**

(1) The Minister charged with responsibility for justice may make regulations generally prescribing further conditions with respect to admissibility of any class of evidence that may be relevant under this Act.

(2) Where a law provides that a rule, regulation, notification, or any other matter be published in the Federal

Government Gazette, the requirement shall be deemed to have been satisfied if the rule, regulation, notification, or any other matter is published in the Federal Government gazette or Electronic Gazette.

256. **Application**

(1) This Act shall apply to all judicial proceedings in or before any court established in the Federal Republic of Nigeria but it shall not apply to –

(a) proceedings before an arbitrator; or

(b) a field general court martial;

(c) judicial proceedings in any civil cause or matter in or before any Sharia Court of Appeal, Customary Court of Appeal, Area Court or Customary Court unless any authority empowered to do so under the Constitution, by order published in the Gazette, confers upon any or all Sharia Courts of Appeal, Customary Courts of Appeal, Area Courts or Customary Courts in the Federal Capital Territory Abuja or a State, as the case may be, power to enforce any or all the provisions of this Act.

(2) In judicial proceedings in any criminal cause or matter in or before an Area Court, the court shall be guided by the provisions of this Act and in accordance with the provisions of the Criminal Procedure Code Law. (3) Notwithstanding anything in this section, an Area Court shall, in judicial proceedings in any criminal cause or matter, be bound by the provisions of sections 134 to 140.

257. **Repeal and savings**

(1) The Evidence Act cap E14, Laws of the Federation of Nigeria, 2004 is hereby repealed.

(2) Nothing in this Act shall affect any proceedings commenced before the coming into force of this Act.

258. **Interpretation**

(1) In this Act, unless where the context otherwise requires –

"audio – visual communication" means being able to see, hear and communicate with another individual in real time, using electronic means;

"Bank" or "banker" means a bank licensed under the Banks and Other Financial Institutions Act 1991 and includes anybody authorized under an enactment to carry on banking business;

"banker's books" (and related expressions) includes ledger, day - books, cash - books, account books and all other books used in banking business;

"Banking business" has the meaning assigned to it in the Banks and Other Financial Institutions Act 1991;

"Cloud Computing" means the delivery of different services through the internet, including data storage, servers, databases, networking and software;

"Computer" means any device for storing and processing information, including mobile phones and any reference to information being derived from it by calculation, comparison or any other process;

"The Constitution" means the Constitution of the Federal Republic of Nigeria 1999;

"Copy of a document" includes -

(a) in the case of a document falling within paragraph (b) but not (c) of the definition of "document" in this subsection, a transcript of the sounds or other data embodied in it;

(b) in the case of a document falling within paragraph (b) but not (c) of that definition, a reproduction or still reproduction of the image or images embodied in it whether enlarged or not;

(c) in the case of a document falling within both those paragraphs, such a transcript together with such a still reproduction; and

(d) in the case of a document not falling within the said paragraph (c) of which a visual image is embodied in a document falling within that paragraph, a reproduction of that image, whether enlarged on not, and any reference to a copy of the material part of a document shall be construed accordingly;

"Computer" means any device for storing and processing information and any reference to information being derived from other information is a reference to its being derived from it by calculation, comparison or any other process;

"court" includes all judges and magistrates and, except arbitrators, all persons legally authorized to take evidence;

"customs" is a rule which, in a particular district, has, from long usage, obtained the force of law;

"digital signature" means an electronically generated signature which is attached to an electronically transmitted document to verify its contents and the sender's identify;

"document" includes –

(a) books, maps, plans, graphs, drawings, photographs, and also includes any matter expressed or described upon any substance by means of letters, figures or marks or by more than one of these means, intended to be used or which may be used for the purpose of recording that matter;

(b) any disc, tape, sound track or other device in which sounds or other data (not being visual images) are embodied so as to be capable (with or without the aid of some other equipment) of being reproduced from it; and

(c) any film, negative, tape or other device in which one or more visual images are embodied so as to be capable (with or without the aid of some other equipment) of being reproduced from it; and

(d) any device by means of which information is recorded, stored or retrievable including computer output.

"Electronic Gazette" means official Gazette published in the electronic form;

"electronic record" means data, record or data generated, image or sound stored, received, or sent in an electronic form or microfilm;

"electronic signature" means authentication of any electronic record by a subscriber by means of the electronic technique specified in the Second Schedule and includes digital signature;

"fact" includes:

(a) anything, state of things, or relation of things, capable of being perceived by the senses; and

(b) any mental condition of which any person is conscious;

"fact in issue" includes any fact from which either by itself or in connection with other facts the existence, non - existence, nature or extent of any right, liability or disability asserted or denied in any suit or proceeding necessarily follows;

"film" includes a microfilm;

"financial institution" has the meaning assigned to "other financial institution" by the Banks and Other Financial Institutions Act, 1991;

"magnetic media" includes cassette tapes, hard disks, floppy disks, video and computer tapes;

"optical media" means DVD, CD and Blu – ray;

"person interested" means any person likely to be personally affected by the outcome of a proceeding;

"Public Service of the Federation or of a State" has the meaning assigned thereto in the Constitution; and "public officer" shall be construed accordingly;

"real evidence" means anything other than testimony admissible hearsay or a document the contents of which are offered as evidence of a fact at a trial, which is examined by the court as a means of proof of such fact;

"statement" includes any representation of fact whether made in words or otherwise; and "wife" and "husband" mean respectively the wife and husband of a marriage validly contracted under the Marriage Act, or under Islamic law or a Customary law applicable in Nigeria, and includes any marriage recognized as valid under the Marriage Act.

(2) In this Act, unless the context otherwise requires, any reference to a section or other provision of the Criminal Code Act or the Criminal Procedure Act shall, as the case may be, be construed as including a reference to the corresponding section or provision of the Criminal Code Law or Penal Code Law or the Criminal Procedure Code Law of a State or, in respects of the Federal Capital Territory, Abuja, the Penal Code Act or the Criminal Procedure Code Act, whichever may be appropriate.

259. **This Act may be cited as the Evidence Act, 2011.**

INDEX

1999 Constitution; 85
Abuja; 95, 214, 235, 237, 241
Abundaga; 108
Adekeye; 90
Afolagbiye, ChiefAwoniy;i 28
Ahmadu, ProfessorM.I.; vi
Aina, MrEdward Oladipo; 42, 55, 68
AIS Bo;x 76
Ajileye, Hon. Justice Omolaye; 64
Amsterdam; 77
Anglo-American; 9
Anyalewechi, Harvey Esq.; 88
Apex Court; 88, 123
Appellant; 49, 52, 57, 66, 67, 68, 69, 70, 71, 73, 77, 78, 86, 88, 96, 103, 108, 109, 111, 117, 122, 132
Area Cour;t 237
Attorney General ofthe Federation; 213, 225
Automated TellerMachine (ATM); viii
Awoniyi, JosephAyinla; 28
Ayaya, Surv. Asuquo; 111
Blu-ray; 240
Bolaji; 81
Borno State Government; 15

Burrill, AlexanderM.; 4
CD; 240
Central Bank; 176
Chairman ofthe Administrative Panel ofInquiry; 15
Chairman ofthe Local Government Council; 181
Civil Procedure Rules; 79
Constitution 189, 215, 237, 238
Court ofAppeal ofNigeria; 64
Cotonou; 77
CounterTerrorism Investigation Department; 95, 102
Court ofAppeal; ix, 70, 72, 74, 101
Cross RiverState; 111
Customary Court 237
Customary Court ofAppeal; 237
Customary law; 206
Dennis, I.H.; 99
Department ofState Services; 95, 102
Deputy Surveyor-General; 111
DirectorofLands; 111
DirectorofOperations; 75, 77
Donald, Justin; 76
DVD; 240
EFCC; 76, 77, 108, 109, 117
Ekwenze, Chinwuba; 67
ElectronicEvidence: Disclosure, Discovery and Admissibility; 51
ElectronicGazette; 237, 239
Enugu; 22
Enugu Campus; 22
Europea; 9
Evidence; 1, 2, 3, 4, 5, 6, 7, 8, 9, 10, 13, 14, 15, 16, 17, 19, 20, 21, 23, 24, 25, 26, 27, 28, 30, 32, 33, 39, 49, 50, 56, 60, 61,

66, 68, 69, 70, 72, 73, 74, 75, 76, 78, 80, 81, 82, 84, 87, 95, 96, 97, 102, 103, 104, 105, 107, 108, 110, 112, 116, 117, 118, 119, 120, 121, 122, 123, 124, 125, 126, 127, 128, 129, 131, 133, 134, 137, 138, 140, 141, 142, 144, 145, 146, 147, 149, 150, 151, 154, 155, 156, 161, 167, 168, 173, 174, 175, 178, 190, 191, 193, 211, 212, 213, 215, 216, 217, 218, 220, 221, 223, 228, 230, 231, 232, 234

Expressio unius est exclusion alterius;59

Facta probantia; 8

Factum probandum; 8

Federal Capital Territory; 214, 235, 237, 241

Federal Gazette; 162, 181, 188, 237

Federal High Court; 214, 235

Federal Inland Revenue Service; 176, 177

Federal RepublicofNigeria; 188, 238

Federal Road Safety Commission; 219

Gadami Beach;77

Galadima; 126

Gazette ofNigeria; 200

Global Satellite Mobile (GSM); 65, 81

Government White Paper; 16

Governor ofthe Central Bank ofNigeria; 162

Governor ofthe Local Government Council; 181

Grand Kadi; 214

Griffith, Lord; 98

Griffiths, Lord; 105

Grundnorm; 46

GSM; 66, 82

Harman, L.J.; 113

High Court 31, 235

High Court ofthe State; 214

Hon, S.T.; 86

House ofAssembly ofa State; 200
Houses ofAssembly ofthe States ofNigeria; 188
Ibadan University library; 88
Idigbe; 72
Imolega, Solomon; 103
Information and Communications Technology; viii
Institute forDevelopment Studies; 22
International Maritime Organisation; 130
Investigating Police Officer; 77
Judges ofthe Superiorand InferiorCourts; vi
Justice ofthe Court ofAppeal ofNigeria; vi
Karibi-Whyte; 70, 74, 114
Kekere-Ekun; 89, 112
Kriti Akti; 77
Langan, St. J.; 112
Laws ofthe Assembly ofa State; 181
Learned Trial Judge; 17
Lex non mogit ad impossibili;34
Lloyd's List Intelligence Report; 75-79, 83, 130
Local Government Council; 181, 182
Maiduguri Metropolitan Council; 15
Malek, HM; 51
Mason, S.; 51
Matazu, ProfessorA.S.R; vi
Maxwell on the Interpretation ofStatutes; 112, 113
Microfinance Bank; 39
MotherVessel; 75
MotorAccount Department; 42, 55
MrAB; 91
MT Althea; 77
MT ASTERIS; 130
MT Bruno; 130

MT Kriti Akti; 75
MTN; 68
National Assembly; 181, 188, 200
National Library; 88, 89
New York; 12
Nigeria; v, viii, ix, x, xi, xii, 22, 46, 76, 83, 86, 88, 90, 91, 168, 181, 182, 183, 188, 200, 237, 238
Nigeria Police Force; 219
Nigerian Consulate; 184
Nigerian Deposit Insurance Corporation; 176, 177
Nigerian Embass;y 184
Nigerian High Commission;184
Nimpar; 84
Nimpar, Y.B.; 21
November; 111
Nweze; 97
Obadina; 15
Obaseki-Adejumo; 108
Obende, S.S.; 21
Odukoya, ChiefT. Ola; 42, 55, 69, 71
Ogakwu; 129
Ogunwumiju, Lordshi;p 83
Onnoghen; 91, 103, 121
Onnogheri; 91
Onyekachi, Umah Esq.; 91
Onyemenam; 109
Open; 16
Opesitan, Bolaj;i 81
Osita, Nnamdi; 67
Pakistan; 77
Parliament Roll; 112
Passion; 51

Peter-Odil;i 84, 132
President ofa Customary Court ofAppea; 214
Rabiu, ProfessorS.O.; vi
Redmayne; 100
Rhodes-Vivour; 121, 123, 130
Royal Assent; 112
Rufai, ProfessorMuftau; vi
Sa'id, ProfessorMansurIbrahim; xii
Said, ProfessorMansurIbrahim; vi
Saidu, Associate ProfessorBalkisu; vi
Saulawa; 45, 46
SETUBA; 130
Sharia Court ofAppeal; 237
SMS; 83, 84
Sokoto State; vi
Sokoto; vi, x, xii
Spare Parts Manager; 55, 68
State Government; 213
State House Assembly; 181
State House ofAssembly; 188
Supreme Cour;t 15, 64, 68, 78, 89, 90, 91, 105
Supreme Court ofNigeria; 1, 2, 90
The Bar; x
The Commonwealth; 182, 188
House ofRepresentatives; 181
Senate; 181
Supreme Court; 41, 51
Umaru, ProfessorM.J.; vi
University ofNigeria; 22
Usman; 101
Usman, Aliyu; 95
Usmanu Danfodio University; xii

Uwais; 55, 68
West African Court ofAppeal; 72
Williams, J; 55, 68

www.ingramcontent.com/pod-product-compliance
Lightning Source LLC
Chambersburg PA
CBHW050523240926
51846CB00003B/664